CW01021100

Handbook of Tyranny

Theo Deutinger

Handbook of Tyranny

Lars Müller Publishers

Introduction

"Where are we now?" asked David Bowie in a song on his second-to-last album. The song describes an old man strolling through Berlin, reflecting upon the changes that took place in 1989. Bowie's question is asked in a time that sees the return of topics and technologies that ought to be long gone, such as a wall dividing a country into east and west. Once, the fall of such a wall heralded a new age and the promise of a peaceful global future. The technology that soon followed—the mobile phone and the World Wide Web—fueled visions of an open, transparent, and mobile society.

There is no single answer to Bowie's question. With *Handbook of Tyranny*, I try to contribute to the many attempts to answer it, while also interpreting the question as a command. That's why the book is born out of curiosity and even more so out of a sense of duty. Tackling the question in my medium—*illustrating* the walls that separate countries, the water cannons directed against protesters, and the modes of capital punishment—gives this book the appearance of an unearthed compendium of blueprints drawn by or for a dictator of our time. For every obstacle to organizing and controlling society, there seems to be a technical solution at hand. The illustrated details—the sheer number and the bluntness of these technologies—profoundly reinforce their cruelty.

To draw is to minimize, realize, and internalize. Just as an atlas explains the world we inhabit, *Handbook of Tyranny* helps the reader to grasp the forms of cruelty in use. The experience is like standing on a watchtower with a pair of binoculars: having an overview but also a zoomed-in view of the essential details. A confrontation with cruelty is necessary first to understand it, and second to react to it. Depicting the magnitude of technology as an instrument of power and showing the myriad forms this can take, *Handbook of Tyranny* provides a basis for everyone who wants to fight tyranny.

Here we are.

Theo Deutinger

■ Jus soli unconditional

■ Jus soli with restrictions

The Tragedy of Territory

"The territorium is the sum of the lands within the boundaries of a community [civitatis]; which some say is so named because the magistrate of a place has the right of terrifying [terrendi], that is, exercising jurisdiction, within its boundaries."
Pomponius' Manual, in the Digest of Justinian, 2nd century AD

Leaving Africa 70 000 years ago was an incredibly successful move by *Homo sapiens*, but it required technology. One of the most crucial tools seems to have been a communications device: the human larynx, more beautifully and mechanistically called the voice box, which developed 100 000 years ago. The voice box was an essential instrument for the planning of the trip and the organization of the 150 to 1000 travelers who would one day be part of a world-dominating species of almost 8 billion.

As the population increased and human intellect expanded, claims to land and truth multiplied. To organize life on planet Earth, humans refined their technology. Intrinsic tools such as the voice box were used to invent laws, political systems, and binary codes so that people and space could be organized, while more extrinsic tools such as stones were later turned into bullets so that space could be dominated. Thus, life consists not just of us (humans) and the space we inhabit (Earth), but also of the technology we develop.

These three elements act in concert. If they didn't, we would pick up a stone, throw it, and kill somebody, just to gain more space. We don't, because we are not just people, but citizens; we are part of a state and consequently inhabitants of a very specific territory. As citizens, we surrender, we disarm and hand over the right to use our weapons (our technology) to the state, so that the state can fight for us and protect us. On the one hand, this makes us weaker as individuals, but on the other hand it prevents us from constantly being at war, defending our personal freedoms, our belongings, and our land. By handing over our individual powers to the state, we sign a social contract, a kind of nonaggression pact with each other.

What is not always clear is that aggression is still involved, since laws will be enforced. With the transfer of individual power to the state, citizens provide the state with the right to strike, arrest, and in some cases kill in their name. Yet hardly any of us remember placing a signature on a contract, since this contract was "signed" purely by the act of birth.

The world today is divided into two legal zones. In states that apply the principle of jus soli, a newborn is said to fall from the mother's womb onto a particular territory; he or she signs a contract with the territory, becoming a citizen of that state. In states that apply jus sanguinis, the newborn falls into the embrace of his or her mother or father; he or she signs a contract with the state and territory of their origin.[1] In both scenarios, the newborn is passive; he or she leaves the mother's body only to fall into the arms of the state.[2]

A birth certificate and proof of citizenship are the first documents newborns receive, which instantly assign them to one of the 203 existing sovereign states.[3]

1 In the "New World," jus soli is applied on a much larger scale than in the "Old World." Jus soli allows a faster integration of newcomers.
2 In fact, the arms of the state are there first. Birth might be the signatory act, but the territory in which it occurs has rules in place prior to conception. Laws on abortion, sex with minors, and in vitro fertilization are all bound to a state.
3 186 sovereign states plus 17 sovereign states with limited recognition (recognized by at least one UN-member state).

The new citizen can call the entire territory of this state his or her homeland, and throughout this territory the law is the same for everybody. All currently existing 203 sovereign states act in accordance with the "territoriality of law," which determines that it is the territory that inherits the law, not the person.

"[…] the shift from the kingdom of the Franks to the Frankish realm, a move from the people to the land; from race to place. [Historian Charles] McIlwain calls this the most important aspect of the Frankish period: 'the change from the personality to the territoriality of law.'"[4]

A shift from the personality of law[5] in the Middle Ages to the territoriality of law in modern times created the possibility of freeing the people from serfdom and slavery, treating everyone equally, and eliminating the influence of race, status, and family background on justice. However, territorial law reinforced the ownership of territory and the division of the earth's surface into the current 203 sovereign states. Today even the remotest corners of the planet are loaded with ownership, laws, and regulations.[6] We can't escape territory; therefore, we can't escape the law.

The territoriality of law works as long as citizens remain within the territory to which they are assigned, when registration, visa laws, and travel regulations are taken into account. Yet the link between territory and citizenship can be broken, resulting in refugees and stateless individuals. Currently there are more than 20 million refugees and 10 million stateless people. The division of the earth's entire surface into territories of states leaves them in complete limbo. They are people without land. There is no ground on which they are allowed to walk, sit or sleep. Theoretically, according to the territoriality of law, these people should not exist, which is why there is no answer to their needs. The world seems to lack land instead of territory.

The history of turning land into territory and people into citizens is directly linked to the history of military technology. Owning or even just maintaining territory is and always has been linked to the ability to defend it. For a long period of human history, city walls protected the most valuable land, property, and people. The building technology and military capacity of the time could not guarantee the protection of larger areas and hence did not allow the establishment of a legal system that covered them. Therefore, the vast areas between cities were something much closer to land than territory – land that belonged to a kingdom or an emperor but whose limits were not unambiguously defined. Borders between kingdoms weren't clear lines either, but were large stretches of marshland, desert or mountains.

Step by step, as surveying technology developed and improved, solid lines were drawn within these stretches of no-man's-land. The cementation of territorial borders and the elimination of the grey zones resulted in the extension of political power right up to the border. In earlier times, the power of the state declined with distance, but today, the technology of surveillance and warfare enables the state to project its power with equal strength throughout its entire territory. In legal terms, the urban prevailed over the rural, and as the land was turned into territory, the people were turned into citizens. The outlaw disappeared with the no-man's-land. Today the territory hunts or harbors the people. One can be hunted as a villain in one territory and hailed as a hero in another, as the story of Julian Assange shows. Since 2012 he's lived in the Ecuadorian embassy in London. This embassy, considered Ecuadorian territory within the capital of the United Kingdom, shelters an Australian from an extradition requested by Sweden. Regardless of the sexual assault allegations against the founder of WikiLeaks, he is for a fact hunted and shunned because of the release of information to the public which states did not want to be revealed – information that potentially threatens their power monopoly and subsequently their territory.

4 Stuart Elden, *The Birth of Territory*, Chicago, 2013.
5 "The use of different bodies of law based on citizenship over a single geographic area reflected the principle of personality, a legal approach from antiquity that runs counter to our modern territorial conception of jurisdiction. Under the personality of law principle, a nation's laws apply only to their citizens such that the law depends on one's 'personal status.' Under the territoriality principle, however, it is location that matters as nations reserve the right to apply their law to anyone within their territory, regardless of citizenship." Aldo S. Zilli, "Rome's Erie Problem: Applying Roman Law to Foreigners" (essay for Prof. David D. Friedman, Santa Clara University, 2010), citing P. G. Monateri, "Black Gaius: A Quest for Multicultural Origins of the 'Western Legal Tradition,'" *Hastings Law Journal* 51 (2000): 479.
6 The prospect that "the moon and other celestial bodies" may be a future "promised land" and not a "promised territory" appears gloomy as well, since the Moon Treaty, which proposes giving the international community jurisdiction over all celestial bodies, has been signed by only 17 nations. Either way, even advocates of the Moon Treaty are proposing a jurisdiction for outer space. There seems to be no other option than the territoriality of law at this moment.

The territory, the state, and its laws are called into question today by their own promises. The Universal Declaration of Human Rights, drafted heroically as a reaction to the negative forces unleashed in two World Wars, is a challenge to the world. As its name indicates, the Universal Declaration of Human Rights goes far beyond the purview of the sovereign state and inevitably had to clash with national laws. Today, people indulge in freedom of speech and freedom of thought, conscience and religion on the Internet, a medium to which the concept of territory is completely foreign.[7] At the same time, more and more people are discovering the right to freedom of movement and are challenging the very countries that drafted, signed, and promoted the Declaration of Human Rights 70 years ago.

While citizens challenge the political system from within, multinational corporations are using the existing economic freedom and the nebulosity of the digital era to test the system from the outside. Where is a company like Facebook truly located, to whom is it responsible, and what does it produce? With little more than 20 000 employees, Facebook serves, influences, and monitors two billion active users or almost one-third of the world's population. In mathematical terms, one Facebook employee is in charge of an army of 100 000 people. If Facebook were a country, it would be the world's largest, but with the smallest administrative body. But Facebook needs no territory, no streets, no schools, and no hospitals. Facebook has no borders.[8]

The power of companies like Facebook is larger than that of some countries. It is no coincidence that Apple's European headquarters are in Ireland, Amazon's seat is in Luxembourg, and IKEA runs a dubious foundation in the Netherlands. Those countries offered the best deal. Laws and regulations are bent to accommodate the multinational corporations that must comply with them. When the inequality in the legal landscape between territories is abused, it suddenly matters.

When the United Nations was founded in 1945, the world was ahead of its time in establishing a specific set of rules intended to be valid throughout an entire territory. Today, the territoriality of law and its technical instruments seem to belong to an outdated model which has little place in a globalized world. Having said that, the internationality which surrounds us daily in the form of clothing sizes, road signs, standardized passports, and digital documents points clearly in the direction of global standards. It seems that we are on our way to becoming global citizens, with the whole world as our territory. We just don't have a road map yet.

7 While the medium itself knows no borders, the states that feel affected by it are eager to restrain its influence by erecting national firewalls. The best known of these is the Great Firewall of China, which blocks access to selected foreign websites and slows down cross-border Internet traffic. Most countries have means of Internet censorship that filter such content as hate speech and child pornography. National firewalls indicate a tendency to turn cyberspace into cyberterritory.
8 Facebook has no borders, but states do, and they use it to keep Facebook out. Currently, Facebook is blocked in China, Iran and North Korea.

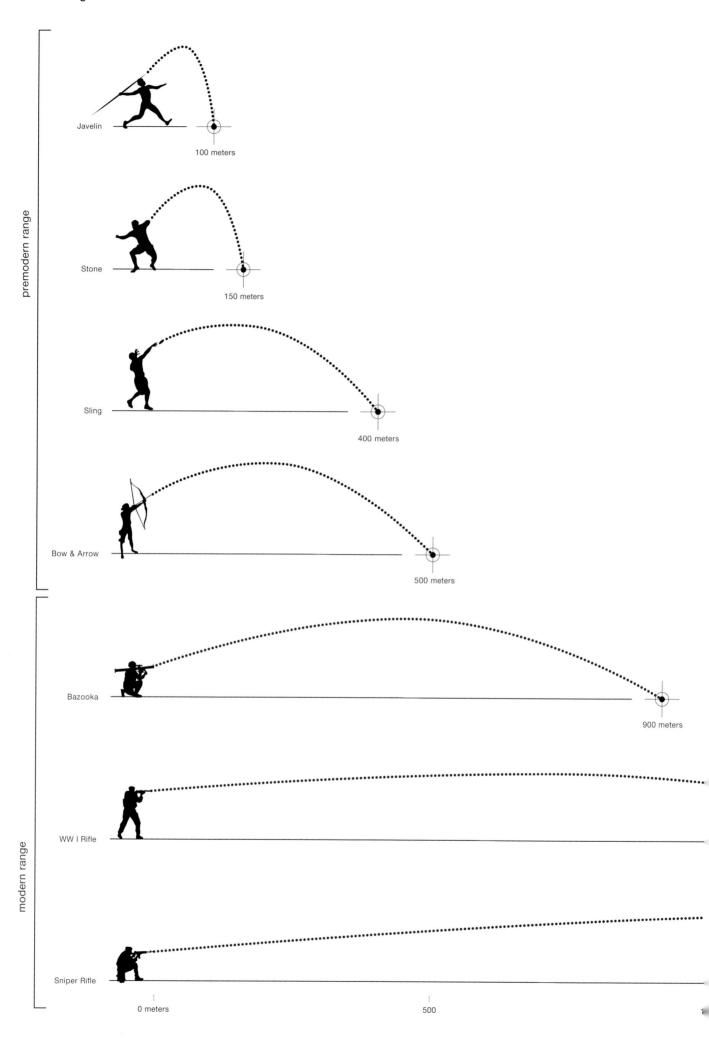

premodern range

Javelin

100 meters

Stone

150 meters

Sling

400 meters

Bow & Arrow

500 meters

modern range

Bazooka

900 meters

WW I Rifle

Sniper Rifle

0 meters

500

Human Range

Humans have developed a number of special abilities, such as the ability to walk continuously on two legs (~7 million years ago), to speak (~2 million years ago), to produce written language (3100 BC), and to engage in complex reasoning. One of the first remarkable skills to set the tone for all future relationships between us and our surroundings was the ability to throw objects accurately and at a distance.

One of the earliest things hominins threw must have been a stone. In fact, the act of throwing turned the stone into a tool. Some 10 000 years ago, a second revolutionary extension of human physical strength was introduced with the invention of the bow and arrow, which increased not only the range but, more importantly, the accuracy that could be delivered. It took another 9000 years for Chinese inventors to introduce the fire lance, a precursor to the cannon. Today, firearms have a range that extends far beyond human sight. Compared to the Stone Age, the area covered by

the range of one person wielding a hand-held weapon has increased from 0.03 km² to 40 km².

The increase in human range has led to the rise of individual power. Today, one person with a firearm covers the same range as 1300 Stone Age people – the size of an army brigade. The result is an increasing overlap in ranges of power. A microstate such as Monaco with its 2 km² territory can be secured by a single person with a firearm, yet its range extends far beyond its borders, deep into French territory.

In peaceful societies, this increasing overlap of human ranges is less apparent. We experience it every day in virtual form via the Internet and mobile phones. The human voice's normal range of 180 meters has been broadened to an extent that covers the entire inhabited world. Imagine the overlap of the catchment areas created by all phone calls, e-mail, and text messages. It is truly gigantic.

06/22/2017 Washington (CNN) A Canadian special operations sniper successfully hit an ISIS fighter from a record-breaking distance of more than two miles away while assisting Iraqi forces in the push to retake Mosul, according to Canadian Special Operations Command.

The unnamed marksman was part of Canada's elite Joint Task Force 2 special operations unit that is currently deployed in an "advise and assist" capacity to help Iraqi security forces battle ISIS from behind the front line in Mosul.
"The Canadian Special Operations Command can confirm that a member of the Joint Task Force 2 successfully hit a target from 3540 meters. For operational security reasons and to preserve the safety of our personnel and our Coalition partners, we will not discuss precise details on when and how this incident took place," the unit said in a written statement....
"The elite sniper was using a McMillan TAC-50 sniper rifle while firing from a high-rise during an operation that took place within the last month in Iraq. It took under 10 seconds to hit the target...."

www.edition.cnn.com

1600 meters

3540 meters

1500   2000

Boundaries of historical ethnicities before colonization—premodern Africa

Current national boundaries—modern Africa

Free Entry

Let us imagine the planet Earth with its 203 sovereign states as a large palace that consists of 203 rooms.[1] As it happens, all 203 rooms of this palace have individual locks, and each room gives away its keys in a very selective manner to the other rooms. The result is a highly unequal distribution of keys throughout the palace. People from the rooms labeled "Germany" and "Singapore" are each in possession of 159 keys, while people from the room labeled "Afghanistan" have keys to only 22 other rooms. The rooms that provide no keys expect each visitor to submit a special request, called a visa.

Consequently, Palace Earth isn't the same size to everybody. With keys to only 22 other rooms, people from the room labeled "Afghanistan" perceive the palace as extremely small. This is reinforced by the fact that none of the neighboring rooms provide keys. To most of the occupants of Afghanistan, Palace Earth is the size of their room, and this room is definitely not the most luxurious or flamboyant room of the palace.

Having the right key is having the right passport—a document that is, in its current state, not even 100 years old. The rapid expansion of railway infrastructure and the increasing wealth of European citizens throughout the mid-nineteenth century resulted in a rapid increase in international travel. A number of nonstandardized travel documents were issued by various European countries at that time, but due to the increasing number of travelers, enforcement was extremely difficult. Generally, it was easy to travel throughout Europe without any document back then:

"Until August 1914 a sensible, law-abiding Englishman could pass through life and hardly notice the existence of the state beyond the post office and the policeman. He could live where he liked and as he liked. He had no official number or identity card. He could travel abroad or leave the country forever without a passport or any sort of official permission," wrote historian A. J. P. Taylor in his classic work *English History 1914–45*.

It was during World War I that European governments introduced passport requirements to secure the borders and prevent people who were useful in warfare from fleeing the country. After the war, the border controls remained while international traffic continued to increase. To recognize the authenticity of the various passports, certain standards were introduced in the Paris Conference on Passports & Customs Formalities and Through Tickets in 1920. This conference gave birth to the passport as we use it today.

Since that time, the importance of the passport only continued to increase. Agreements on freedom of movement, such as that establishing the Schengen zone in Europe, are a reaction to ever-stricter border controls. Twenty-six European countries abolished border controls entirely and adopted a common visa policy in order to maximize the flow of people and goods. Abolishing the border controls between the countries led to the reinforcement of the so-called Schengen border, the line between Schengen and non-Schengen states.

The strength of the passport seems to be a matter of trust in the people from the specific countries. The Schengen countries trust in their members and in their common security system. Yet above all, the passport system is a matter of wealth. Rich countries deny access to people from poor countries even if they only want to come for the purpose of tourism. Wealthy individuals

1 186 sovereign states plus 17 sovereign states with limited recognition (recognized by at least one UN-member state)

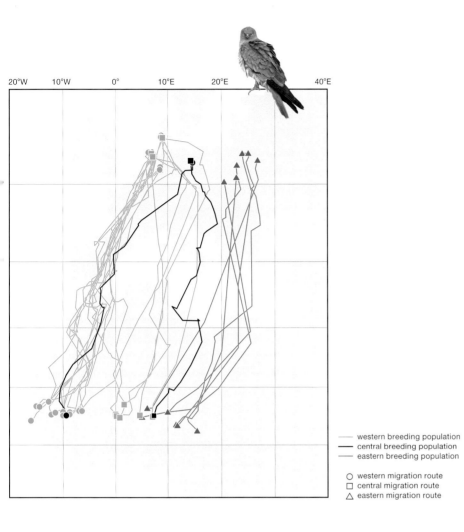

Migration routes of adult Montagu's harriers for autumn (n = 27). Grey tones indicate different breeding populations (light grey: western; black: central; dark grey: eastern). Symbols refer to migration routes (circle: western; square: central; triangle: eastern). For individuals tracked during several years, only one representative track is shown per season. Maps are in Mercator projection.

— western breeding population
— central breeding population
— eastern breeding population

○ western migration route
□ central migration route
△ eastern migration route

from countries with weak passports have an easy way out of this dilemma: buying citizenship. For €1.5 million, a Singapore passport can be bought, and with it the freedom to travel visa-free to 159 countries.[2]

Within this sea of restrictions there are 14 countries that show that a different world is possible.[3] These 14 countries welcome every citizen from any country in the world with a valid passport without any visa restrictions: Comoros, Côte d'Ivoire, Guinea-Bissau, Madagascar, Maldives, Mauritania, Micronesia, Mozambique, Samoa, Seychelles, Timor-Leste, Togo, Tuvalu and Uganda. Frankly, these 14 countries are predestined to serve as global meeting points. It is time the United Nations recognizes and honors this by moving there or at least opening an office in one of these 14 countries. Preferably an office that deals with the "human right to freedom of movement" introduced as part of the Universal Declaration of Human Rights, a common standard for all UN members in 1948:

Article 13 of the Universal Declaration on Human Rights:[4]
Everyone has the right to freedom of movement and residence within the borders of each state.
Everyone has the right to leave any country, including his own, and to return to his country.

If Article 13 of the Universal Declaration of Human Rights were taken seriously, Palace Earth would have doors without locks. Just one rule would need to be applied: please knock before entering.

2 Buying a Singapore passport: S$2.5 million (€1.56 million), www.passports.io/singapore
3 Countries that their holders can visit unconditionally without a visa, with visa on arrival or Electronic Travel Authorization (eTA).
4 United Nations

Germany
159 countries

Singapore
159 countries

South Korea
158 countries

France
157 countries

Italy
157 countries

Japan
157 countries

United States of America
157 countries

Austria
156 countries

Belgium
156 countries

Switzerland
156 countries

Canada
155 countries

Ireland
155 countries

New Zealand
154 countries

Czech Republic
153 countries

Iceland
153 countries

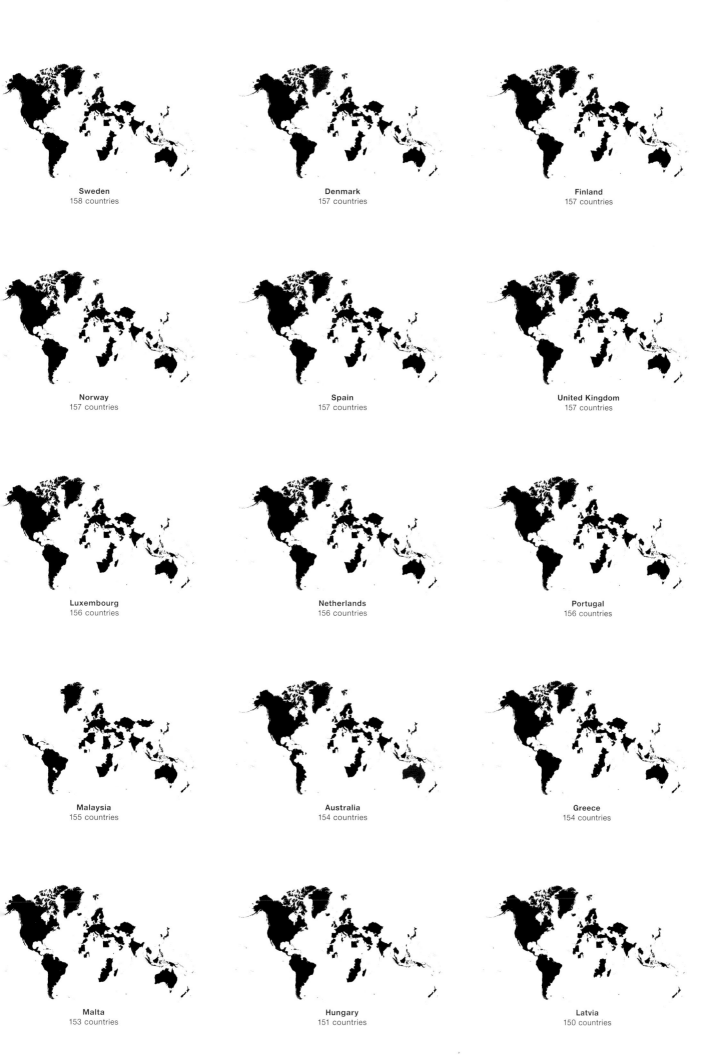

Sweden
158 countries

Denmark
157 countries

Finland
157 countries

Norway
157 countries

Spain
157 countries

United Kingdom
157 countries

Luxembourg
156 countries

Netherlands
156 countries

Portugal
156 countries

Malaysia
155 countries

Australia
154 countries

Greece
154 countries

Malta
153 countries

Hungary
151 countries

Latvia
150 countries

Lithuania
150 countries

Poland
150 countries

Slovakia
150 countries

Cyprus
147 countries

Brazil
145 countries

Argentina
144 countries

Chile
143 countries

Romania
143 countries

Hong Kong
142 countries

Barbados
136 countries

Brunei
136 countries

Mexico
132 countries

Uruguay
129 countries

United Arab Emirates
128 countries

Saint Kitts and Nevis
126 countries

Slovenia
150 countries

Estonia
149 countries

Liechtenstein
148 countries

Bulgaria
144 countries

Croatia
144 countries

Monaco
144 countries

Andorra
140 countries

San Marino
140 countries

Israel
138 countries

Bahamas
131 countries

Vatican City
131 countries

Seychelles
130 countries

Antigua and Barbuda
125 countries

St. Vincent and the Grenadines
124 countries

Peru
123 countries

Trinidad and Tobago
123 countries

Costa Rica
122 countries

Mauritius
122 countries

Grenada
119 countries

Macao
119 countries

Ukraine
119 countries

Dominica
115 countries

El Salvador
113 countries

Honduras
113 countries

Serbia
112 countries

Guatemala
111 countries

Tonga
109 countries

Colombia
106 countries

Marshall Islands
105 countries

Moldova
105 countries

Venezuela
122 countries

Taiwan
121 countries

Saint Lucia
120 countries

Panama
117 countries

Paraguay
117 countries

Vanuatu
116 countries

Samoa
113 countries

Solomon Islands
113 countries

Tuvalu
113 countries

Kiribati
108 countries

Macedonia (FYROM)
108 countries

Russian Federation
107 countries

Montenegro
105 countries

Turkey
105 countries

Nicaragua
104 countries

Georgia
103 countries

Micronesia
102 countries

Bosnia and Herzegovina
101 countries

Kuwait
86 countries

Belize
84 countries

Timor-Leste
84 countries

Jamaica
78 countries

Equador
77 countries

Bahrain
76 countries

Kazakhstan
71 countries

Nauru
71 countries

Oman
71 countries

Papua New Guinea
69 countries

Saudi Arabia
69 countries

Suriname
69 countries

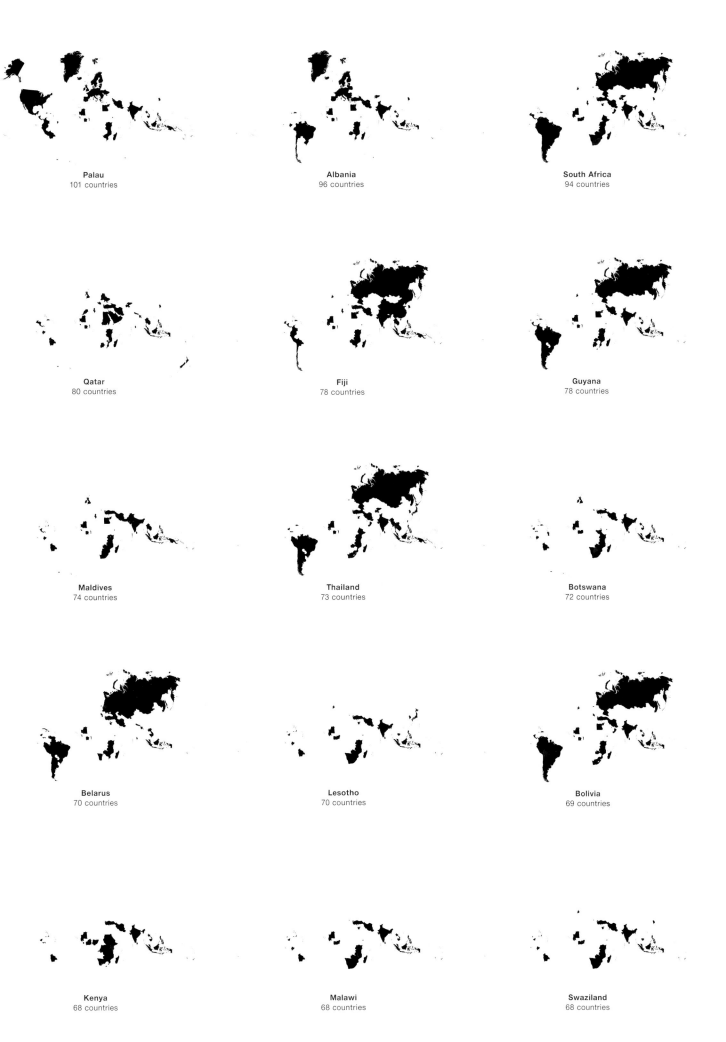

Palau
101 countries

Albania
96 countries

South Africa
94 countries

Qatar
80 countries

Fiji
78 countries

Guyana
78 countries

Maldives
74 countries

Thailand
73 countries

Botswana
72 countries

Belarus
70 countries

Lesotho
70 countries

Bolivia
69 countries

Kenya
68 countries

Malawi
68 countries

Swaziland
68 countries

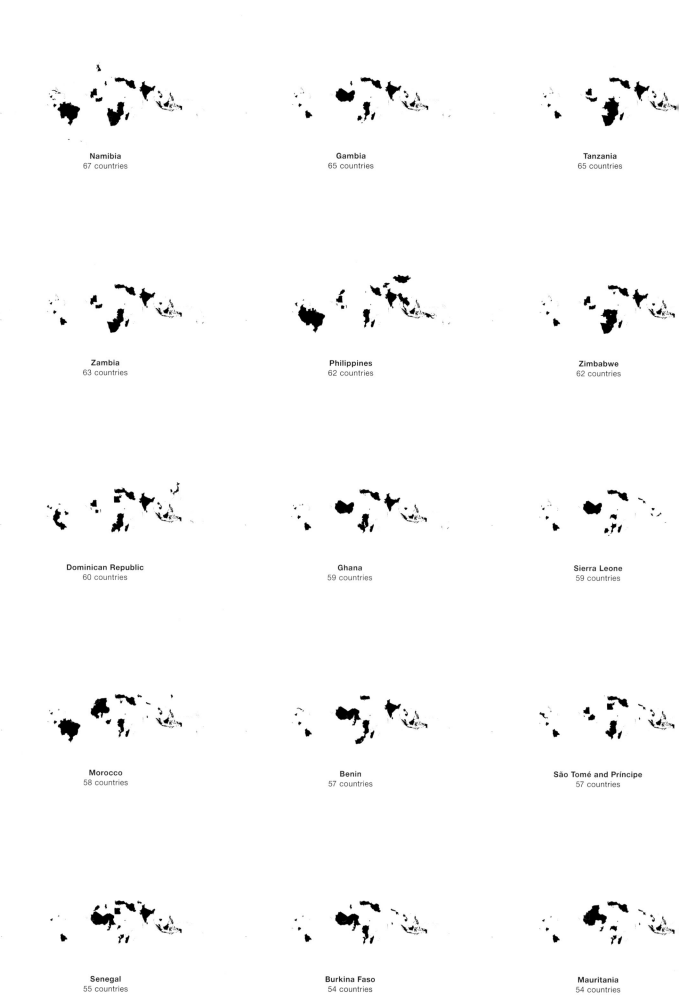

Namibia
67 countries

Gambia
65 countries

Tanzania
65 countries

Zambia
63 countries

Philippines
62 countries

Zimbabwe
62 countries

Dominican Republic
60 countries

Ghana
59 countries

Sierra Leone
59 countries

Morocco
58 countries

Benin
57 countries

São Tomé and Príncipe
57 countries

Senegal
55 countries

Burkina Faso
54 countries

Mauritania
54 countries

Azerbaijan
63 countries

Cape Verde
63 countries

Tunisia
63 countries

Indonesia
61 countries

Uganda
61 countries

Cuba
60 countries

Armenia
58 countries

China
58 countries

Kyrgyzstan
58 countries

Mongolia
56 countries

Côte d'Ivoire
55 countries

Guinea
55 countries

Tajikistan
54 countries

Uzbekistan
54 countries

Haiti
53 countries

Mozambique
53 countries

Rwanda
53 countries

Gabon
52 countries

Egypt
51 countries

Mali
51 countries

Niger
51 countries

Chad
49 countries

Guinea-Bissau
49 countries

Turkmenistan
49 countries

Burundi
47 countries

Cameroon
47 countries

Central African Republic
47 countries

Liberia
46 countries

Congo
45 countries

Djibouti
44 countries

Madagascar
52 countries

Togo
52 countries

Comoros
51 countries

Bhutan
50 countries

India
50 countries

Cambodia
49 countries

Vietnam
49 countries

Algeria
47 countries

Angola
47 countries

Equatorial Guinea
47 countries

Jordan
47 countries

Laos
46 countries

Nigeria
44 countries

Congo (Dem. Rep.)
42 countries

Kosovo
41 countries

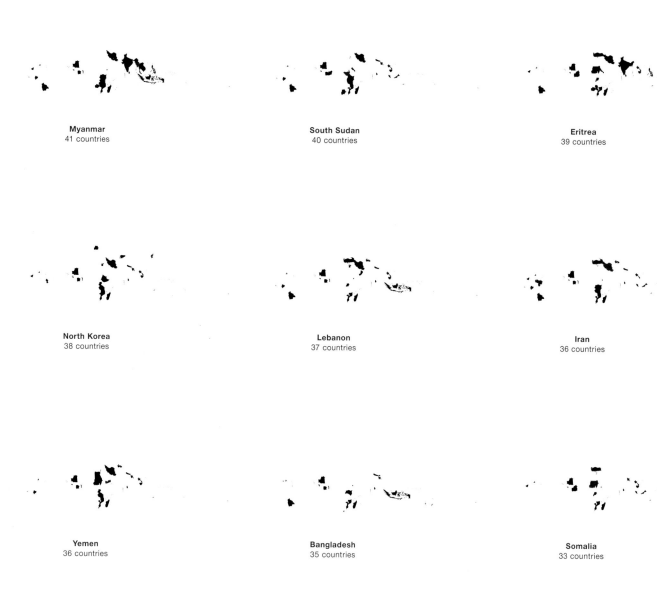

Myanmar
41 countries

South Sudan
40 countries

Eritrea
39 countries

North Korea
38 countries

Lebanon
37 countries

Iran
36 countries

Yemen
36 countries

Bangladesh
35 countries

Somalia
33 countries

Afghanistan
22 countries

Ethiopia
39 countries

Palestinian Territories
39 countries

Libya
38 countries

Nepal
36 countries

Sri Lanka
36 countries

Sudan
36 countries

Syria
30 countries

Iraq
26 countries

Pakistan
25 countries

Germany

Germany
159 countries

Afghanistan

Afghanistan
22 countries

Visa World

Visa-Free World

moa

Guinea-Bissau
Mauritania
Togo
Côte d'Ivoire
Uganda
Maldives
Comoros
Madagascar
Mozambique
Timor-Leste
Micronesia
Tuvalu

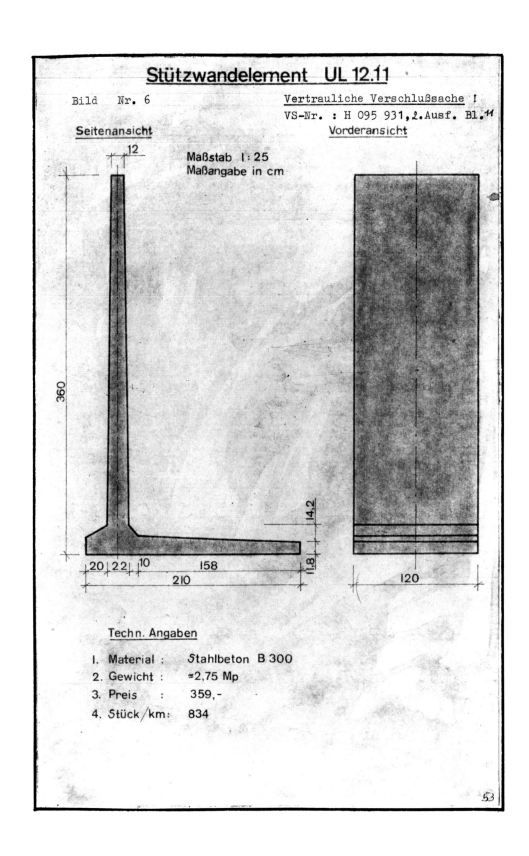

Prefabricated concrete element used for the construction
of the Berlin Wall

Walls & Fences

With the fall of the Iron Curtain in 1989, the world celebrated the end of the Cold War and presumed the end of idiotic wall-building activities which had proven to be ineffective to the utmost. Paradoxically, the fall of the Iron Curtain marked not the end, but the beginning of a global wall-building hype which materialized in the form of about 20 000 km of wire, concrete, steel, sand, stone, and mesh; anything to keep peoples out—or in. Currently there are 66 barriers between nation-states. From this list, 50 barriers with a total length of 18 000 km have been built after the year 2000.

Land survey techniques in the eighteenth century reduced the borderland to a border line, and allowed for the first time the exact demarcation of a territory. What is a seemingly small technical invention that allowed refinement, eventually helped to give birth to the modern nation-state, which uses the map as a political tool to link people to space, hence territory.

Today, border lines are exposed to forces that blur them again. The virtualization of information, money, and goods (movies, text, sound, etc.) continuously undermines state authority. As a countermeasure, walls and fences are erected predominantly to control the flow of what can hardly be virtualized: the flow of people. Yet even Israeli experts, the world's leading wall-construction specialists, admit that physical barriers are most effective as symbols. The symbolism the wall-builders present is worth noticing. Entire states are about to lock themselves in: Turkey is already quite far along and Israel is almost done, while Morocco and Saudi Arabia are on their way. On the other hand, Gaza, the West Bank, and Bangladesh are entirely locked out. The actions taken by EU countries and the United States, which are about to close off an entire continent, are the most shocking, since it's they who promote themselves as the democratic avant-garde of the world. The symbols tell a different story.

For companies, fences, and walls are big business. In 2015, Hungary paid €94 million for its 175 km border fence topped with concertina wire.[1] The Belgian company Betafence[2] built the barrier between Hong Kong and Shenzhen (2007), another between the United Arab Emirates and Oman, and parts of the fence between the United States and Mexico. Yet today's security technology is on the brink of the next revolution. With the application of intrusion-detection sensors, night-vision cameras, and 24/7 drone surveillance, so-called "smart walls"[3] are about to appear, reducing walls and fences to pure icons or warning signs. India operates a so-called "laser wall"[4] on its border to Pakistan in Punjab, and Israel is about to install a "smart wall" by Elbit Systems along its Gaza border. "Smart walls" broaden the border line into a borderland again, since they make it possible to identify potential targets kilometers away, before they get close to the border.

However smart and invisible border-protection technology might become, the symbolism of the wall will always remain. This symbolic value has been greatly emphasized by the president of the United States of America, Donald Trump, who describes his proposed wall between the US and Mexico as "impenetrable, physical, tall, powerful, beautiful."[5] "Impenetrable" aside, these adjectives better suit the description of a monument than an element of border security. Thus the wall, if it is ever built, will be the aesthetic legacy of a dictator.

1 www.reuters.com
2 www.betafence.com
3 timesofindia.indiatimes.com
4 www.ft.com
5 www.washingtonpost.com

Anti-vehicle barriers

Anti-vehicle barriers are the softest version of border demarcation design. In most cases, no foundation is needed and the design is based on natural materials.

The oldest and simplest kind of border barrier is the ditch, the layout of which varies according to the type of vehicle by which the border needs to be protected. According to a US Army manual, a ditch 3.3 meters wide cannot be "bridged" by tanks alone, and a ditch 1.5 meters deep in consolidated, firm soil cannot be crossed by tanks or other vehicles without the aid of bridging or earthmoving equipment.

A more sophisticated barrier design is reinforced earth. For example, on the border between Afghanistan and Pakistan, the HESCO bastion (MIL™) is part of the border design. In the late 1980s, the British company HESCO designed this collapsible wire-mesh container covered with heavy-duty fabric liner. Filled with soil and stacked on top of one another, they can form a massive wall cheaply and quickly.

The varying terrain along the Mexican-United States border demands a variety of border design options. The most challenging surfaces are the ever-changing Algodones Dunes in California. The PV-4 fence is a floating fence that is installed on site by using a forklift on top of sand dunes. The "sand dragon," as it's been dubbed, can be repositioned by machine to the appropriate border line whenever the dunes have shifted.

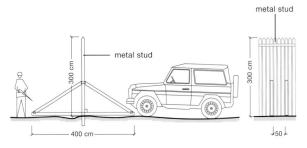

1a USA-Mexico. PV-4 metal "floating fence" designed especially for areas with sand dunes. Anti-smuggling and anti–illegal immigration barrier.

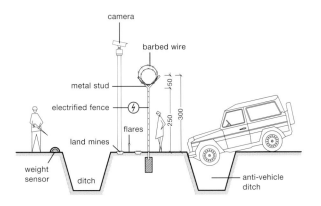

2 Ukraine-Russia. Two anti-vehicle ditches with barbed-wire electrified fence in between. Features land mines, flares, cameras and weight sensor alarms. Conflict-zone barrier aimed to deter terrorism and weapons smuggling.

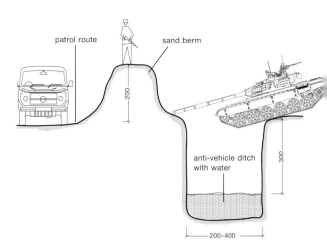

5 Tunisia-Libya. Sand banks and water ditches. Anti-terrorism barrier.

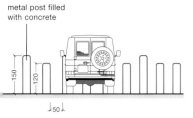

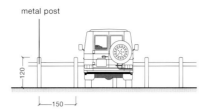

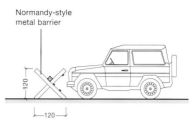

1b USA-Mexico. Metal posts filled with concrete. Anti-smuggling and anti–illegal immigration barrier.

1c USA-Mexico. Metal post barrier. Anti-smuggling and anti–illegal immigration barrier.

1d USA-Mexico. Normandy-style metal barrier. Anti-smuggling and anti–illegal immigration barrier.

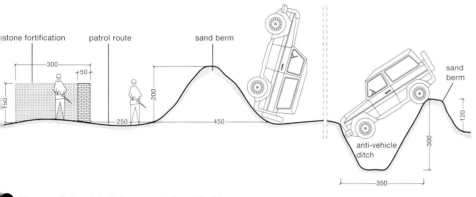

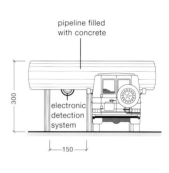

3 Morocco-Sahrawi Arab Democratic Republic (Western Sahara). Sand berms with stone fortifications and ditches. Anti-smuggling and anti–illegal immigration barrier.

4 Saudi Arabia-Yemen. Huge pipelines filled with concrete equipped with an electronic detection system. Anti-infiltration and anti-terrorism barrier.

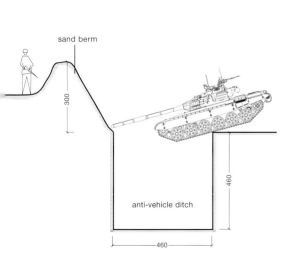

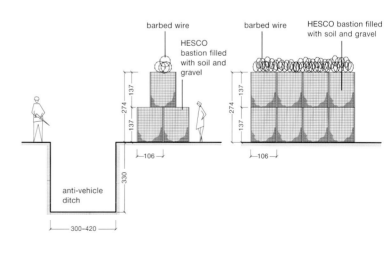

6 Kuwait-Iraq. Anti-vehicle ditch and sand berms. Anti-terrorism barrier.

7 Pakistan-Afghanistan. HESCO bastion prefabricated wall with barbed wire and anti-vehicle ditch. Anti-smuggling and anti–illegal immigration barrier.

Fences

The construction of a wall or fence between two countries is mostly based on fundamental economic and/or political differences. One example of how political changes directly lead to border fencing is the fence between Morocco and the Spanish territories of Ceuta & Melilla. Since Spain joined the European Union in 1989 and the Schengen Treaty came into force in 1995, fences have been erected between Spain and Morocco, between Africa and Europe. Today this system of fences is the most extreme border-protection system of the EU Schengen zone. Adding the surveillance road to the fencing system, the entire structure is about 12 meters wide.

The world's most heavily guarded border is the Demilitarized Zone (DMZ) between North and South Korea, which was created as the result of an agreement between North Korea, China, and the United Nations in 1953. The system of fences is part of the 4 km wide zone, which is practically a no-go area over the length of 250 km, cutting the peninsula in half. The non-interference of humans has resulted in an inadvertent park which is now recognized as one of the world's best-preserved natural habitats in the temperate zone.

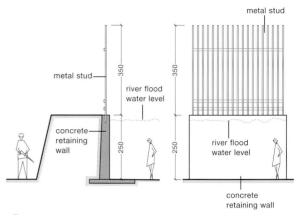

8a USA-Mexico. Metal fence on top of concrete retaining wall. Anti-smuggling and anti–illegal immigration barrier.

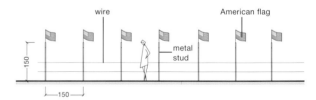

8e USA-Mexico. Wire fence with metal studs and American flags. Anti-smuggling and anti–illegal immigration barrier.

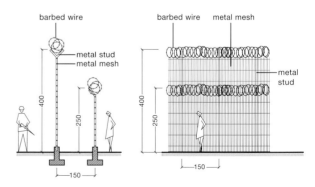

11 UK-France (Great Wall of Calais). Double metal mesh fence fixed on Y-shaped metal studs on one side and vertical metal studs on the other, with barbed wire on top. Anti–illegal immigration barrier.

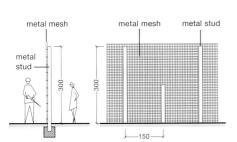

8b USA-Mexico. Metal mesh fence fixed on metal studs. Anti-smuggling and anti–illegal immigration barrier.

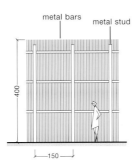

8c USA-Mexico. Metal bar fence fixed on metal studs. Anti-smuggling and anti–illegal immigration barrier.

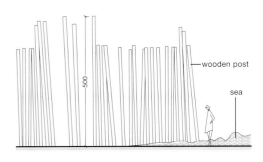

8d USA-Mexico. Wooden pole fence. Anti-smuggling and anti–illegal immigration barrier.

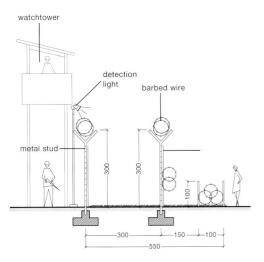

9 USA-Cuba (Guantanamo Bay). Double metal mesh fence fixed on Y-shaped metal studs with barbed wire. The fence is covered with a nontransparent fabric, possibly to eliminate visibility through it. Features watchtowers, security lights, cameras, and gravel surfaces that allow patrols to listen to any intruders. Border security and detention center perimeter security barrier.

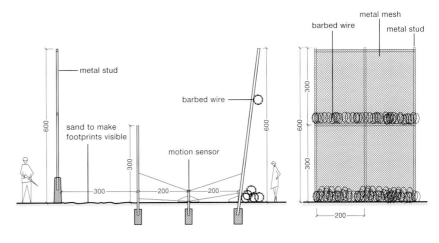

10 Spain-Morocco (Ceuta/Melilla). Triple-layered metal mesh fence fixed on metal studs with barbed wire, motion detectors, and a strip of sand that helps detect intruders by revealing footsteps. Anti–illegal immigration and anti-smuggling barrier.

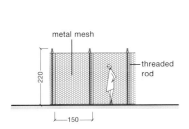

12 Austria-Slovenia. Hexagonal metal mesh fence fixed on steel-threaded rods. Anti–illegal immigration barrier.

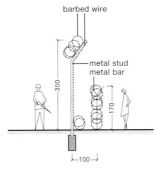

13 Hungary-Serbia. Double metal mesh fence with barbed wire. Anti–illegal immigration barrier.

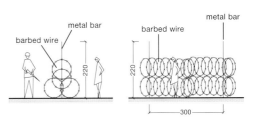

14a Slovenia-Croatia. Barbed wire fixed on metal bars. Anti–illegal immigration barrier.

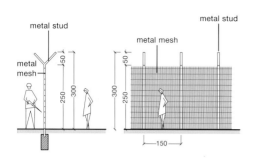

14b Slovenia-Croatia. Metal mesh fence fixed on Y-shaped metal studs. Anti–illegal immigration barrier.

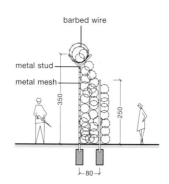

15a Bulgaria-Turkey. Double metal mesh fence fixed on Y-shaped metal studs on one side and vertical metal studs on the other. Barbed wire is placed on top of both fences as well as between them. Anti–illegal immigration barrier.

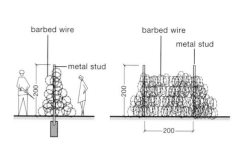

15b Bulgaria-Turkey. Barbed-wire fence fixed on metal studs. Anti–illegal immigration barrier.

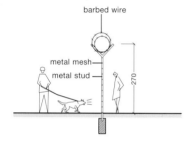

19 Latvia-Russia. Metal mesh fence fixed on Y-shaped metal studs with barbed wire. Anti–illegal immigration barrier.

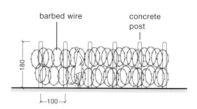

20a Russia-Poland. Barbed-wire fence fixed on concrete posts. Anti–illegal immigration barrier.

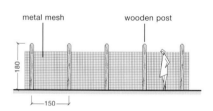

20b Russia-Poland. Barbed-wire fence fixed on wooden posts. Anti–illegal immigration barrier.

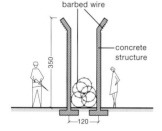

24 Kenya-Somalia. Double metal mesh fence fixed on prefabricated concrete posts with barbed wire in between. Anti-terrorism barrier.

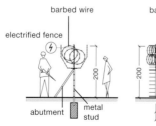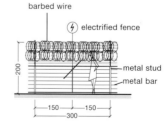

25 Botswana-Zimbabwe. Electrified (turned off) metal mesh fence with barbed wire fixed on metal studs. Anti–illegal immigration and animal control barrier.

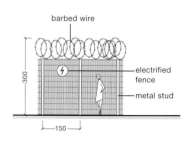

26 South Africa-Zimbabwe. Electrified (35 000-volt) metal mesh fence with barbed wire and patrol route. Anti–illegal immigration and anti-smuggling barrier.

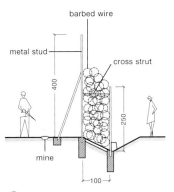

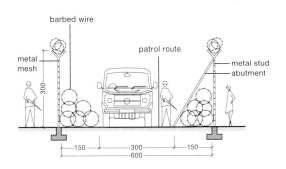

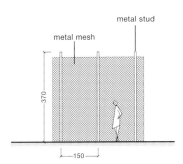

16 Greece-Turkey. Double metal mesh fence with barbed wire fixed on metal studs. Features extensive minefields. Border security and anti–illegal immigration barrier.

17 Macedonia-Greece. Double metal mesh fence fixed on Y-shaped metal studs. Features a patrol route and is heavily protected with barbed wire. Anti–illegal immigration barrier.

18 Norway-Russia. Metal mesh fence fixed on metal studs. Anti–illegal immigration and anti-smuggling barrier.

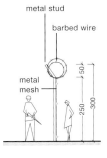
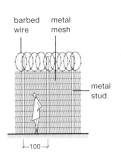

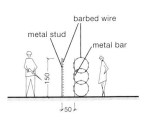

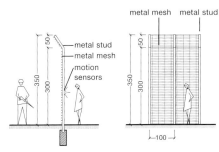

21 Ukraine-Russia. Metal mesh fence with barbed wire on top fixed on metal studs. Conflict zone barrier aimed at deterring terrorism and weapons smuggling.

22 Russia-Georgia (Abkhazia/South Ossetia). Double barbed-wire fence fixed on metal bars and studs. Illegal occupation barrier in violation of human rights.

23 Morocco-Algeria. Metal mesh fence fixed on metal studs. Features motion sensors. Conflict and anti-terrorism barrier.

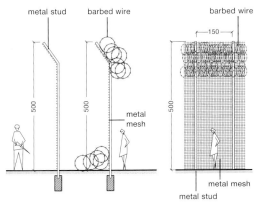

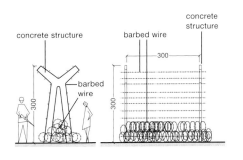

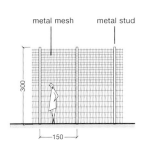

27 Israel-Egypt. Double fence with barbed wire fixed on metal studs. Anti–illegal immigration barrier.

28 Turkey-Syria. Barbed-wire fence fixed on prefabricated concrete posts. Anti–illegal immigration and anti-terrorism barrier.

29 Israel-Jordan. Metal mesh fence fixed on metal studs. Anti-terrorism and anti–illegal immigration barrier.

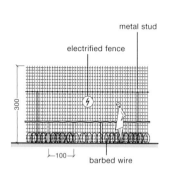

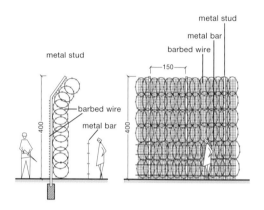

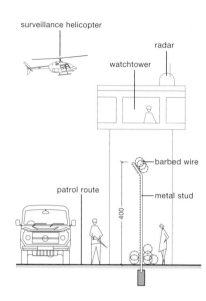

30 Israel-Gaza strip. Electrified metal mesh fence with barbed wire fixed on metal studs. Anti–illegal immigration barrier.

31 Israel-Syria. Metal mesh fence fixed on metal studs with barbed wire. Anti–illegal immigration and anti-terrorism barrier.

32 Jordan-Syria and Iraq. Metal mesh fence fixed on metal studs with barbed wire. The barrier features watchtowers equipped with radar, patrol routes, and helicopter patrols. Anti–illegal immigration and anti-terrorism barrier.

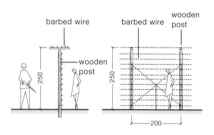

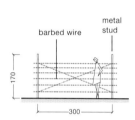

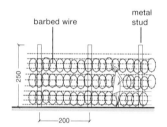

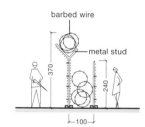

35 Tajikistan-Afghanistan. Barbed-wire fence fixed on T-shaped wooden posts. Anti-smuggling barrier.

36 Kazakhstan-Uzbekistan. Barbed-wire fence fixed on metal studs. Anti-smuggling barrier.

37 Uzbekistan-Kyrgyzstan. Barbed-wire fence fixed on concrete posts. Conflict zone and anti-smuggling barrier.

38 India-Pakistan (Kashmir). Double metal mesh fence fixed on Y-shaped metal studs and vertical metal studs. Disputed territory and anti–illegal immigration barrier.

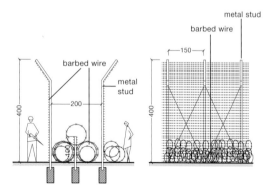

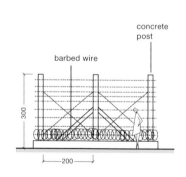

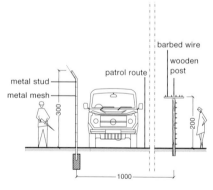

41 India-Bangladesh. Double metal mesh fence fixed on metal studs with barbed wire. Border security and anti–illegal immigration barrier.

42 Myanmar-Bangladesh. Barbed-wire fence fixed on concrete posts. Anti–illegal immigration and anti-smuggling barrier.

43 Russia-Mongolia. Double metal mesh fence fixed on metal studs on one side and T-shaped wooden posts on the other. Anti–illegal immigration barrier.

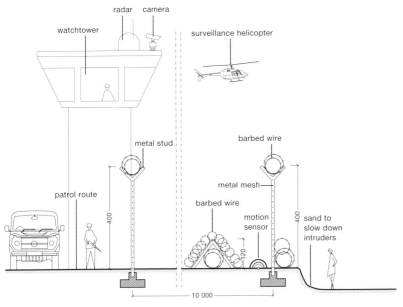

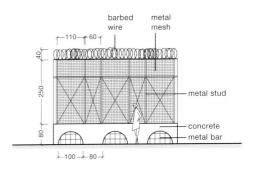

33 Saudi Arabia-Iraq. Double metal mesh fence fixed on Y-shaped metal studs with barbed wire on top. The distance between the two fences is 100 meters. Between the two fences, there is another razor-wire pyramid and underground motion detectors. On the Saudi Arabian side, there are watchtowers equipped with cameras and radar. There are frequent helicopter patrols over the border area. Conflict zone, anti–illegal immigration and anti-terrorism barrier.

34 UAE-Oman. Metal mesh fence with concrete base and barbed wire on top. Anti-smuggling, anti-terrorism and anti–illegal immigration barrier.

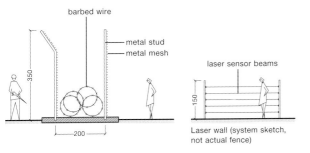

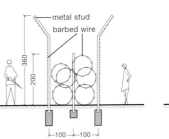

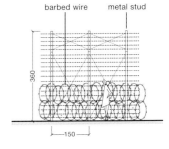

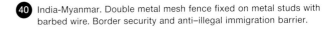

39 India-Pakistan. Double metal mesh fence with barbed wire fixed on metal studs. According to sources, in 2016, India started equipping the barrier with laser-based motion-detection technology. Conflict zone, anti-terrorism and anti–illegal immigration barrier.

40 India-Myanmar. Double metal mesh fence fixed on metal studs with barbed wire. Border security and anti–illegal immigration barrier.

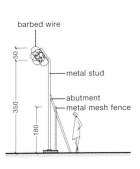

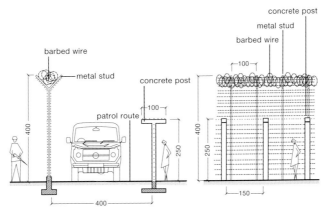

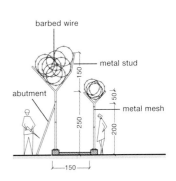

44 China-Hong Kong. Metal mesh fence fixed on metal studs with barbed wire. Anti–illegal immigration barrier.

45 China-North Korea. Double metal mesh fence fixed on Y-shaped metal studs on one side and T-shaped concrete posts on the other, with barbed wire and patrol route. Border security and anti–illegal immigration barrier.

46 Korea (DMZ). Double metal mesh fence with barbed wire fixed on Y-shaped metal studs. Features a patrol route between the two fences. Conflict zone barrier.

Walls

Walls are the longest-lasting and most expensive border barriers, as well as the most symbolic, physically and rhetorically. Walls don't just appear; they generally replace preexisting fences to reinforce a political conflict. It is highly doubtful that walls are more effective than fences at keeping people out. They do, however, signal to outsiders that they are excluded not only from entering but also from seeing the walled territory. In densely populated areas, walls have been preferred to fences since they are more effective at preventing targeted shooting.

Contemporary walls are made of reinforced concrete or steel, as in the case of the Israel–Gaza Strip wall. Most of the reinforced concrete walls are prefabricated T- or L-shaped elements that are linked by a step joint and topped with barbed wire. The most famous prefab concrete wall, the Berlin Wall, known as "UL 12.11," was L-shaped, 3.6 m in height, with a 1.2 m wide base. To link the 2750 kg elements and to make climbing more difficult, the elements were connected by a 4-meter-long asbestos pipe at the top.

The steel wall between Egypt and Gaza is an exception. Built in 2009 by Egypt with the help of the US, this sheet piling system has a visible height of 8 meters while extending 18 meters below the surface. The main reason for choosing this wall design was to disrupt the smuggling business between the two territories via tunnels. Currently Israel is upgrading its barrier to Gaza with a slurry wall that extends tens of meters underground in order to block Palestinians from digging their way into the country and carrying out attacks.

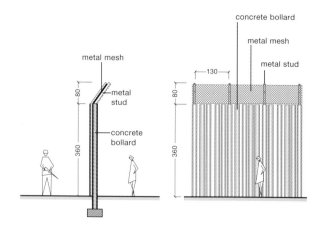

47a USA-Mexico. Concrete bollards with barbed wire on top. Anti-smuggling and anti–illegal immigration barrier.

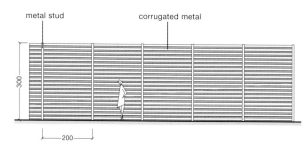

47d USA-Mexico. Horizontally aligned corrugated metal sheet wall. Anti-smuggling and anti–illegal immigration barrier.

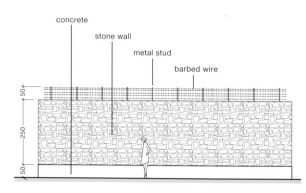

50a Cyprus UN Buffer Zone (Cyprus Green Line). Stone wall with concrete base and barbed wire on top. Demilitarized zone barrier.

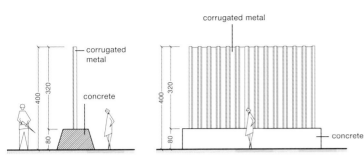

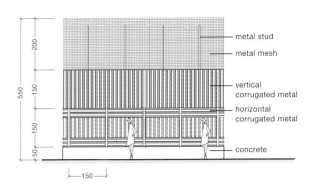

47b USA-Mexico. Concrete base with corrugated metal barrier. Anti-smuggling and anti–illegal immigration barrier.

47c USA-Mexico. Wall barrier constructed using multiple corrugated metal sheets in both vertical and horizontal alignment. Features a metal mesh fence on top. Anti-smuggling and anti–illegal immigration barrier.

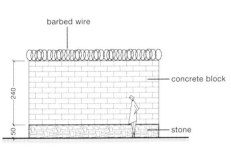

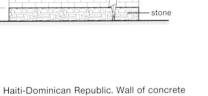

48 Haiti-Dominican Republic. Wall of concrete blocks with stone base and barbed wire on top. Demilitarized zone barrier.

49 UK-France (Great Wall of Calais). Concrete-panel wall with barbed wire. Anti–illegal immigration barrier.

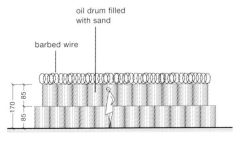

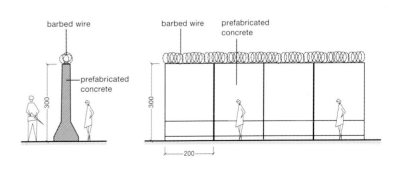

50b Cyprus UN Buffer Zone (Cyprus Green Line). Sand-filled oil drums wall with barbed wire on top. Demilitarized zone barrier.

51a Turkey-Syria. Prefabricated concrete wall with barbed wire on top. Anti–illegal immigration and anti-terrorism barrier.

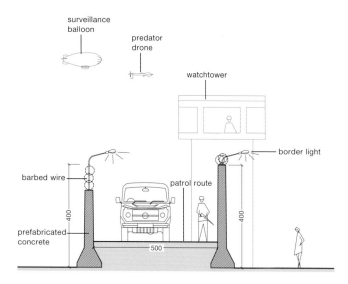

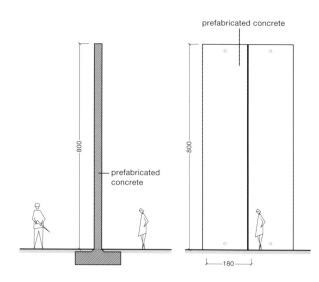

51b Turkey-Syria (proposed). Double prefabricated concrete wall barrier with patrol route between the two walls. Features barbed wire on top, border lights, Predator drones, surveillance balloons and watchtowers. Anti–illegal immigration and anti-terrorism barrier.

52 Israel-Lebanon. Prefabricated concrete wall barrier. Anti-terrorism barrier.

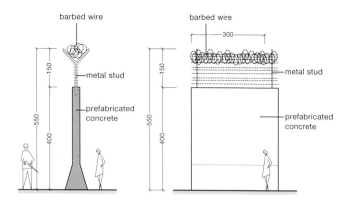

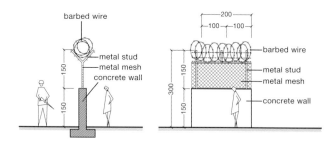

55 Iran-Pakistan. Reinforced concrete barrier with barbed-wire extension. Border barrier and anti–illegal immigration barrier.

56 Malaysia-Thailand. Reinforced concrete wall with metal mesh fence and barbed wire on top. Anti-terrorism barrier.

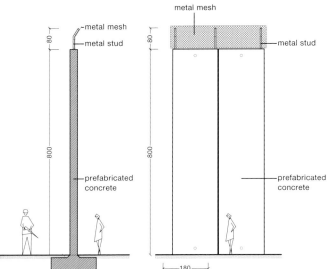

53 Israel-West Bank. Prefabricated concrete wall barrier with metal mesh extension. Anti-terrorism barrier.

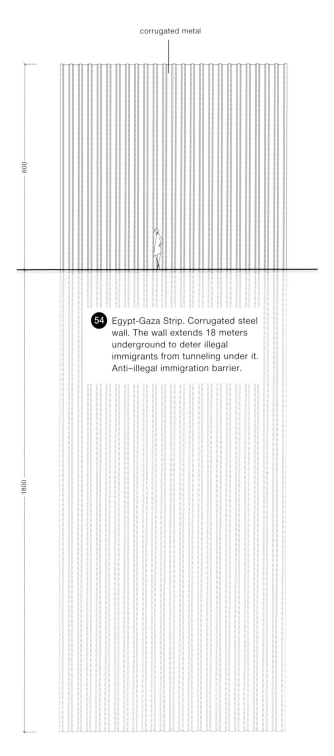

54 Egypt-Gaza Strip. Corrugated steel wall. The wall extends 18 meters underground to deter illegal immigrants from tunneling under it. Anti–illegal immigration barrier.

49

The reasons for building a fence or wall along a border are manifold.

To Thailand and Malaysia, it is all about combating transnational crime and smuggling, which is also the case for most of the walls between Afghanistan and its neighbors as well as those between India and Bangladesh. The barriers built very recently in southeastern Europe are predominantly meant to stop illegal immigration. The fences in eastern and northeastern Europe were erected out of fear that "little green men"– disguised Russian soldiers, wearing unmarked green army uniforms but carrying modern Russian military weapons–could stage a coup similar to the annexation of the Crimea.[1] Barriers in northern Africa and the Middle East are predominantly against radical Islamic groups such as ISIL.

The most discussed of all barriers is the one along the border between the United States and Mexico, whose oldest segment, the "Tortilla Wall," was built in 1994. Due to the very diverse landscape it passes through, its relatively long construction period, and the strong local influence on its materialization, the US-Mexico border barrier is the most diverse of all. According to government reports, there are 567 km of primary fencing, 58 km of secondary fencing, and 481 km of vehicle-barrier fencing between the two countries.[2] This adds up to more than 1100 km of fencing–about one-third the length of the 3201 km border.

The United States is also busy helping to separate nation-states abroad. The fences and barriers along the Jordan-Iraq and Jordan-Syria borders (2008–2014)[3] were financed by the US, as was the wall between Egypt and Gaza (2009).[4] Gaza is the world's most severely fenced-out territory. Its 1.85 million inhabitants, or more accurately prisoners, are 100% cut off from the neighboring states of Egypt and Israel. The West Bank is very close to following this fate.

Its prison guard, Israel, is achieving the same through self-enclosure: since construction of the wall between Israel and the West Bank began in 2000, Israel has fortified about 80% of its land borders. The country is using its walls and fences not only for self-protection, but also for a land grab. In the West Bank, only 15% of the wall follows the Green Line, the demarcation line set out in the 1949 Armistice Agreements between the armies of Israel and those of its neighbors, while 85% of it cuts at times 18 kilometers deep into the West Bank.[5] The International Court of Justice found the barrier to be a violation of international law, and the United Nations General Assembly adopted a resolution that condemned the barrier by a vote of 150–6 with 10 abstentions.[6]

1 www.theatlantic.com
2 www.theguardian.com
3 news.vice.com
4 en.wikipedia.org
5,6 www.un.org

Legend

India–Myanmar   The first mentioned country is the country that builds / builds the barrier

———————— border barrier erected before 2000

━━━━━━━━ border barrier erected after 2000

··············· border barrier under construction

– – – – – – – partial border barrier

Anti-Vehicle Barriers

1. USA–Mexico
2. Ukraine–Russia
3. Morocco–Sahrawi
4. Saudi Arabia–Yemen
5. Tunisia–Libya
6. Kuwait–Iraq
7. Pakistan–Afghanistan

Fence Barriers

8. USA–Mexico
9. USA–Cuba
10. Spain–Morocco (C & M)
11. UK–France (Calais)
12. Austria–Slovenia
13. Hungary–Croatia & Serbia
14. Slovenia–Croatia
15. Bulgaria–Turkey
16. Greece–Turkey
17. Macedonia–Greece

18. Norway–Russia
19. Latvia–Russia
20. Russia–Poland
21. Ukraine–Russia
22. Russia–Georgia (A. & S.O)
23. Morocco–Algeria
24. Kenya–Somalia
25. Botswana–Zimbabwe
26. South Africa–Zimbabwe
27. Israel–Egypt

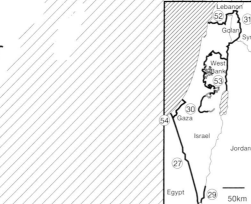

Wall Barriers

47 USA–Mexico
48 Haiti–Dominican Rep.
49 UK–France (Calais)
50 Cyprus UN Buffer Zone
51 Turkey–Syria
52 Israel–Lebanon
53 Israel–West Bank / Jordan
54 Egypt–Gaza Strip
55 Iran–Pakistan
56 Malaysia–Thailand

**Other Barriers
(no visuals available)**

57 Algeria–Libya
58 Estonia–Russia
59 Lithuania–Russia
60 Turkey–Iran, Armenia & Iraq
61 Uzbekistan–Afghanistan
62 India–Bhutan
63 China–Vietnam

28 Turkey–Syria
29 Israel–Jordan
30 Israel–Gaza Strip
31 Israel–Syria
32 Jordan–Syria & Iraq
33 Saudi Arabia–Iraq
34 UAE–Oman
35 Tajikistan–Afghanistan
36 Kazakhstan–Uzbekistan
37 Uzbekistan–Kyrgyzstan

38 India–Pakistan (Kashmir)
39 India–Pakistan
40 India–Myanmar
41 India–Bangladesh
42 Myanmar–Bangladesh
43 Russia–Mongolia
44 Hong Kong–China
45 North Korea–China
46 DMZ Korea

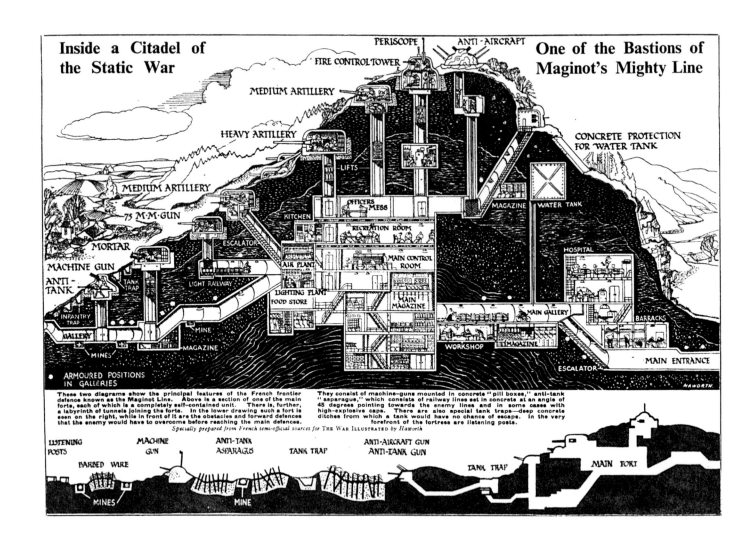

Section through a Maginot Line fort positioned along
the French border to Germany, 1939

Bunker Buster

With the introduction of zeppelins and airplanes, war expanded into the vertical realm. On board these aircraft were bombs meant to destroy the population and cities of an adversary. In response to the means of attack rising into the air, defense went underground. Underground air-raid shelters appeared as a new architectural form in the years prior to World War II. The air-raid shelter made it possible to hide the population beneath concrete ceilings and walls built to be impenetrable to bombs—at least until such time as bunker-busting bombs were developed, specifically for the purpose of killing those hiding underground.

Civilians used to be the ones who hid in bunkers. Increasingly, however, it's contemporary warriors who occupy them, having retreated from the battlefield and traded their guns for computers. To hit a bunker is to win a military jackpot, eliminating drone pilots, cyberwarriors, and military command all at once. These ever deeper and ever more reinforced bunker installations are designed by engineers and architects. Their safety and design are measured against their biggest threat, the bunker busters.

A bunker buster is a bomb that is able to delay its explosion until after it has penetrated layers of earth or concrete with the help of a timer and a propeller. More advanced bombs detect the sound of impact and delay detonation until a specific number of floors in a structure have been penetrated. Although the first earth-penetrating weapons were used in World War II by the British army, the first real bunker busters didn't appear on the scene until the early 1990s. During Operation Desert Storm (1991), there was a sudden need for a deep-penetration bomb. Within just 28 days, the laser "Guided Bomb Unit-28" (GBU-28) was developed. The bomb was nicknamed "The Saddam-izer,"[1] referring to its initial target: Saddam Hussein's bunker.

Despite their high amount of collateral damage, bunker buster usage is in full swing. The West has recently accused Russia and the Syrian government of dropping the Russian-designed bunker buster KAB-1500L-Pr on Aleppo,[2] while the Royal Air Force has been using an Enhanced Paveway III (equivalent to BLU-109 Penetrator) against Islamic State fighters in Iraq.[3] And the collateral damage is about to increase. In November 2015, a test of the B61-12, a nuclear bunker buster, was conducted by the US Army.[4] Being able to penetrate the ground reduces the risk of radioactive fallout, thereby lowering the threshold for its actual usage. The bunker buster is about to open a back door to the use of nuclear warheads by blurring the sharp line between conventional weapons and weapons of mass destruction.

The withdrawal of armies from the planet's surface into the air or the ground literally leaves civilians alone in the middle. The fact that cities are the contemporary battlegrounds seems to prove that the only bulwark that armies hesitate to break through is the human shield.

1 www.fas.org, www.ipfs.io
2 www.defense-aerospace.com
3 www.telegraph.co.uk
4 www.fas.org

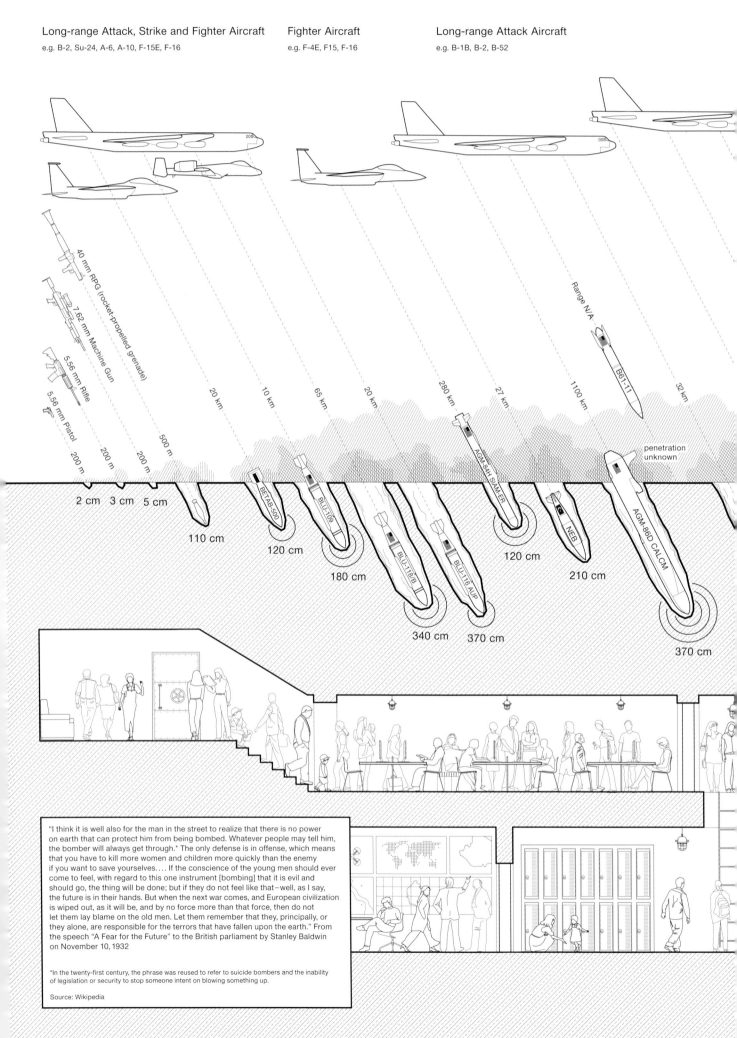

Bunker Buster

Long-range Attack, Strike and Fighter Aircraft
e.g. B-2, Su-24, A-6, A-10, F-15E, F-16

Fighter Aircraft
e.g. F-4E, F15, F-16

Long-range Attack Aircraft
e.g. B-1B, B-2, B-52

40 mm RPG (rocket-propelled grenade)

7.62 mm Machine Gun

5.56 mm Rifle

5.56 mm Pistol

Range N/A

B61-11

20 km

10 km

65 km

20 km

280 km

27 km

1100 km

32 km

500 m

200 m

200 m

200 m

penetration unknown

2 cm   3 cm   5 cm

BETAB-500

BLU-109

AGM-84H SLAM-ER

NEB

AGM-86D CALCM

BLU-118/B

BLU-116 AUP

110 cm

120 cm

180 cm

120 cm

210 cm

340 cm

370 cm

370 cm

"I think it is well also for the man in the street to realize that there is no power on earth that can protect him from being bombed. Whatever people may tell him, the bomber will always get through.* The only defense is in offense, which means that you have to kill more women and children more quickly than the enemy if you want to save yourselves.... If the conscience of the young men should ever come to feel, with regard to this one instrument [bombing] that it is evil and should go, the thing will be done; but if they do not feel like that—well, as I say, the future is in their hands. But when the next war comes, and European civilization is wiped out, as it will be, and by no force more than that force, then do not let them lay blame on the old men. Let them remember that they, principally, or they alone, are responsible for the terrors that have fallen upon the earth." From the speech "A Fear for the Future" to the British parliament by Stanley Baldwin on November 10, 1932

*In the twenty-first century, the phrase was reused to refer to suicide bombers and the inability of legislation or security to stop someone intent on blowing something up.

Source: Wikipedia

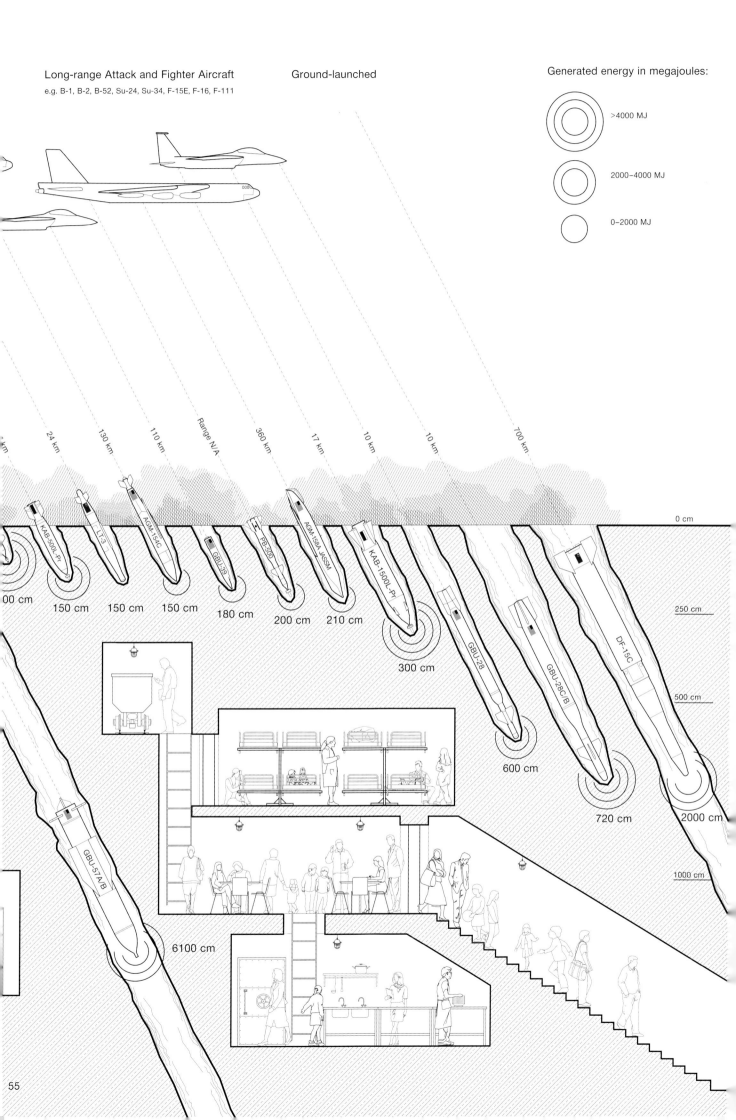

Long-range Attack and Fighter Aircraft
e.g. B-1, B-2, B-52, Su-24, Su-34, F-15E, F-16, F-111

Ground-launched

Generated energy in megajoules:

>4000 MJ

2000–4000 MJ

0–2000 MJ

24 km

130 km

110 km

Range N/A

360 km

17 km

10 km

10 km

700 km

0 cm

KAB-500L-Pr

LT-3

AGM-154C

GBU-39

PB500U

AGM-158A JASSM

KAB-1500L-Pr

GBU-28

GBU-28C/B

DF-15C

00 cm

150 cm

150 cm

150 cm

180 cm

200 cm

210 cm

250 cm

300 cm

500 cm

600 cm

720 cm

2000 cm

GBU-57A/B

1000 cm

6100 cm

Terrorist Groups

Currently, more than 180 designated terrorist organizations exist around the world.[1] Unlike criminal organizations such as the Mafia, whose main objective is economic profit, terrorist organizations target the power monopoly of nation-states. Flags, coats of arms, and sometimes even an anthem are essential means of expressing this opposition and of communicating the way in which it is to be carried out.

Flags of terrorist organizations are blunt and iconographic, loaded with historical and cultural meaning. A flag is in its essence the visualized battle cry of a movement. It is meant to unite followers and scare opponents. The ISIL flag, for example, is black because this is the Sunni color as opposed to green, which has been used predominantly by Shiites since the twelfth century. With an Arabic inscription, the ISIL flag clearly addresses a very specific group of readers who understand its message: "There is no god but Allah," a declaration of faith used across Islam and known as the shahada. Underneath in a white circle, which is meant to resemble the Prophet's seal, "Muhammad is the messenger of God" is written.

In the new millennium, black has become the prevailing color of terror. Use of the communist red, sometimes in combination with the hammer and sickle, is fading. Since the end of the Cold War, belief in the communist ideal has waned, and terrorist organizations have had to gather around other ideologies. Religion came in handy because it comprises large groups and is highly charged with emotion and resentment against members of other religions. Add to this mixture a common threat or enemy, and the perfect ingredients for founding a terrorist organization are assembled.

An essential tool for a political movement is propaganda. Connecting half of the world's population, the Internet is a fantastic instrument for a global movement such as the terrorist group ISIL. Similar to the case with tech start-ups, nobody knows how small an organization's human resources are, but its reach and impact are able to change the way the world is thinking. Just as Facebook's 20 658 employees[2] influence the lives of two billion people, ISIL's 10 000 to 200 000 members—nobody knows exactly how many there are—communicate fear to the entire world. ISIL is using almost every communications tool the Internet provides, from Twitter and Facebook to YouTube, LiveLeak, and radio stations. Following a terror attack, confirmation of ISIL involvement is eagerly awaited by the mainstream press around the world. This amplifies the terrorists' message by giving it the same amount of attention as the release of a new smartphone.

One cornerstone of terrorist propaganda has always been the proclamation of a common heroic goal. This goal must be so sublime that it is worth dying for. World domination by the just and righteous is a goal that has often been professed by major terrorist groups, heralding the promise: "If we win, the whole world will be like us." Though terrorism may be the most extreme and violent version of political opposition, it itself does not allow any disagreement. Radical terrorist groups follow a political agenda based on the staunch belief that their group is good and all others are bad. In the end, all terrorist groups are faced with the same dilemma: how to explain convincingly that it is righteous to kill.

Addressing all Muslims enables ISIL to go beyond the idea of territory and consequently beyond the idea of the nation-state. The legal concept of ISIL

1 en.wikipedia.org
Designated as terrorist groups by 21 nation-states, plus the EU and the United Nations. The process of designating terrorist organizations is not standardized and varies considerably among these countries.
2 newsroom.fb.com/company-info

The Seal of Muhammad as used in the flag of the Islamic State of Iraq and the Levant

mimics the laws of religions and therefore refers to the "personality of law." No matter the territory, even if it is the Moon, the law is always within the person. The results are a society heavily segregated in men, women, believers and nonbelievers, each with a different set of rules. While the West is struggling with the forces released by the World Wide Web which undermine nation-states and the territorial nature of their laws, Islamist terrorist groups are targeting these nation-states with the outdated concept of personal law. Both threats are real and dangerous. While the virtual world still keeps the promise of the unknown, religion has already proven itself incapable of leading the way to a peaceful future.

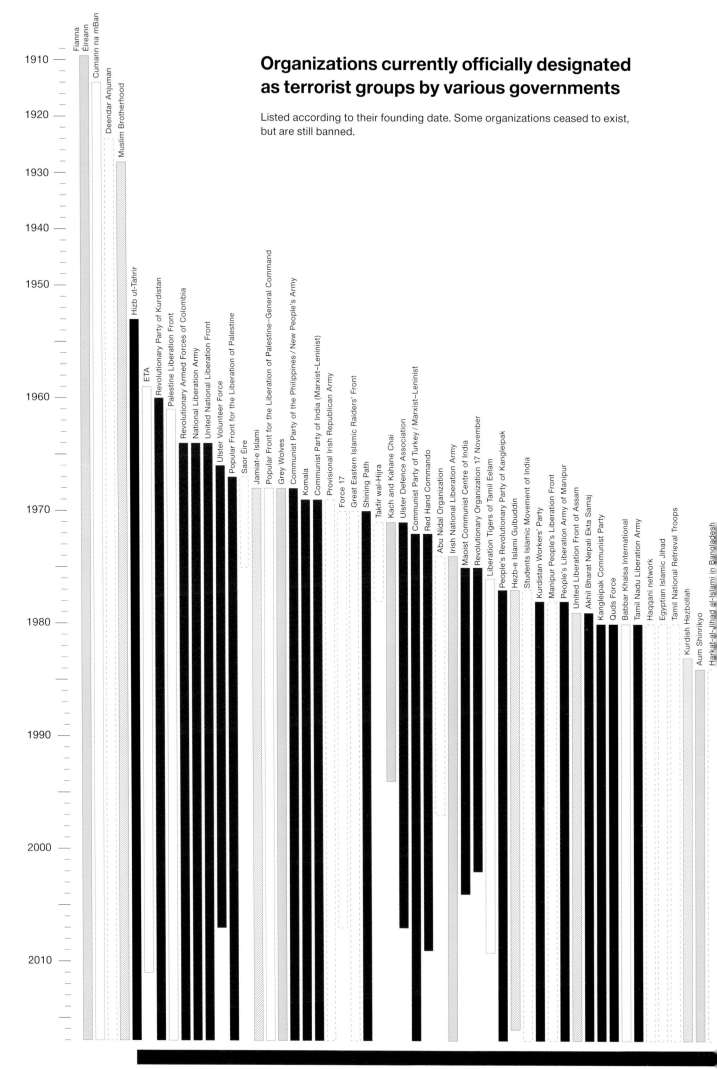

Organizations currently officially designated as terrorist groups by various governments

Listed according to their founding date. Some organizations ceased to exist, but are still banned.

1910
1920
1930
1940
1950
1960
1970
1980
1990
2000
2010

Fianna Éireann
Cumann na mBan
Deendar Anjuman
Muslim Brotherhood
Hizb ut-Tahrir
ETA
Revolutionary Party of Kurdistan
Palestine Liberation Front
Revolutionary Armed Forces of Colombia
National Liberation Army
United National Liberation Front
Ulster Volunteer Force
Popular Front for the Liberation of Palestine
Saor Éire
Jamiat-e Islami
Popular Front for the Liberation of Palestine–General Command
Grey Wolves
Communist Party of the Philippines / New People's Army
Komala
Communist Party of India (Marxist–Leninist)
Provisional Irish Republican Army
Force 17
Great Eastern Islamic Raiders' Front
Shining Path
Takfir wal-Hijra
Kach and Kahane Chai
Ulster Defence Association
Communist Party of Turkey / Marxist–Leninist
Red Hand Commando
Abu Nidal Organization
Irish National Liberation Army
Maoist Communist Centre of India
Revolutionary Organization 17 November
Liberation Tigers of Tamil Eelam
People's Revolutionary Party of Kangleipak
Hezb-e Islami Gulbuddin
Students Islamic Movement of India
Kurdistan Workers' Party
Manipur People's Liberation Front
People's Liberation Army of Manipur
United Liberation Front of Assam
Akhil Bharat Nepali Ekta Samaj
Kangleipak Communist Party
Quds Force
Babbar Khalsa International
Tamil Nadu Liberation Army
Haqqani network
Egyptian Islamic Jihad
Tamil National Retrieval Troops
Kurdish Hezbollah
Aum Shinrikyo
Harkat-al-Jihad al-Islami in Bangladesh

58

red | before 1989

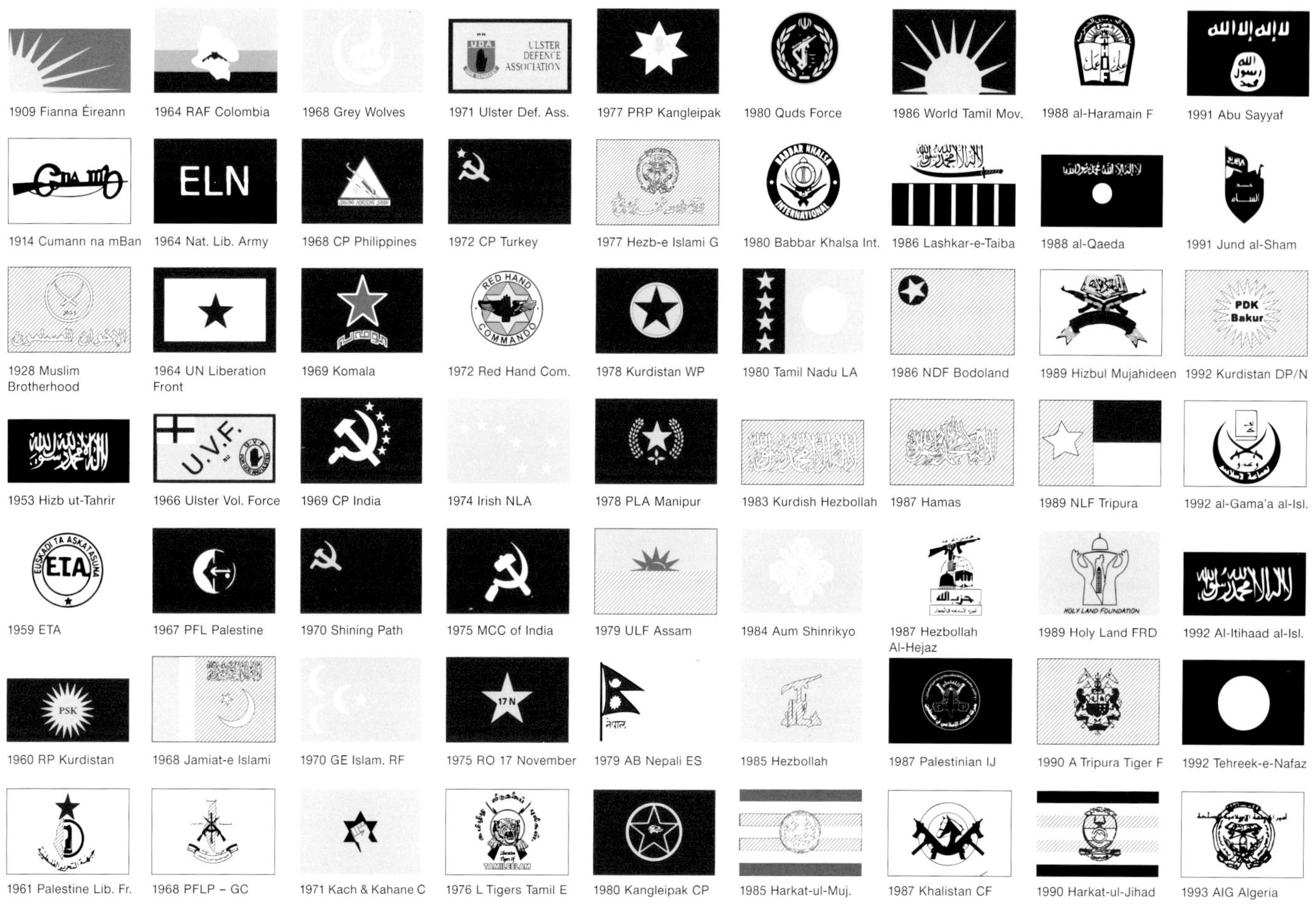

1909 Fianna Éireann · 1964 RAF Colombia · 1968 Grey Wolves · 1971 Ulster Def. Ass. · 1977 PRP Kangleipak · 1980 Quds Force · 1986 World Tamil Mov. · 1988 al-Haramain F · 1991 Abu Sayyaf

1914 Cumann na mBan · 1964 Nat. Lib. Army · 1968 CP Philippines · 1972 CP Turkey · 1977 Hezb-e Islami G · 1980 Babbar Khalsa Int. · 1986 Lashkar-e-Taiba · 1988 al-Qaeda · 1991 Jund al-Sham

1928 Muslim Brotherhood · 1964 UN Liberation Front · 1969 Komala · 1972 Red Hand Com. · 1978 Kurdistan WP · 1980 Tamil Nadu LA · 1986 NDF Bodoland · 1989 Hizbul Mujahideen · 1992 Kurdistan DP/N

1953 Hizb ut-Tahrir · 1966 Ulster Vol. Force · 1969 CP India · 1974 Irish NLA · 1978 PLA Manipur · 1983 Kurdish Hezbollah · 1987 Hamas · 1989 NLF Tripura · 1992 al-Gama'a al-Isl.

1959 ETA · 1967 PFL Palestine · 1970 Shining Path · 1975 MCC of India · 1979 ULF Assam · 1984 Aum Shinrikyo · 1987 Hezbollah Al-Hejaz · 1989 Holy Land FRD · 1992 Al-Itihaad al-Isl.

1960 RP Kurdistan · 1968 Jamiat-e Islami · 1970 GE Islam. RF · 1975 RO 17 November · 1979 AB Nepali ES · 1985 Hezbollah · 1987 Palestinian IJ · 1990 A Tripura Tiger F · 1992 Tehreek-e-Nafaz

1961 Palestine Lib. Fr. · 1968 PFLP – GC · 1971 Kach & Kahane C · 1976 L Tigers Tamil E · 1980 Kangleipak CP · 1985 Harkat-ul-Muj. · 1987 Khalistan CF · 1990 Harkat-ul-Jihad · 1993 AIG Algeria

Harkat-ul-Mujahideen
World Tamil Movement
Lashkar-e-Taiba
National Democratic Front of Bodoland
Irish People's Liberation Organisation
Jamaat al Dawa al Quran
Hamas
Hezbollah Al-Hejaz
Palestinian Islamic Jihad
Khalistan Commando Force
al-Haramain Foundation
al-Qaeda
Khalistan Zindabad Force
Al-Umar-Mujahideen
Hizbul Mujahideen
National Liberation Front of Tripura
Holy Land Foundation for Relief and Development
All Tripura Tiger Force
Harkat-ul-Jihad al-Islami
Committee for Charity and Solidarity with Palestine
Moroccan Islamic Combatant Group
Abu Sayyaf
Jund al-Sham
Kurdistan Democratic Party/North
al-Gama'a al-Islamiyya / al-Jama'a al-Islamiyya
Al-Itihaad al-Islamiya
Tehreek-e-Nafaz-e-Shariat-e-Mohammadi
Society of the Revival of Islamic Heritage
Armed Islamic Group of Algeria
Dukhtaran-e-Millat
Izz ad-Din al-Qassam Brigades
Aden-Abyan Islamic Army
Jamiat ul-Ansar
Jemaah Islamiyah
Vanguards of Conquest
Revolutionary People's Liberation Party-Front
Marxist–Leninist Communist Party
Palestinian Relief Development Fund–Interpal
Taliban
Continuity Irish Republican Army
Houthis
Osbat al-Ansar
Kanglei Yawol Kanna Lup
Sipah-e-Sahaba Pakistan
Libyan Islamic Fighting Group
Tanzim
East Turkestan Information Center
Lashkar-e-Jhangvi
Loyalist Volunteer Force
East Turkestan Islamic Party
al-Aqsa Foundation
United Self-Defense Forces of Colombia
Stichting Al Aqsa
Real Irish Republican Army
Islamic Movement of Uzbekistan
Red Hand Defenders
Al-Badr
Jamaat-ul-Mujahideen Bangladesh
Orange Volunteers
Ansar al-Sharia (Tunisia)

al-Aqsa Martyrs' Brigades
East Turkestan Liberation Organization
Jaish-e-Mohammed
Khuddam ul-Islam / Jaish-e-Mohammed
Ansar al-Islam
Ergenekon
Islamic Jihad Union
Boko Haram
Hofstad Network
Harakat-Ul-Mujahideen/Alami
Kata'ib Hezbollah
Revolutionary Struggle
Jundallah
Jamaat Ansar al-Sunna
Jamiat al-Islah al-Idzhtimai
Balochistan Liberation Army
Party of Free Life of Kurdistan
Kurdistan Freedom Falcons
World Uygur Youth Congress
Al Ghurabaa
The Saved Sect
Army of the Men of the Naqshbandi Order
Army of Islam
Al-Shabaab
Caucasus Emirate
al-Qaeda in the Islamic Maghreb
Tehrik-i-Taliban Pakistan
Indian Mujahideen
Conspiracy of Fire Nuclei
Jamaah Ansharut Tauhid
Abdullah Azzam Brigades
al-Qaeda in the Arabian Peninsula
Mujahidin Indonesia Timur
Movement for Oneness and Jihad in West Africa
Ansaru
Ansar Bait al-Maqdis
Yarmouk Martyrs Brigade
Jaish al-Muhajireen wal-Ansar
Ansar Dine
Mujahideen Shura Council in the Environs of Jerusalem
Ansar al-Sharia (Libya)
Al-Nusra Front / Jabhat Fateh al-Sham
Al-Mourabitoun
Ajnad Misr
al-Qaeda in the Indian Subcontinent
Lugansk People's Republic
Donetsk People's Republic
Islamic State of Iraq and the Levant–Yemen Province
Islamic State of Iraq and the Levant–Libya Province
Harakat Sham al-Islam
Jund al-Aqsa
Jund al-Khilafah
Jamaat-ul-Ahrar
Islamic State of Iraq and the Levant–Caucasus Province
Islamic State of Iraq and the Levant–Khorasan Province

green | 1989–2001

black | after 2001

1993 Dukhtaran-e-Millat

1995 Libyan Isl. FG

1998 Red Hand Def.

2002 Islamic Jihad Un.

2004 PFL Kurdistan

2007 al-Qaeda IM

2011 MO Jihad WA

2012 A al-Sharia (Lib.)

2014 Donetsk PR

1993 al-Qassam Brig.

1996 Lashkar-e-Jhangvi

1998 Al-Badr

2002 Boko Haram

2004 Kurd. FF

2007 T.-i-Taliban Pak.

2011 A Bait al-Maqdis

2012 Al-Nusra Front

2014 ISIL Yemen

1994 RPL Party–Front

1996 Loy. Vol. Force

2000 A al-Sharia (Tun.)

2003 Kata'ib Hezbollah

2004 W Uygur YC

2008 C Fire Nuclei

2012 Ansaru

2013 ISIL

2014 ISIL Libya

1994 Marx.–Leninist CP

1997 E Turkestan IP

2000 al-Aqsa MB

2003 Rev. Struggle

2006 AM Naqshbandi

2008 JA Tauhid

2012 Yarmouk Martyrs B

2013 Al-Mourabitoun

2014 Harakat Sham

1994 PRDF – Interpal

1997 al-Aqsa Found.

2000 E Turkestan LO

2003 Jundallah

2006 Army of Islam

2009 Abd Azzam B

2012 Jaish al-Muhajireen

2013 Ajnad Misr

2014 Jund al-Aqsa

1994 Taliban

1997 USDF Colombia

2000 Jaish-e-Moh.

2003 JA al-Sunna

2006 Al-Shabaab

2009 al-Qaeda AP

2012 Ansar Dine

2014 al-Qaeda IS

2015 ISIL Caucasus

1995 SSP

1998 Isl. M Uzbekistan

2001 Ansar al-Islam

2004 Balochistan LA

2007 Caucasus Emirate

2010 Mujah. Ind. Timur

2012 MSCE Jerusalem

2014 Lugansk PR

2015 ISIL Khorasan

1993 Dukhtaran-e-Millat

1995 Libyan Isl. FG

1998 Red Hand Def.

2002 Islamic Jihad Un.

2004 PFL Kurdistan

2007 al-Qaeda IM

2011 MO Jihad WA

2012 A al-Sharia (Lib.)

2014 Donetsk PR

1993 al-Qassam Brig.

1996 Lashkar-e-Jhangvi

1998 Al-Badr

2002 Boko Haram

2004 Kurd. FF

2007 T.-i-Taliban Pak.

2011 A Bait al-Maqdis

2012 Al-Nusra Front

2014 ISIL Yemen

1994 RPL Party–Front

1996 Loy. Vol. Force

2000 A al-Sharia (Tun.)

2003 Kata'ib Hezbollah

2004 W Uygur YC

2008 C Fire Nuclei

2012 Ansaru

2013 ISIL

2014 ISIL Libya

1994 Marx.–Leninist CP

1997 E Turkestan IP

2000 al-Aqsa MB

2003 Rev. Struggle

2006 AM Naqshbandi

2008 JA Tauhid

2012 Yarmouk Martyrs B

2013 Al-Mourabitoun

2014 Harakat Sham

1994 PRDF – Interpal

1997 al-Aqsa Found.

2000 E Turkestan LO

2003 Jundallah

2006 Army of Islam

2009 Abd Azzam B

2012 Jaish al-Muhajireen

2013 Ajnad Misr

2014 Jund al-Aqsa

1994 Taliban

1997 USDF Colombia

2000 Jaish-e-Moh.

2003 JA al-Sunna

2006 Al-Shabaab

2009 al-Qaeda AP

2012 Ansar Dine

2014 al-Qaeda IS

2015 ISIL Caucasus

1995 SSP

1998 Isl. M Uzbekistan

2001 Ansar al-Islam

2004 Balochistan LA

2007 Caucasus Emirate

2010 Mujah. Ind. Timur

2012 MSCE Jerusalem

2014 Lugansk PR

2015 ISIL Khorasan

Terrorist Groups

1909 Fianna Éireann	1964 RAF Colombia	1968 Grey Wolves	1971 Ulster Def. Ass.	1977 PRP Kangleipak	1980 Quds Force	1986 World Tamil Mov.	1988 al-Haramain F	1991 Abu Sayyaf
1914 Cumann na mBan	1964 Nat. Lib. Army	1968 CP Philippines	1972 CP Turkey	1977 Hezb-e Islami G	1980 Babbar Khalsa Int.	1986 Lashkar-e-Taiba	1988 al-Qaeda	1991 Jund al-Sham
1928 Muslim Brotherhood	1964 UN Liberation Front	1969 Komala	1972 Red Hand Com.	1978 Kurdistan WP	1980 Tamil Nadu LA	1986 NDF Bodoland	1989 Hizbul Mujahideen	1992 Kurdistan DP/N
1953 Hizb ut-Tahrir	1966 Ulster Vol. Force	1969 CP India	1974 Irish NLA	1978 PLA Manipur	1983 Kurdish Hezbollah	1987 Hamas	1989 NLF Tripura	1992 al-Gama'a al-Isl.
1959 ETA	1967 PFL Palestine	1970 Shining Path	1975 MCC of India	1979 ULF Assam	1984 Aum Shinrikyo	1987 Hezbollah Al-Hejaz	1989 Holy Land FRD	1992 Al-Itihaad al-Isl.
1960 RP Kurdistan	1968 Jamiat-e Islami	1970 GE Islam. RF	1975 RO 17 November	1979 AB Nepali ES	1985 Hezbollah	1987 Palestinian IJ	1990 A Tripura Tiger F	1992 Tehreek-e-Nafaz
1961 Palestine Lib. Fr.	1968 PFLP – GC	1971 Kach & Kahane C	1976 L Tigers Tamil E	1980 Kangleipak CP	1985 Harkat-ul-Muj.	1987 Khalistan CF	1990 Harkat-ul-Jihad	1993 AIG Algeria

1909 Fianna Éireann	1964 RAF Colombia	1968 Grey Wolves	1971 Ulster Def. Ass.	1977 PRP Kangleipak	1980 Quds Force	1986 World Tamil Mov.	1988 al-Haramain F	1991 Abu Sayyaf
1914 Cumann na mBan	1964 Nat. Lib. Army	1968 CP Philippines	1972 CP Turkey	1977 Hezb-e Islami G	1980 Babbar Khalsa Int.	1986 Lashkar-e-Taiba	1988 al-Qaeda	1991 Jund al-Sham
1928 Muslim Brotherhood	1964 UN Liberation Front	1969 Komala	1972 Red Hand Com.	1978 Kurdistan WP	1980 Tamil Nadu LA	1986 NDF Bodoland	1989 Hizbul Mujahideen	1992 Kurdistan DP/N
1953 Hizb ut-Tahrir	1966 Ulster Vol. Force	1969 CP India	1974 Irish NLA	1978 PLA Manipur	1983 Kurdish Hezbollah	1987 Hamas	1989 NLF Tripura	1992 al-Gama'a al-Isl.
1959 ETA	1967 PFL Palestine	1970 Shining Path	1975 MCC of India	1979 ULF Assam	1984 Aum Shinrikyo	1987 Hezbollah Al-Hejaz	1989 Holy Land FRD	1992 Al-Itihaad al-Isl.
1960 RP Kurdistan	1968 Jamiat-e Islami	1970 GE Islam. RF	1975 RO 17 November	1979 AB Nepali ES	1985 Hezbollah	1987 Palestinian IJ	1990 A Tripura Tiger F	1992 Tehreek-e-Nafaz
1961 Palestine Lib. Fr.	1968 PFLP – GC	1971 Kach & Kahane C	1976 L Tigers Tamil E	1980 Kangleipak CP	1985 Harkat-ul-Muj.	1987 Khalistan CF	1990 Harkat-ul-Jihad	1993 AIG Algeria

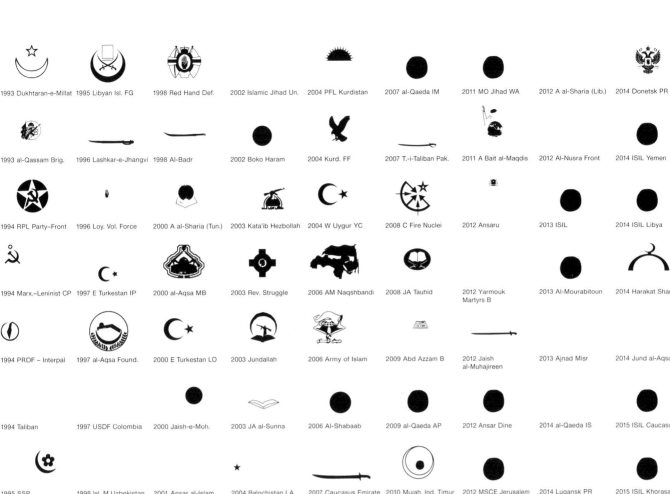

1993 Dukhtaran-e-Millat | 1995 Libyan Isl. FG | 1998 Red Hand Def. | 2002 Islamic Jihad Un. | 2004 PFL Kurdistan | 2007 al-Qaeda IM | 2011 MO Jihad WA | 2012 A al-Sharia (Lib.) | 2014 Donetsk PR

1993 al-Qassam Brig. | 1996 Lashkar-e-Jhangvi | 1998 Al-Badr | 2002 Boko Haram | 2004 Kurd. FF | 2007 T.-i-Taliban Pak. | 2011 A Bait al-Maqdis | 2012 Al-Nusra Front | 2014 ISIL Yemen

1994 RPL Party–Front | 1996 Loy. Vol. Force | 2000 A al-Sharia (Tun.) | 2003 Kata'ib Hezbollah | 2004 W Uygur YC | 2008 C Fire Nuclei | 2012 Ansaru | 2013 ISIL | 2014 ISIL Libya

1994 Marx.–Leninist CP | 1997 E Turkestan IP | 2000 al-Aqsa MB | 2003 Rev. Struggle | 2006 AM Naqshbandi | 2008 JA Tauhid | 2012 Yarmouk Martyrs B | 2013 Al-Mourabitoun | 2014 Harakat Sham

1994 PRDF – Interpal | 1997 al-Aqsa Found. | 2000 E Turkestan LO | 2003 Jundallah | 2006 Army of Islam | 2009 Abd Azzam B | 2012 Jaish al-Muhajireen | 2013 Ajnad Misr | 2014 Jund al-Aqsa

1994 Taliban | 1997 USDF Colombia | 2000 Jaish-e-Moh. | 2003 JA al-Sunna | 2006 Al-Shabaab | 2009 al-Qaeda AP | 2012 Ansar Dine | 2014 al-Qaeda IS | 2015 ISIL Caucasus

1995 SSP | 1998 Isl. M Uzbekistan | 2001 Ansar al-Islam | 2004 Balochistan LA | 2007 Caucasus Emirate | 2010 Mujah. Ind. Timur | 2012 MSCE Jerusalem | 2014 Lugansk PR | 2015 ISIL Khorasan

1993 Dukhtaran-e-Millat | 1995 Libyan Isl. FG | 1998 Red Hand Def. | 2002 Islamic Jihad Un. | 2004 PFL Kurdistan | 2007 al-Qaeda IM | 2011 MO Jihad WA | 2012 A al-Sharia (Lib.) | 2014 Donetsk PR

1993 al-Qassam Brig. | 1996 Lashkar-e-Jhangvi | 1998 Al-Badr | 2002 Boko Haram | 2004 Kurd. FF | 2007 T.-i-Taliban Pak. | 2011 A Bait al-Maqdis | 2012 Al-Nusra Front | 2014 ISIL Yemen

1994 RPL Party–Front | 1996 Loy. Vol. Force | 2000 A al-Sharia (Tun.) | 2003 Kata'ib Hezbollah | 2004 W Uygur YC | 2008 C Fire Nuclei | 2012 Ansaru | 2013 ISIL | 2014 ISIL Libya

1994 Marx.–Leninist CP | 1997 E Turkestan IP | 2000 al-Aqsa MB | 2003 Rev. Struggle | 2006 AM Naqshbandi | 2008 JA Tauhid | 2012 Yarmouk Martyrs B | 2013 Al-Mourabitoun | 2014 Harakat Sham

1994 PRDF – Interpal | 1997 al-Aqsa Found. | 2000 E Turkestan LO | 2003 Jundallah | 2006 Army of Islam | 2009 Abd Azzam B | 2012 Jaish al-Muhajireen | 2013 Ajnad Misr | 2014 Jund al-Aqsa

1994 Taliban | 1997 USDF Colombia | 2000 Jaish-e-Moh. | 2003 JA al-Sunna | 2006 Al-Shabaab | 2009 al-Qaeda AP | 2012 Ansar Dine | 2014 al-Qaeda IS | 2015 ISIL Caucasus

1995 SSP | 1998 Isl. M Uzbekistan | 2001 Ansar al-Islam | 2004 Balochistan LA | 2007 Caucasus Emirate | 2010 Mujah. Ind. Timur | 2012 MSCE Jerusalem | 2014 Lugansk PR | 2015 ISIL Khorasan

stars

hammer & sickle

hands

crescent

geography

arabic

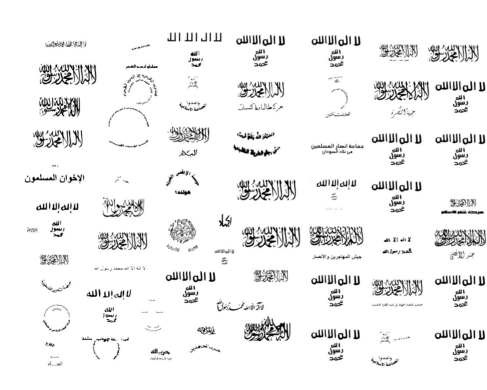

latin

animals   book   cross   book & weapons

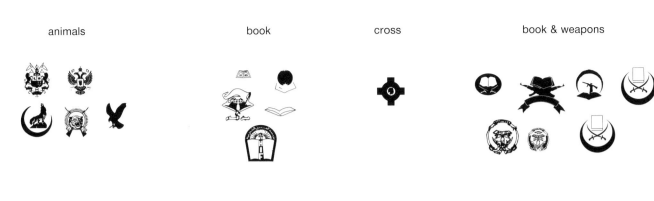

sphere / seal   weapons   unidentified

mixed   other

Currently recognized terrorist groups with main area of operations

Colombia
National Liberation Army
Revolutionary Armed Forces of Colombia
United Self-Defense Forces of Colombia

Peru
Shining Path

Ireland
Fianna Éireann
Cumann na mBan
Ulster Volunteer Force
Saor Éire
Provisional Irish Republican Army
Ulster Defence Association
Red Hand Commando
Irish National Liberation Army
Irish People's Liberation Organisation
Continuity Irish Republican Army
Loyalist Volunteer Force
Real Irish Republican Army
Orange Volunteers
Red Hand Defenders

Spain
ETA

Ukraine
Donetsk People's Republic
Lugansk People's Republic

Greece
Revolutionary Organization 17 November
Revolutionary Struggle
Conspiracy of Fire Nuclei

Turkey
Communist Party of Turkey
Marxist–Leninist Communist Party
Revolutionary People's Liberation
  Party–Front
Ergenekon

Kurdistan
Revolutionary Party of Kurdistan
Komala
Kurdistan Workers' Party
Kurdish Hezbollah
Kurdistan Democratic Party/North
Kurdistan Freedom Falcons
Party of Free Life of Kurdistan

Russia
People's Congress of Ichkeria and
  Dagestan
Islamic State of Iraq & the Levant–
  Caucasus Province
Supreme Military Majlis ul-Shura of the
  United Mujahideen Forces of Caucasus
Caucasus Emirate

Maghreb
Movement for Oneness and Jihad W. Africa
Al-Mourabitoun
Ansar al-Sharia (Tunisia)
Ansar Dine
Moroccan Islamic Combatant Group

Algeria
Armed Islamic Group of Algeria
Jund al-Khilafah

Libya
Libyan Islamic Fighting Group
Ansar al-Sharia (Libya)
Islamic State of Iraq & the Levant–
  Libya Province
Islamic State of Iraq & the Levant–
  Khorasan Province

Egypt
al-Gama'a al-Islamiyya /al-Jama'a
  al-Islamiyya
Vanguards of Conquest
Ajnad Misr
Ansar Bait al-Maqdis

Somalia
Al-Itihaad al-Islamiya

Nigeria / Chad / Niger
Boko Haram

Syria
Al-Nusra Front / Jabhat Fateh al-Sham
Jaish al-Muhajireen wal-Ansar
Yarmouk Martyrs Brigade
Islamic State of Iraq and the Levant
Harakat Sham al-Islam
Jund al-Aqsa
Abdullah Azzam Brigades

Israel
Kach and Kahane Chai

Lebanon
Hezbollah
Hezbollah (Military Wing)
Hezbollah (External Security Organization)
Osbat al-Ansar

Palestine
Palestine Liberation Front
Popular Front for the Liberation of Palestine
Popular Front for the Liberation of
  Palestine–General Command
Force 17
Abu Nidal Organization
Hamas
Palestinian Islamic Jihad
Holy Land Foundation for Relief and
  Development
Committee for Charity & Solidarity with
  Palestine
Izz ad-Din al-Qassam Brigades
Palestinian Relief Development
  Fund–Interpal
al-Aqsa Foundation
Stichting Al Aqsa
al-Aqsa Martyrs' Brigades
Tanzim
Mujahideen Shura Council in the Environs
  of Jerusalem
Palestine al-muslima

Iraq
Ansar al-Islam
Jamaat Ansar al-Sunna
Army of the Men of the Naqshbandi Order

Yemen
Aden-Abyan Islamic Army
Houthis
Islamic State of Iraq & the Levant–
  Yemen Province

Arab Peninsula
Hezbollah Al-Hejaz
al-Qaeda in the Arabian Peninsula

Iran
Quds Force
Kata'ib Hezbollah

Afghanistan-centered
radical Muslims
Jamiat-e Islami
Hezb-e Islami Gulbuddin
Haqqani network
Jamaat al Dawa al Quran
Taliban
Jamaat-ul-Ahrar
Islamic Movement of Uzbekistan

East Turkestan
East Turkestan Islamic Party
East Turkestan Information Center
East Turkestan Liberation Organization
World Uygur Youth Congress

Kashmir / Khalistan
Al-Umar-Mujahideen
Babbar Khalsa International
International Sikh Youth Federation
Khalistan Zindabad Force
Lashkar-e-Taiba
Khalistan Commando Force
Hizbul Mujahideen
Dukhtaran-e-Millat
Jamiat ul-Ansar
Khuddam ul-Islam / Jaish-e-Mohammed
Jaish-e-Mohammed
Al-Badr

India
Communist Party of India
  (Marxist–Leninist)
Maoist Communist Centre of India
Students Islamic Movement of India
Indian Mujahideen
al-Qaeda in the Indian Subcontinent
Tamil Nadu Liberation Army

Pakistan
Harkat-ul-Mujahideen
Sipah-e-Sahaba Pakistan
Lashkar-e-Jhangvi
Harakat-Ul-Mujahideen/Alami
Jundallah
Tehrik-i-Taliban Pakistan
Jamaat Ul-Furquan
Balochistan Liberation Army

Sri Lanka
Liberation Tigers of Tamil Eelam
Tamil National Retrieval Troops
World Tamil Movement

Manipur
United National Liberation Front
People's Revolutionary Party of Kangleipak
Manipur People's Liberation Front
People's Liberation Army of Manipur
Kangleipak Communist Party
Kanglei Yawol Kanna Lup

Tripura
National Liberation Front of Tripura
All Tripura Tiger Force

Bangladesh
Harkat-ul-Jihad al-Islami
Harkat-al-Jihad al-Islami in Bangladesh
Jamaat-ul-Mujahideen Bangladesh

Assam
United Liberation Front of Assam
National Democratic Front of Bodoland

Philippines
Communist Party of the Philippines–
  New People's Army
Abu Sayyaf

Indonesia
Jamaah Ansharut Tauhid
Mujahidin Indonesia Timur

United Muslim World
Muslim Brotherhood
Hizb ut-Tahrir
Takfir wal-Hijra
Egyptian Islamic Jihad
al-Qaeda
Jund al-Sham
Jemaah Islamiyah
Islamic Jihad Union
Al-Shabaab
Army of Islam
al-Qaeda in the Islamic Maghreb

Pan-Turkism
Grey Wolves

Caliphat
Great Eastern Islamic Raiders' Front

No clear territorial claim
Deendar Anjuman
Akhil Bharat Nepali Ekta Samaj
Aum Shinrikyo
al-Haramain Foundation
Society of the Revival of Islamic Heritage
Tehreek-e-Nafaz-e-Shariat-e-Mohammadi
Jamiat al-Islah al-Idzhtimai
Al Ghurabaa
Hofstad Network
The Saved Sect

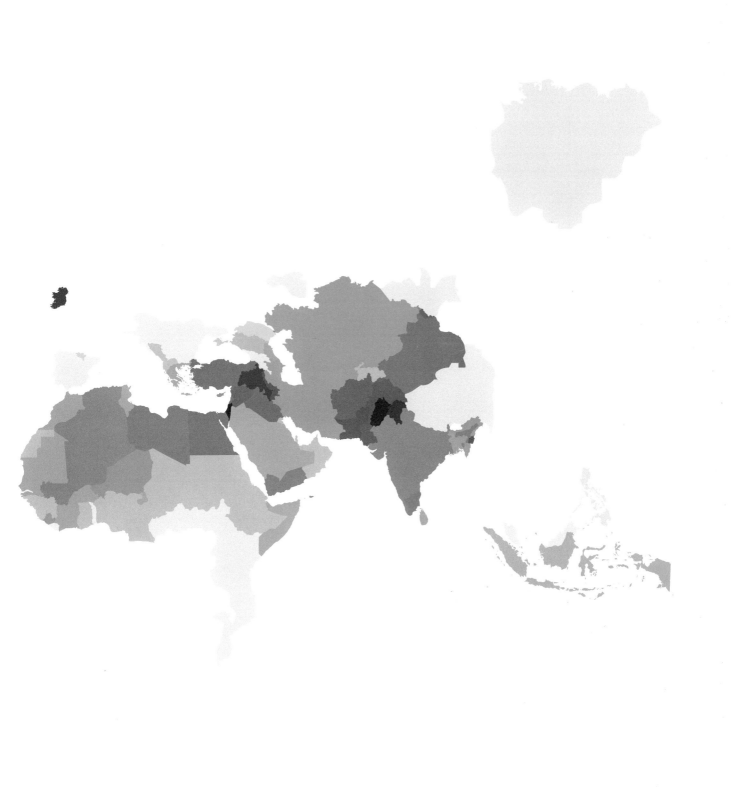

The darker the area, the more terrorist groups claim the territory.

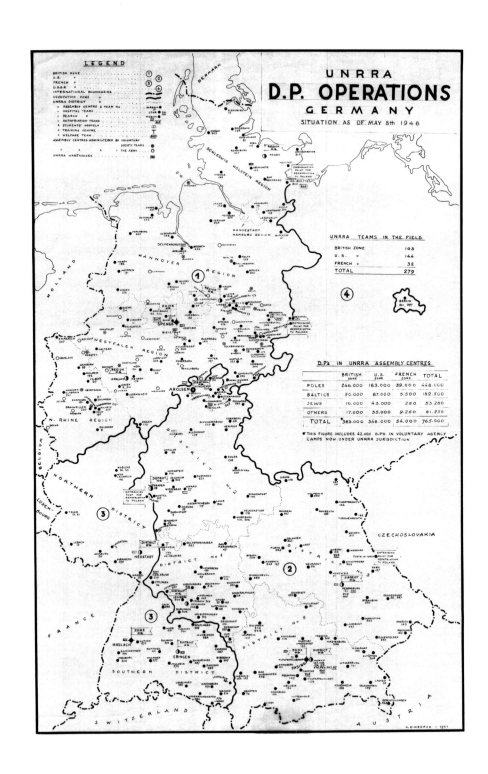

Displaced persons camps (DP camps) operated by the United Nations Relief
and Rehabilitation Administration (UNRRA) in Germany in 1946

Refugee Camps

The division of our planet's surface into territories through the process of nation-building assigned every human being to a specific territory. Theoretically, a neatly organized world should grant specific rights to those within each territory. In practice, however, millions of people are forced out of their assigned territories each year by catastrophes, famine or war. They flee to foreign territories and find themselves refugees. Today one-fourth of these people—some 8.1 million persons—have ended up in camps.[1]

Refugee camps are instant cities, built rapidly to deal with emergencies. An example is Zaatari (Jordan),[2] which opened in July 2012. Within one year, it had become one of the world's largest refugee camps, housing 150 000 people. By 2016, its population had stabilized at about 80 000. If acknowledged as such, Zataari would be Jordan's tenth-largest city, similar in size to Aqaba, a city that was founded around 4000 BC. In order to cope with such extreme situations, the United Nations High Commissioner for Refugees (UNHCR) published a *Handbook for Emergencies,* which includes 11 pages on planning strategies for refugee camps.[3] The handbook is an attempt to organize unpredictable situations. Take, for instance, this sentence on page 239: "As it is difficult to predict the life span of a refugee camp, it is best to plan on a cost-effective, long-term basis." This advice contradicts the precepts of most host countries, which state that no house or fixed structure may be erected in a refugee camp, to prevent the camp from turning into a city. The result is a vast sea of shacks and tents whose durability is limited on purpose.

It's easy to see how refugee camps can become arenas of political struggle. With the help of planning instruments, life there is suspended, sometimes for years. Self-settled camps tend to be built near established towns or villages in order to use existing infrastructure. Planned camps, on the other hand, are often positioned far away from cities to avoid conflicts, to allow for easier expansion of the camp perimeter, and, most importantly, to facilitate supervision of the refugees. In line with UNHCR's recommendation to avoid camps bigger than 20 000 inhabitants, multiple camps are built close together, forming clusters. The internal zoning of planned camps follows safety regulations that reflect the dual standing of the refugee as both victim and possible threat (to other refugees). Peacekeepers' quarters and service buildings are located along the periphery, where they have a good connection to the world outside, but their strategic position is also intended to secure the camp. Ethnic groups are allocated different sections of the camp to reduce the possibility of internal conflict.

As temporary as the structure often is, one never knows how long a camp will exist. The United Nations' oldest refugee camps are the ones that arose when Palestinians were displaced by the founding of the state of Israel in 1948.[4] These 70-year-old camps, like the Khan Younis camp in Gaza, which houses more than 80 000 people,[5] look nothing like the camps described above; these camps are cities with houses made of brick and concrete. But even if one makes the structure of a camp as solid as a rock, it will appear temporary to its inhabitants as long as they keep dreaming of a safe return to their homeland.

1 popstats.unhcr.org
2 www.citymetric.com
3 www.ifrc.org
4 www.unrwa.org
5 www.unrwa.org

Planned / prearranged shelter / cluster expansion

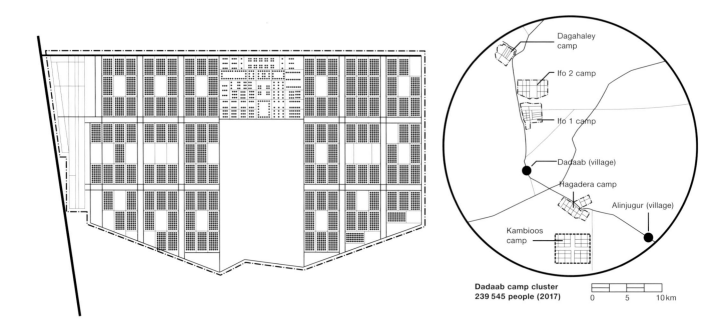

Dadaab camp cluster
239 545 people (2017)

0   5   10 km

Ifo 2 camp, Kenya – 35 046 people
Planned refugee camp demarcated into 18 sections with
implemented orthogonal grid and zoning. Created in 2011 as the
last camp of the Dadaab cluster for refugees fleeing from the
Somali Civil War.

Planned / prearranged shelter / cluster new

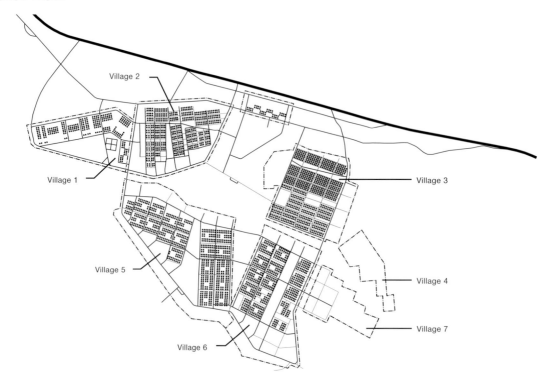

Azraq camp, Jordan – 52 152 people
Planned refugee camp divided into 7 villages with implemented
orthogonal grid and zoning. Created in 2014 for refugees fleeing
from the Syrian Civil War.

Planned / self-made shelter

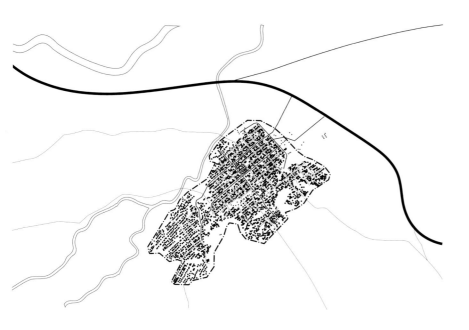

Melkadida camp, Ethiopia–31 616 people
Refugee camp with implemented zoning and rough orthogonal grid.
Created in 2010 for refugees fleeing from the Somali Civil War.

Planned / self-made shelter / cluster

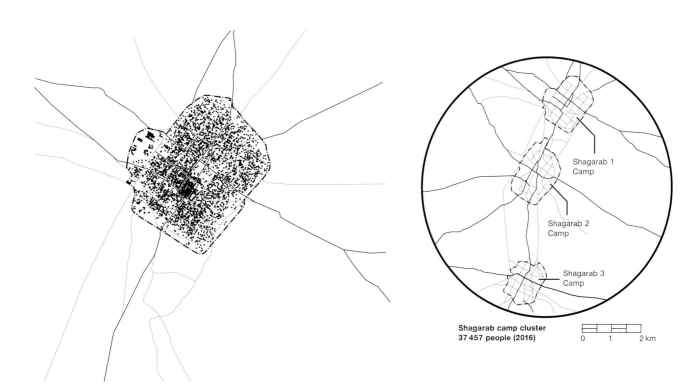

Shagarab 1
Camp

Shagarab 2
Camp

Shagarab 3
Camp

Shagarab camp cluster
37 457 people (2016)

0   1   2 km

Shagarab 1 camp, Sudan–21 239 people
Cluster of three successively developed camps, with implemented
zoning and rough orthogonal grid. Created in the early 1980s for
refugees from Eritrea fleeing from the Eritrean War of Independence
and the civil oppression that followed.

Planned & self-settled /
attached to hosting town

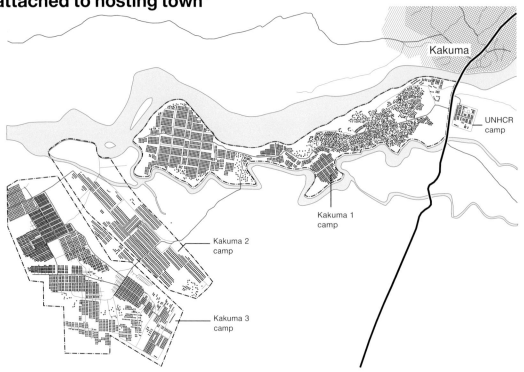

Kakuma camp, Kenya – 154 947 people
Created in 1992 to host refugees mostly from Sudan, South Sudan,
and Somalia. Successively developed refugee camp adjacent to
a host town. In the new sections of the refugee camp, an orthogonal
grid was implemented.

Self-settled / enclave in hosting town

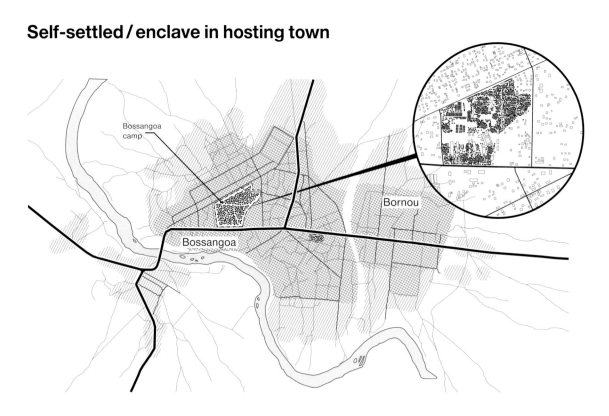

Bossangoa IDP camp, Central African Republic – 38 000 people
Citizens have been relocated in two camps of antithetical religious
groups because of the ongoing civil war. Two very dense camps
surround areas adjacent to a cathedral and a school within an existing
urban structure.

Self-settled / no hosting town

Mae La camp, Thailand – 37 408 people
Localized along transit road to border crossing with dense camp
fabric following hilly topography. Created in 1996 as a result of
Burmese internal ethnic conflicts.

Self-settled / swallowing hosting town

Autochthon villages

Doro camp, South Sudan – 52 742 people
Improvised refugee camp structure which gradually surrounded
existing villages. Created in 2011 as a result of internal conflicts in
Sudan.

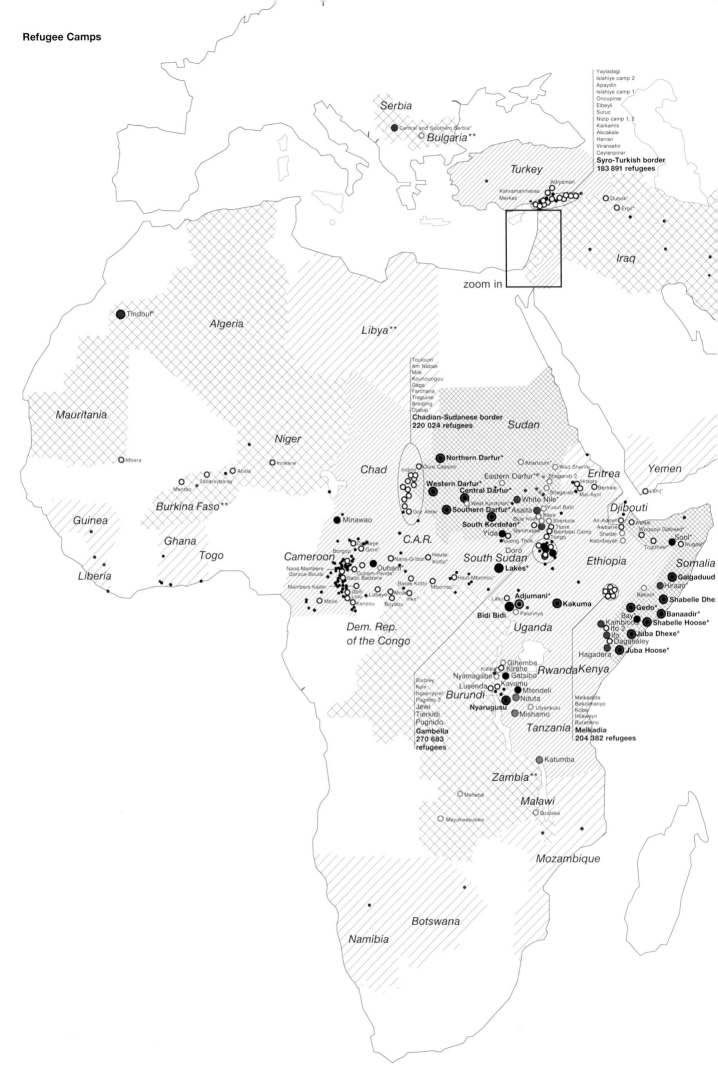

Serbia

Bulgaria**

Central and Southern Serbia*

Turkey

Yayladagi
Islahiye camp 2
Apaydin
Islahiye camp 1
Oncupinar
Elbeyli
Suruc
Nizip camp 1, 2
Karkamis
Akcakale
Harran
Viransehir
Ceylanpinar
**Syro-Turkish border
183 891 refugees**

Adiyaman

Kahramanmaras
Merkez

Duhok*

Erbil*

Iraq

zoom in

Tindouf*

Algeria

Libya**

Yemen

Touloum
Am Nabak
Mile
Kounoungou
Gaga
Farchana
Treguine
Bredjing
Djabal
**Chadian-Sudanese border
220 024 refugees**

Sudan

Mauritania

Niger

Mbera

Intikane

Abala

Tabareybarey

Mentao

Burkina Faso**

Chad

Iridimi

Oure Cassoni

Northern Darfur*

Khartoum

Wad Sherife

Eastern Darfur*

Shagarab 2

Eritrea

Hitsats

Berhale

Western Darfur*

Central Darfur*

West Kordofan*

Southern Darfur*

White Nile*

Shagarab 1

Mai-Ayni

Asaita

Djibouti

Guinea

Ghana

Togo

Liberia

Minawao

Cameroon

Dabanga
Gore*

Borgop

Nana Mambere
Garoua-Boulai

Ouham-Pende*

Gado Badzere

Mambere Kadei

Gbiti
Lolo

Kenzou

Lobaye*

Boyabu

Mbile

C.A.R.

Nana-Gribizi*

Haute-
Kotto*

Basse Kotto*

Mole
Inke*

Haut-Mbomou*

Mbomou*

Goz Amer

South Kordofan*

Yida

Aluong Thok

South Sudan

Doro

Kaya

Yusuf Batil

Blue Nile*

Bambasi Camp

Sherkole

Tsore

Gendrassa

Tongo

Lakes*

Ethiopia

Ali-Addeh
Awbarre
Sheder

Kebribeyah

Waqooyi Galbeed

Togdheer

Sool*

Nugaal*

Somalia

Galgaduud

Hiraan

Bakool

Gedo*

Shabelle Dhe

Banaadir*

Shabelle Hoose*

Bay

Kambioos

Ifo 2
Ifo

Dagahaley

Hagadera

Juba Dhexe*

Juba Hoose*

Lasu

Adjumani*

Palorinya

Kakuma

Bidi Bidi

Kenya

Uganda

Dem. Rep.
of the Congo

Kiziba

Gihembe

Kirehe

Nyamagabe

Gatsibo

Kavumu

Rwanda

Lusenda

Mtendeli

Burbley
Kule
Nguenyyiel
Pugnido 2
Jewi
Tierkidi
Pugnido
**Gambella
270 683
refugees**

Burundi

Nduta

Nyarugusu

Mishamo

Ulyankulu

Tanzania

Melkadida
Bokolmanyo
Kobe
Hilaweyn
Buramino
**Melkadia
204 382 refugees**

Katumba

Zambia**

Meheba

Malawi

Dzaleka

Mayukwayukwa

Mozambique

Botswana

Namibia

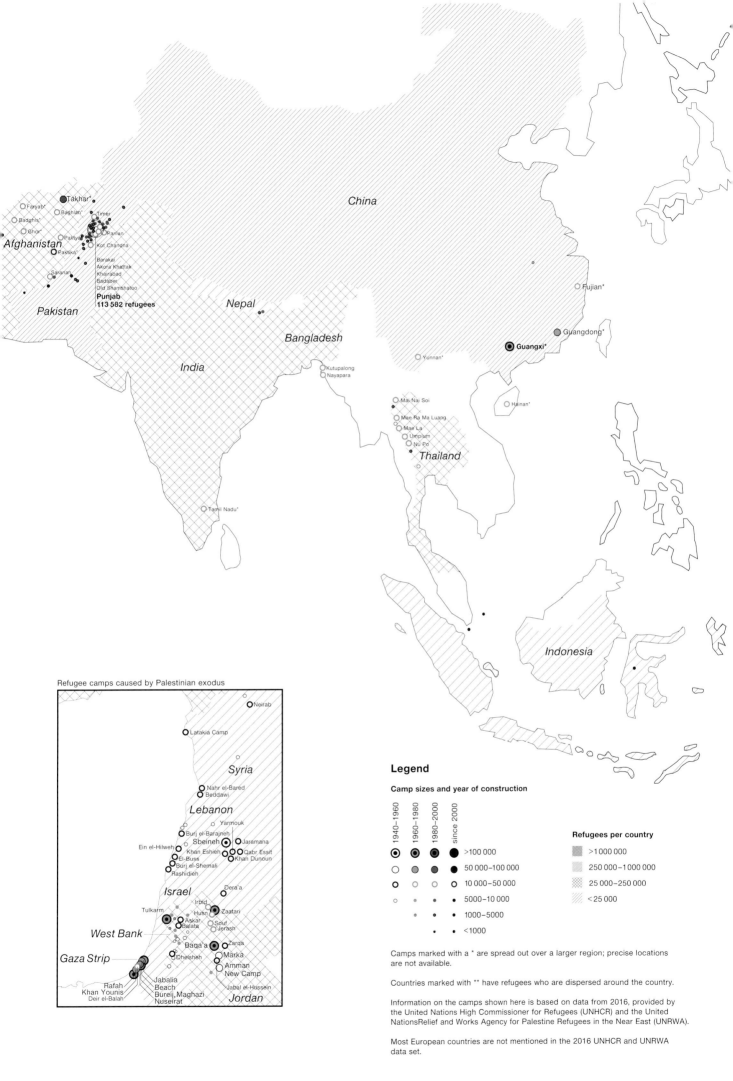

Legend

Camp sizes and year of construction

	1940–1960	1960–1980	1980–2000	since 2000	
	◉	◉	●	●	>100 000
	○	◐	◑	●	50 000–100 000
	○	○	○	○	10 000–50 000
	○	●	●	●	5000–10 000
	·	·	·	·	1000–5000
		·	·	·	<1000

Refugees per country

- >1 000 000
- 250 000–1 000 000
- 25 000–250 000
- < 25 000

Camps marked with a * are spread out over a larger region; precise locations are not available.

Countries marked with ** have refugees who are dispersed around the country.

Information on the camps shown here is based on data from 2016, provided by the United Nations High Commissioner for Refugees (UNHCR) and the United NationsRelief and Works Agency for Palestine Refugees in the Near East (UNRWA).

Most European countries are not mentioned in the 2016 UNHCR and UNRWA data set.

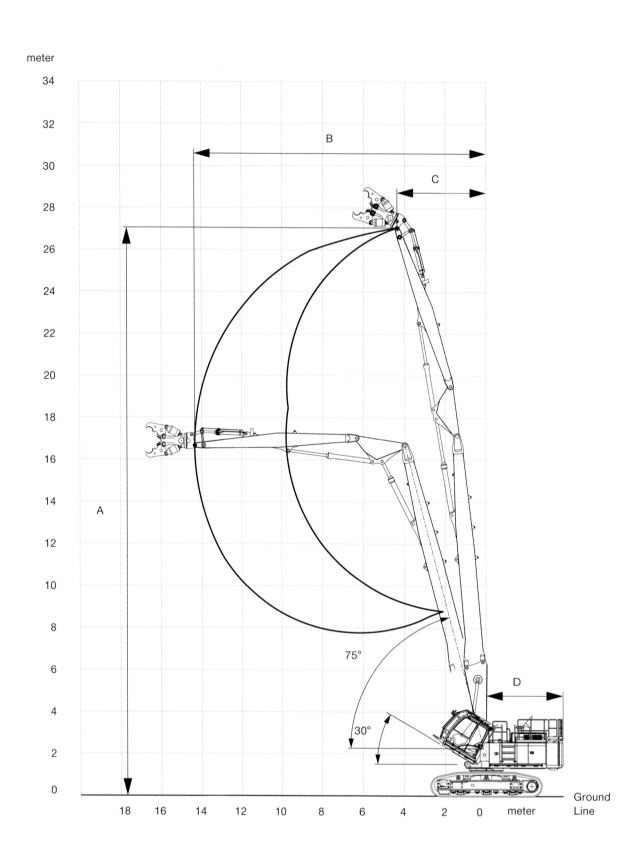

meter

34

32

30

28

26

24

22

20

18

16

14

12

10

8

6

4

2

0

A

B

C

D

75°

30°

18 16 14 12 10 8 6 4 2 0 meter

Ground
Line

Hitachi ZAXIS-5 high-reach demolition machine with
concrete cracker

Total Demolition

Architects, structural engineers, and their clients build for eternity. In the world of accountants, however, buildings are written off rather quickly. In the United States, commercial buildings have a financial life span of 39 years,[1] while in the Netherlands and Germany their life expectancy ranges from 30 to 50 years.[2] In the Netherlands, more than 10 000 apartments are torn down annually;[3] buildings seem to be treated no differently than printers or company cars. The wrecking ball hangs as the proverbial sword of Damocles over almost any building nowadays, with little regard for even magnificent architecture.

Aside from economic reasons, demolition sometimes results from political motivation, for example as historic cleansing by a new regime in power. The most outrageous act by a democratic nation in this regard has certainly been the demolition of the Palace of the Republic (Palast der Republik) in Berlin, which housed the parliament of the German Democratic Republic. This modernist building from the 1970s had to make space for a heinous reconstruction of the Prussian-era Berlin Palace (Stadtschloss). The cost of demolishing the Palace of the Republic eventually amounted to €119 million.[4] To complete the historic tragedy, steel from the Palace of the Republic was used for the construction of the world's tallest building, the Burj Khalifa.[5]

While the fake Stadtschloss is expected to open soon, the largest demolition project in modern history is just about to start in Moscow. The city's mayor, Sergei Sobyanin, has promised that Moscow's "Khrushchevki," which encompass 16 million m² of residential real estate and house one million people, will be torn down.[6] Khrushchevki are mass-produced five-story apartment blocks, constructed between the late 1950s and the early 1980s. Khrushchevki were designed for a life span of 25 years as an interim habitat, to be replaced eventually by the buildings of the true socialist paradise.

Thus, it is certainly not the quality of housing which makes the endeavor so questionable; it is the scale, the nondemocratic nature of the decision, and the uncertainty that replaces the old housing and at what cost. As Moscow has expanded, the land occupied by the low-rise Khrushchevki has become increasingly valuable. Replacing them with high-rise apartments sounds like a promising deal. Muscovites sense a secret pact between politicians and the real estate market as the true intention behind this enormous operation. The Khrushchevki, so it is feared, will now be replaced by the capitalist paradise of the real estate brokers.

Following protests, the city gave in and promised residents the chance to vote against the demolition of their own houses. Surprisingly to many, two weeks before the deadline, President Putin himself signed a law concerning the housing renovation in all districts of Moscow, including the demolition of Khrushchevki and the resettlement of their inhabitants. Consequently, only 169 of the 5144 houses are excluded from demolition.

A building is not just brick and mortar, but a medium charged with economic, cultural, and political value. The decision to destroy these buildings specifically targets one of these values. The promise of higher profits, changes in people's lifestyles, and new political regimes turn out to be the most powerful opponents of built objects. Yet economic bubbles can burst, lifestyles take sudden nostalgic turns (as with loft apartments in old factories), and political regimes can change all too soon.

1 www.finweb.com
2 www.arno.uvt.nl, www.steuertipps.de
3 www.eib.nl
4 www.morgenpost.de
5 www.dw.com
6 www.wikimedia.org, meduza.io, www.mos.ru, daily.afisha.ru

Total Demolition

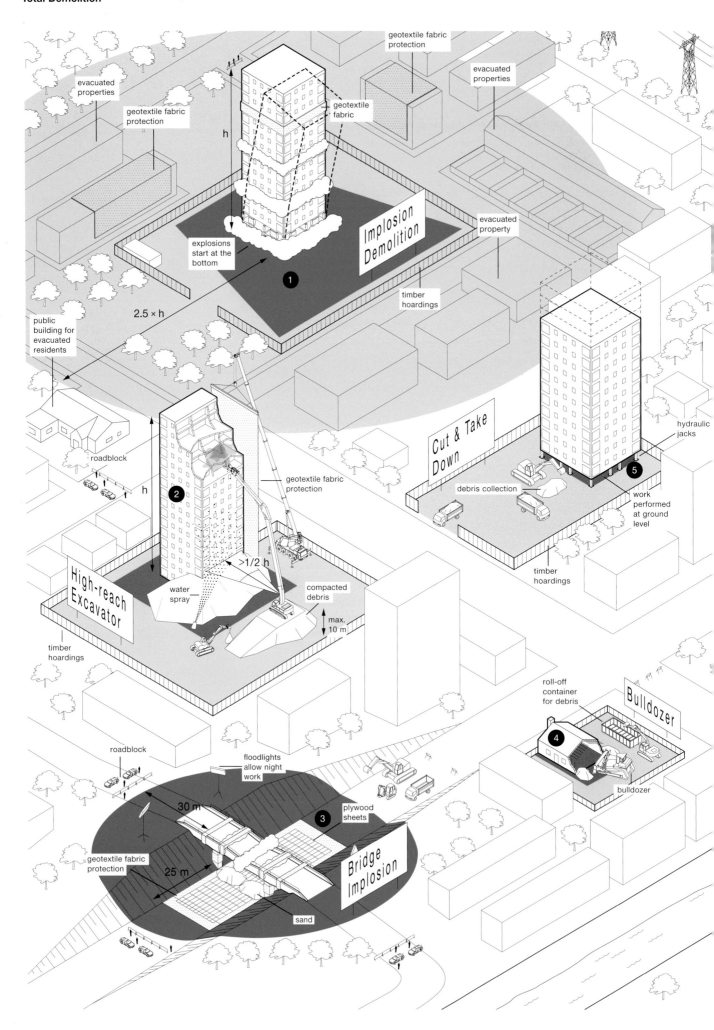

evacuated properties

geotextile fabric protection

geotextile fabric protection

evacuated properties

geotextile fabric

h

Implosion Demolition

explosions start at the bottom

❶

2.5 × h

evacuated property

timber hoardings

public building for evacuated residents

roadblock

h

❷

geotextile fabric protection

High-reach Excavator

water spray

>1/2 h

compacted debris

max. 10 m

timber hoardings

Cut & Take Down

❺

hydraulic jacks

debris collection

work performed at ground level

timber hoardings

roll-off container for debris

Bulldozer

❹

bulldozer

roadblock

floodlights allow night work

30 m

❸

plywood sheets

geotextile fabric protection

25 m

Bridge Implosion

sand

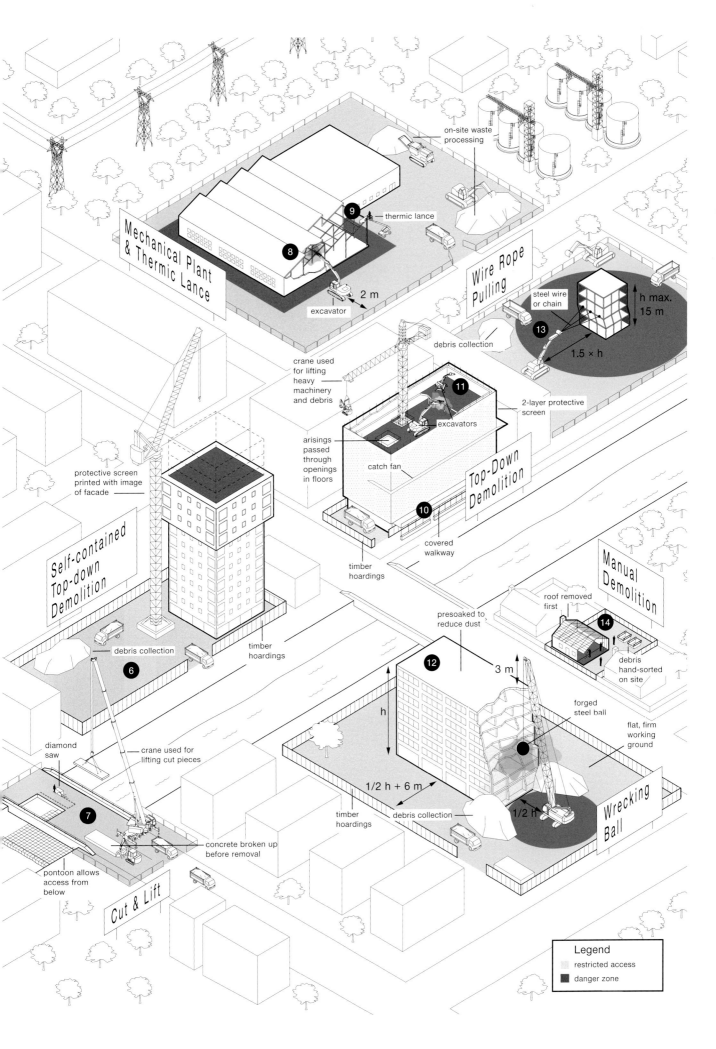

Mechanical Plant & Thermic Lance

thermic lance

9

8

excavator

2 m

on-site waste processing

Wire Rope Pulling

steel wire or chain

13

h max. 15 m

1.5 × h

debris collection

crane used for lifting heavy machinery and debris

11

2-layer protective screen

excavators

arisings passed through openings in floors

catch fan

Top-Down Demolition

covered walkway

10

protective screen printed with image of facade

Self-contained Top-down Demolition

timber hoardings

6

debris collection

timber hoardings

Manual Demolition

roof removed first

14

debris hand-sorted on site

presoaked to reduce dust

3 m

12

h

1/2 h + 6 m

timber hoardings

debris collection

1/2 h

forged steel ball

flat, firm working ground

Wrecking Ball

diamond saw

crane used for lifting cut pieces

7

concrete broken up before removal

pontoon allows access from below

Cut & Lift

Legend
restricted access
danger zone

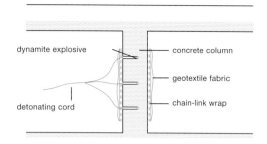

1 Implosion demolition. Explosives are detonated on lower and upper floors to create a controlled collapse. Reduces cost and time when demolishing hazardous multistory structures.

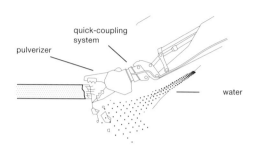

2 High-reach excavator. Used for controlled deconstruction of tall or multistory structures. Boom lengths vary in size from 19 to over 50 m.

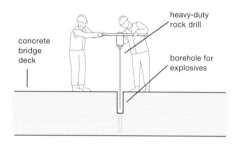

3 Bridge implosion. Common method of bridge demolition, used for adaptability and flexibility. Explosives placed in boreholes are used to create a controlled collapse.

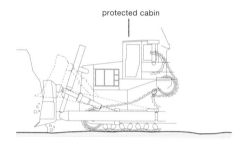

4 Bulldozer. Used to demolish smaller buildings of 1–2 stories. Used to knock down the building and also to clear debris from the site.

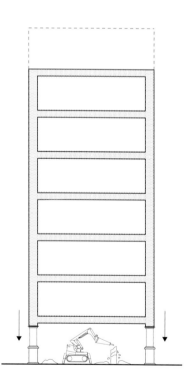

5 Cut and take down. Progressive demolition occurs at ground level while the building is lowered on computer-controlled hydraulic jacks, one floor at a time. Noise and dust pollution are greatly reduced.

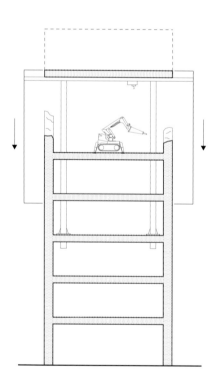

6 Self-contained top-down demolition. An exoskeleton enclosing the top three floors is attached to the building by a hydraulic system and lowered as the structure is progressively demolished from within.

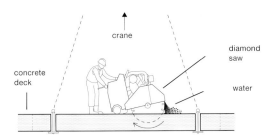

7   Cut and lift. Bridge is cut into sections and removed by crane. Cutting is done using diamond saws or high-pressure water jets.

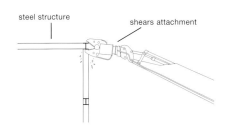

8   Mechanical plant. The most common method, involving progressive demolition using excavators with attachments such as shears, pulverizers, and grapples.

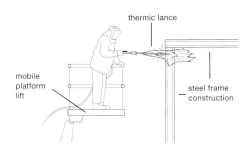

9   Thermic lance. Intense temperatures from a thermochemical reaction are used to cut through almost any material, particularly steel, cast iron, and concrete.

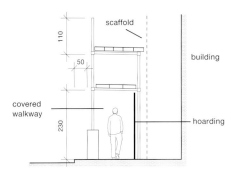

10   Top-down. Traditional demolition method on a constricted site. Progressive demolition performed by a combination of machine and hand demolition.

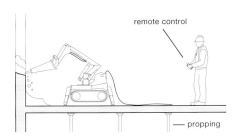

11   Robotic demolition. Remote-controlled powerful hydraulic excavator. Ideal where falling debris is a risk, as no human needs to be in close proximity.

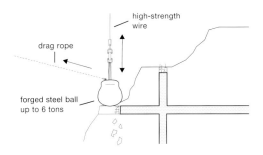

12   Wrecking ball. Progressive demolition used for multistory structures that have suffered structural damage. Force can be applied from above or from the side.

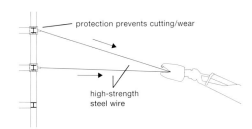

13   Wire rope pulling. A form of deliberate collapse, using wire ropes fixed to key structural elements, pulled by excavator or winch.

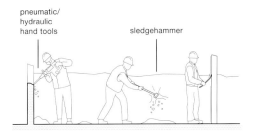

14   Demolition by hand. Used to demolish smaller buildings, delicate structures, or when the building is to be completely dismantled into its component parts for reuse.

CAMDEN bench

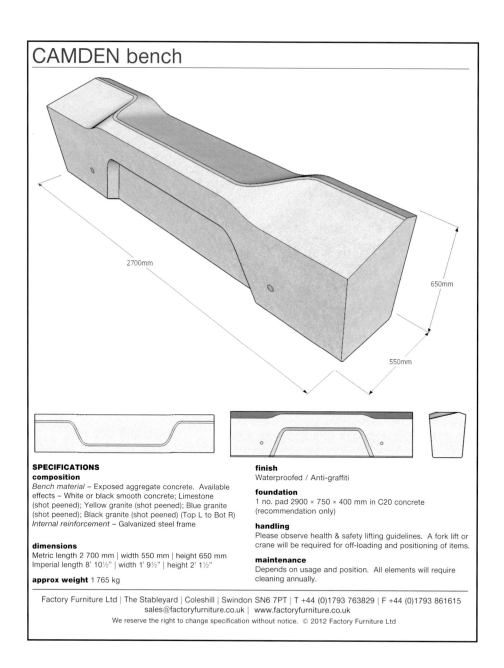

2700mm

650mm

550mm

SPECIFICATIONS

composition

Bench material – Exposed aggregate concrete. Available effects – White or black smooth concrete; Limestone (shot peened); Yellow granite (shot peened); Blue granite (shot peened); Black granite (shot peened) (Top L to Bot R) *Internal reinforcement* – Galvanized steel frame

dimensions

Metric length 2 700 mm | width 550 mm | height 650 mm
Imperial length 8' 10½" | width 1' 9½" | height 2' 1½"

approx weight 1 765 kg

finish

Waterproofed / Anti-graffiti

foundation

1 no. pad 2900 × 750 × 400 mm in C20 concrete (recommendation only)

handling

Please observe health & safety lifting guidelines. A fork lift or crane will be required for off-loading and positioning of items.

maintenance

Depends on usage and position. All elements will require cleaning annually.

Factory Furniture Ltd | The Stableyard | Coleshill | Swindon SN6 7PT | T +44 (0)1793 763829 | F +44 (0)1793 861615
sales@factoryfurniture.co.uk | www.factoryfurniture.co.uk
We reserve the right to change specification without notice. © 2012 Factory Furniture Ltd

The "Camden Bench" street furniture design by Factory Furniture

"Behold the Camden Bench. This pale, amorphous lump of sculpted concrete is designed to resist almost everything in a city that it might come into contact with. Named for the London authority that commissioned it, the Camden Bench has a special coating which makes it impervious to graffiti and vandalism. The squat, featureless surface gives drug dealers nowhere to hide their secret caches. The angled sides repel skateboarders and flyposters, litter, and rain. The cambered top throws off rough sleepers. In fact, it is specially crafted to make sure that it is not used as anything except a bench. This makes it a strange artifact, defined far more by what it is not than what it is. The Camden Bench is a concerted effort to create a nonobject."

Frank Swain, Designing the Perfect Anti-Object, www.medium.com

Defensive City

The age of fortress cities is long gone. Protective borders designed to fend off outside enemies have evolved from urban perimeters to national and even supranational boundaries, as in the case of the Schengen Area. Defensive measures adopted by today's cities mainly target the enemy within. Besides the threat of terrorist attacks, there is a much less violent "enemy" to the city: the ordinary citizen.

Unwanted Behavior

"Unwanted behavior" is the accusatory basis for the implementation of subtle design elements that try to influence the use of public space without being noticed. Since unwanted behavior is not yet a crime, preventive measures are the only way to avert it. Spray-painting a work of art on a wall is not the only example of unwanted behavior; others include lying down, sitting, standing in a group, and walking. These are activities that take place in public spaces— the same spaces advertised in real estate brochures as vivid, dynamic, and bustling with life.

It's a battle of realities. The general public does not want a Saturday morning at the shops to be marred by the reality of homeless people, nor to see the vomit spewed by their own kids the day before congealing in the corner of their favorite store. But the same general public likes to contribute to the image of an open, welcoming, and unconstrained city. Thus, the smaller and less conspicuous the city's protective elements, the better. Park benches with armrests at 50 cm intervals seem pleasant and thoughtfully designed, until you get tired and try to lie down on them. Little metal brackets along the edges of sidewalks look like ornaments but are, in fact, anti-skating devices. Opera music played outside a clothing store appears to be a sophisticated touch, but it's meant to deter youngsters who might want to hang out there. In our electronic future, designs will get smaller and ever more virtual. Crowd scanners, as well as motion and position detectors, have already been tested. It won't be long before an intelligent sidewalk tells you to get up and walk—no spikes needed.

It's the city government that implements preventive designs, but only by popular demand. The city against unwanted behavior is the Western, capitalist city—a clean and bloodless construct that works optimally only until shops close. Statistically, though, we feel safer. The question is: Are we willing to exchange feeling safe for being more alive?

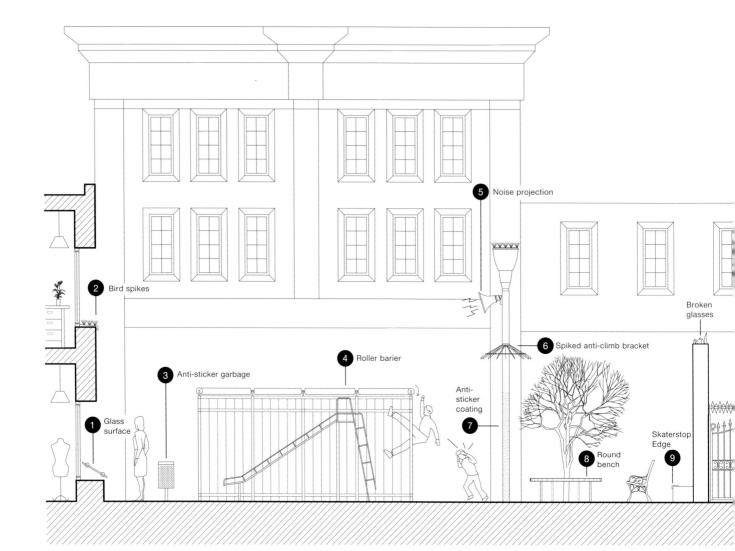

Labels in the illustration:
1 Glass surface
2 Bird spikes
3 Anti-sticker garbage
4 Roller barier
5 Noise projection
6 Spiked anti-climb bracket
7 Anti-sticker coating
8 Round bench
9 Skaterstop Edge
Broken glasses

One strategy is difficult to illustrate, since it is a strategy of absence—for example, the absence of the bench.[1] To remove benches entirely from public spaces has proven to be much more effective against unwanted behavior than any anti-homeless, anti-skating or anti-loitering design. A "positive" side effect of removing benches is the cost savings in acquiring and maintaining street furniture. On top of this, café and restaurant owners are all in favor of bench-free streets and squares since they regard every seat taken on a public bench as a seat lost on their terrace. A win-win situation for politics and businesses does not inevitably result in a resounding success for the people. With the bench, public life—and, if we believe Edwin Heathcote, democracy—is retreating from public space:

"Indeed, the bench and, perhaps in particular, the park bench, has become the symbol of the democratic city—of free, accessible and equitable public space provided by the city for its citizens. It is a place to be private in public, a small space in the melee of the metropolis where it is acceptable to do nothing, to consume nothing, to just be. A truly free bench."[2]

1 www.nrpa.org
2 Edwin Heathcote, in "Public Benches: The Seat of Civilization," *Financial Times*, June 19, 2015, www.ft.com

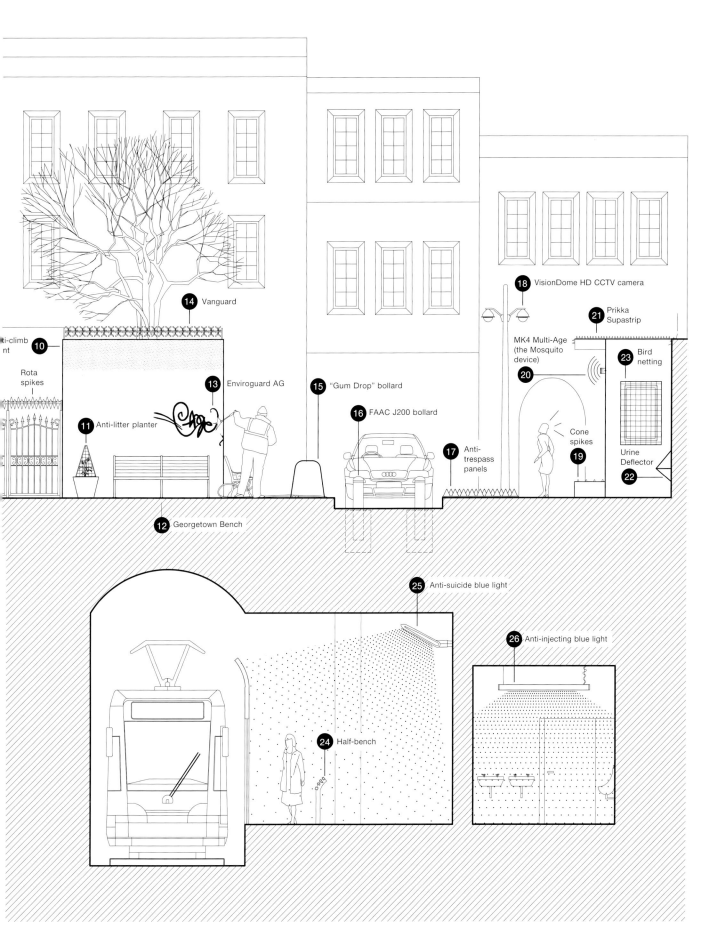

14 Vanguard

10 ti-climb
nt

Rota
spikes

13 Enviroguard AG

15 "Gum Drop" bollard

11 Anti-litter planter

16 FAAC J200 bollard

17 Anti-
trespass
panels

12 Georgetown Bench

18 VisionDome HD CCTV camera

21 Prikka
Supastrip

MK4 Multi-Age
(the Mosquito
device)

20

23 Bird
netting

Cone
spikes

19

Urine
Deflector

22

25 Anti-suicide blue light

26 Anti-injecting blue light

24 Half-bench

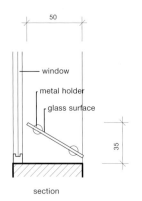

section

1 Glass surface, London, UK. Glass surface with metal holders: addition on window ledges to deter people from sitting or littering.

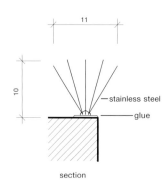

section

2 Bird spikes. Weatherproof stainless steel spikes to deter birds from nesting on ledges, flat roofs, lampposts, etc.

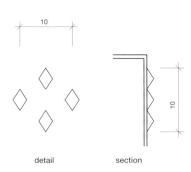

detail   section

3 Anti-sticker litter basket, Linz, Austria. Metal litter basket with diamond-shaped bumps to prevent people from affixing stickers and posters.

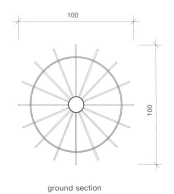

ground section

6 Spiked anti-climbing bracket. Weatherproof spiked bracket made out of steel and galvanized components used in poles, lampposts, trees, etc., to deter people from climbing.

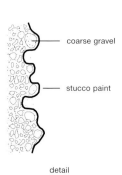

detail

7 Anti-sticker coating, Eindhoven, Netherlands. The AS 2010 Sticker and poster deterrent.

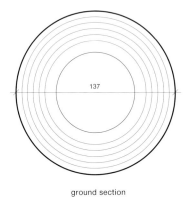

ground section

8 Round bench. Round, backless, galvanized steel bench used to protect plants but also to deter people from lying down.

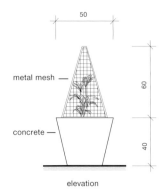

elevation

11 Anti-litter planter, NYC, USA. Concrete-base planter with metal mesh extension to prevent people from littering or sitting on its edges.

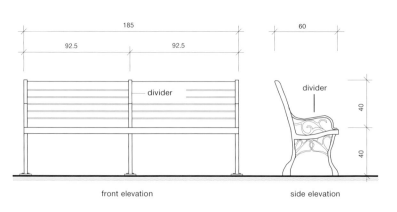

front elevation   side elevation

12 Georgetown Bench. 100% recycled iron and plastic. As the company states, the bench is "designed to face contemporary urban realities with a center arm that discourages overnight stays."

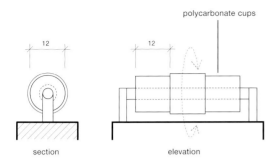

polycarbonate cups

12

12

section   elevation

4 Roller barrier, Philadelphia, USA. Recycled polycarbonate cups are installed as rollers around an aluminium tube to deter people from climbing over walls and fences. Designed especially for playgrounds, schools, mental institutions, and youth detention centers.

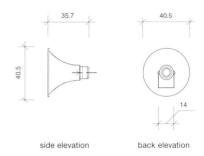

35.7   40.5

40.5

14

side elevation   back elevation

5 Noise projection, San Francisco, USA. Loud construction noises from speakers outside buildings to keep homeless people from sleeping between 11 p.m. and 7 a.m.

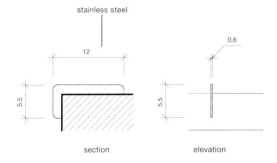

stainless steel

12   0.6

5.5   5.5

section   elevation

9 SkateStop Edge, Melbourne, Australia. Stainless-steel skate deterrent.

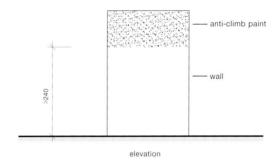

anti-climb paint

wall

>240

elevation

10 Anti-climbing paint. A thick, oily, slippery, nondrying coating for ledges, fences, and walls. It deters potential intruders by making surfaces virtually unclimbable, while rubbing off on hands and clothing. Can be applied to brickwork, concrete, plastic, metal or wood.

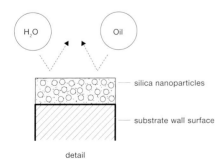

H_2O Oil

silica nanoparticles

substrate wall surface

detail

13 Enviroguard AG, Edinburgh, UK. Nontoxic coating for all types of walls. Graffiti damage can be removed from any surface without chemicals by using pressured hot water at 1000 to 1500 psi and 85°C.

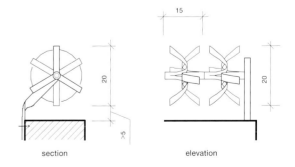

15

20   20

>5

section   elevation

14 Vanguard. Split and formed aluminum tubing used to deter people from climbing over a wall or fence. Vanguard works more as a visual deterrent; it is unlikely to cause life-threatening or serious injury.

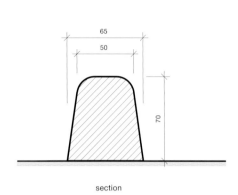

section

15 "Gum Drop" bollard, New York City, USA. Concrete bollards placed on the sidewalk to prevent street vendors from parking their carts.

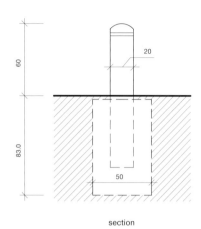

section

16 FAAC J200 bollard. Metal cylindrical bollard resistant to impact and weather. Provided with a piston mechanism with which it can be moved on command to deter unwanted traffic.

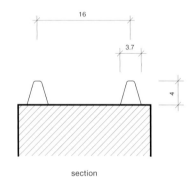

section

19 Cone spikes, London, UK. Metal cone-shaped spikes used to deter people from sitting or sleeping on ledges.

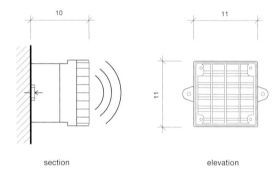

section   elevation

20 MK4 Multi-Age (the Mosquito device), Manchester, UK. Plastic speaker that produces a high-frequency sound (8–17 kHz) to deter people from loitering in public spaces. 17 kHz sound is used against teenagers (aged 13–25), while 8 kHz is used against people of all ages.

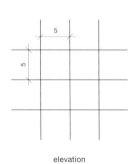

elevation

23 Bird netting. High-density, UV-resistant polyethylene net that forms a strong, impenetrable bird barrier.

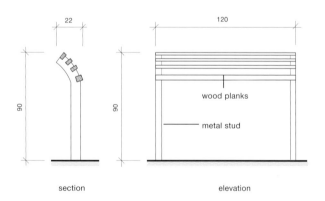

section   elevation

24 Half bench, Rotterdam, Netherlands. Metal and wood bench that discourages citizens from staying for too long and does not allow sleeping.

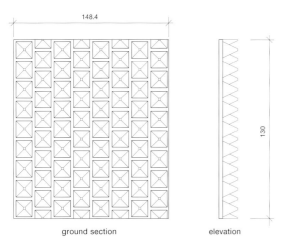

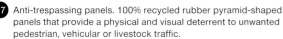

ground section   elevation

17 Anti-trespassing panels. 100% recycled rubber pyramid-shaped panels that provide a physical and visual deterrent to unwanted pedestrian, vehicular or livestock traffic.

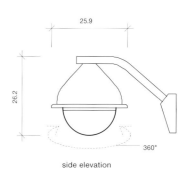

side elevation

18 VisionDome HD CCTV camera, Broadway, UK. 360° high-resolution camera disguised as a street lamp.

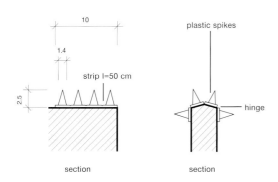

section   section

21 Prikka SupaStrip. Robust UV (ultraviolet)-balanced, weatherproof, recycled plastic-hinged spikes to deter climbing on walls and flat roofs. Causes maximum discomfort but minimum harm. Also useful against cats and birds.

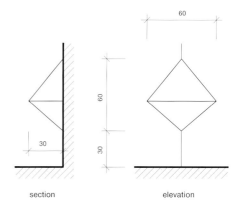

section   elevation

22 Urine deflector, Frankfurt, Germany. Steel profile used in public spaces to deter public urination. Similar devices in London date back to the nineteenth century.

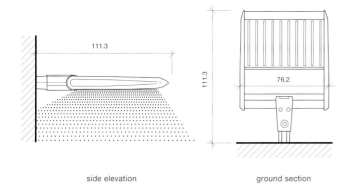

side elevation   ground section

25 Anti-suicide blue light, Tokyo, Japan. Blue LEDs are used to prevent people from committing suicide in train or subway stations. A research paper published in the Journal of Affective Disorders four years after the first lights were installed found that there was an 84% decrease in suicides at stations with blue lights.

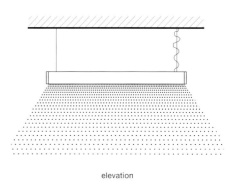

elevation

26 26 Anti-injecting blue light, the Hague, Netherlands. Black-light blue fluorescent light bulbs are used in public restrooms to deter people from using intravenous drugs, as they make it harder for users to see their veins.

Vehicle as Weapon

Using a motor vehicle as a weapon is, despite the headlines in recent years, not a new phenomenon. In Israel, the first vehicle ramming attack was carried out in 1987 by a Palestinian.[3] Since then, this mode of terror increased and started to appear in cities around the world. In July 2016, Europe's most tragic terrorist event happened in Nice, France, when a truck was deliberately driven into a crowd celebrating Bastille Day. This resulted in 87 deaths and 434 people injured.[4] The terror organization ISIL claimed responsibility for the attack.

It is exactly this organization that propagates the idea of using vehicles as deadly devices through its magazines *Rumiyah* and *Dabiq*. "Though being an essential part of modern life, very few actually comprehend the deadly and destructive capability of the motor vehicle and its capacity [for] reaping large numbers of casualties if used in a premeditated manner" can be read in the third issue (fall 2016) of *Rumiyah*.[5] The article describes in detail which vehicles are ideal (older models with a steel frame, as they are heavy and fast-moving) and which vehicles should be avoided (cars and load-bearing trucks with load compartments). The rising popularity of using vehicles as weapons is rooted in a combination of factors: they are cheap, require little expertise, and can be piloted single-handedly, while the damage to the morale of the urban population is large, since any truck or any car could be a threat at any time. The knowledge that terrorists prefer to target crowded places, such as shopping malls, parades or markets, induces a general feeling of fear and uneasiness in the urban public. That's why the main ram-proof measures in urban areas focus on the built environment in crowded places.

Generally, people want to feel safe but do not want to be confronted with safety measures. Additionally, people want to have an untroubled, barrier-free urban experience, while the ram-proof city asks for height differences—the installation of heavy blockades and bollards. The art of designing a ram-proof city is the art of concealing. The first step is to separate pedestrians from vehicle lanes by clearly defined pathways. In a second step, a defensive line of vertical elements is placed between vehicles and pedestrians. Large historical statues and landmarks, planters, rocks, trees, fountains, light poles, bus shelters, and even contemporary art can be part of this ram-proof landscape.

As the threat remains, our cities will increasingly become ram-proof and therefore ever more cluttered with obstacles that are camouflaged as art, nature or furniture. Street profiles will change to prevent vehicles from accelerating rapidly; more stairs and steps will appear. Interestingly enough, this recent development toward a ram-proof city directly contradicts the emptying out of public space as described above. In this tragic need to design a protective city lies the potential for a more livable, pedestrian-friendly, and diverse city.

3 www.terrorism-info.org
4 www.theguardian.com
5 *Rumiyah* no. 3, November 2016
azelin.files.wordpress.com

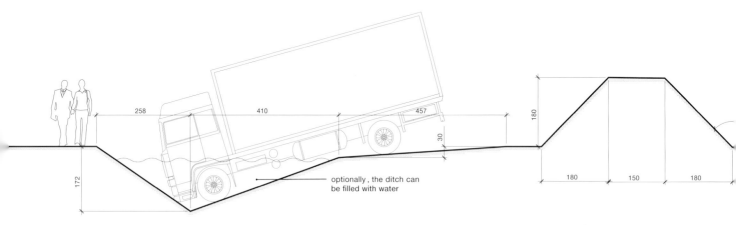

258   410   457   180

172   30   180   150   180

optionally, the ditch can be filled with water

1 Anti-vehicle ditch. Ditches offer a simple method of securing a lengthy perimeter against moving vehicles. Trapezoidal ditches should be avoided since vehicles could drive in and out of the ditch in a slow attack.

Water. A channel can be designed to be an effective trap. In combination with walls, it can be engineered to stop a vehicle. Water can also be used in the form of lakes and fountains.

2 Berm. Berms are more intrusive than ditches, since they can easily hinder the view and therefore help to fragment public space.

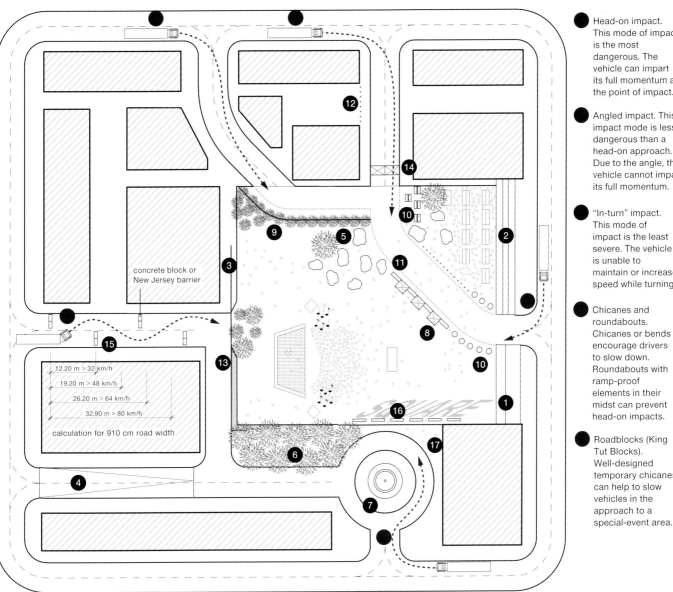

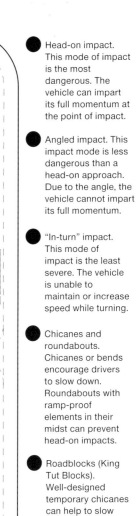

Head-on impact. This mode of impact is the most dangerous. The vehicle can impart its full momentum at the point of impact.

Angled impact. This impact mode is less dangerous than a head-on approach. Due to the angle, the vehicle cannot impart its full momentum.

"In-turn" impact. This mode of impact is the least severe. The vehicle is unable to maintain or increase speed while turning.

Chicanes and roundabouts. Chicanes or bends encourage drivers to slow down. Roundabouts with ramp-proof elements in their midst can prevent head-on impacts.

Roadblocks (King Tut Blocks). Well-designed temporary chicanes can help to slow vehicles in the approach to a special-event area.

concrete block or New Jersey barrier

12.20 m > 32 km/h
19.20 m > 48 km/h
26.20 m > 64 km/h
32.90 m > 80 km/h
calculation for 910 cm road width

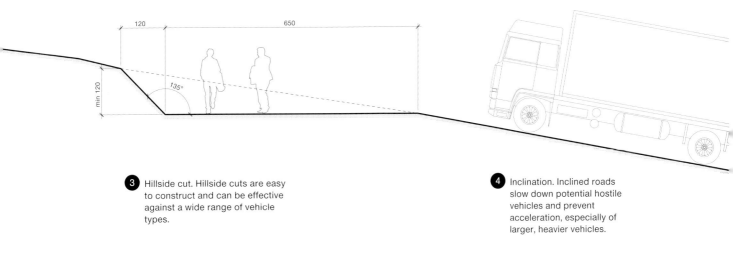

3 Hillside cut. Hillside cuts are easy to construct and can be effective against a wide range of vehicle types.

4 Inclination. Inclined roads slow down potential hostile vehicles and prevent acceleration, especially of larger, heavier vehicles.

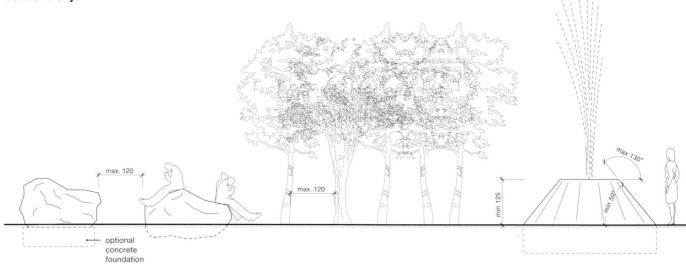

5 Rocks. Rocks are a landscape design element; they may serve as seating but also as engineered barriers.

6 Trees. Forest or densely packed trees form a natural barrier. Gaps between trees may require additional measures. The use of individual trees is not generally recommended.

7 Features with sloped pedestal. For elements with a sloped base, specific heights and angles need to be taken into account so that the measure can be effective.

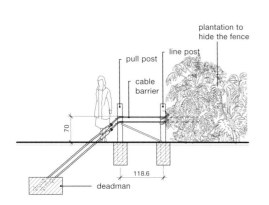

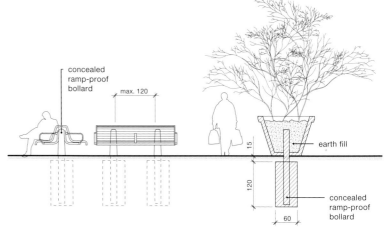

9 Fences. Cable restraints that stop the vehicle are hidden among vegetation. The cable is held in place by bollards and is anchored to the ground by a "deadman."

10 Hidden bollards (in planters and street furniture). Crash-rated bollards can be concealed between benches and in planters to minimize visual obstruction, save space, and secure the terrain.

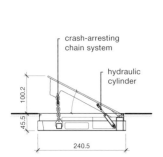

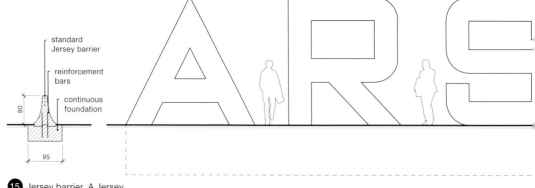

14 Wedge barrier. The barrier ramp is flush with the roadway and does not obstruct pedestrian or vehicular traffic when not active. The system can rise in less than two seconds.

15 Jersey barrier. A Jersey barrier or Jersey wall is a modular concrete barrier that separates lanes of traffic. When used as a permanent measure, the Jersey wall is reinforced by a concrete foundation.

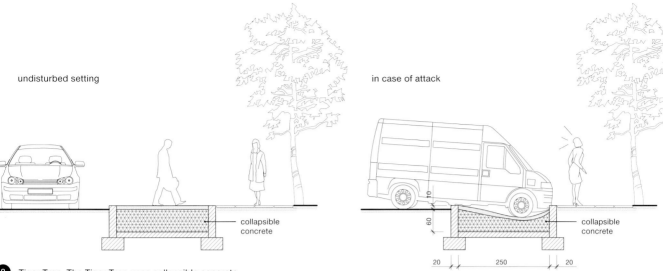

undisturbed setting   in case of attack

collapsible concrete

collapsible concrete

8 Tiger Trap. The Tiger Trap uses collapsible concrete technology below at-grade paving or planting. Under the weight of a vehicle, the material collapses and is stopped by a wall.

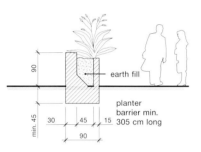

earth fill

planter barrier min. 305 cm long

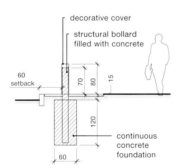

decorative cover

structural bollard filled with concrete

continuous concrete foundation

60 setback

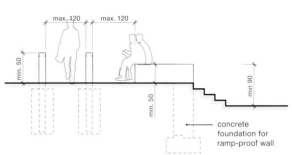

concrete foundation for ramp-proof wall

11 Planter barrier. Engineered planters have below-grade reinforcements and become fixed elements of the design. Planters located on the surface rely on friction to stop or delay a vehicle.

12 Bollard. Cylindrical vehicle barrier made of steel or concrete. Bollards prevent vehicles from passing, but allow the entrance of pedestrians and bicycles. A bollard system connects all bollards underground with one continuous beam.

13 Stairs and retention walls. Stairs and walls are effective measures that can be incorporated in the design. Sufficient heights and angles have to be taken into account.

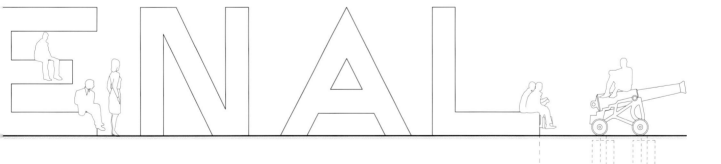

16 Advertisement. In the case of the Emirates Stadium in London, the name of the Arsenal soccer club functions as a massive shield at a critical access point. The letters can allegedly stop a seven-ton truck.

17 Icons and art in public space. For example, cannons, which feature in the Arsenal soccer club's insignia, are used as disguised "tank traps" to stop car bombers.

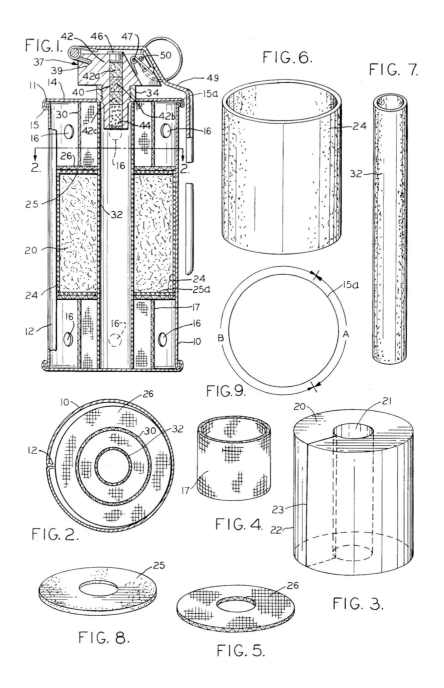

Illustration attached to a US patent for a tear gas grenade
by Michael K. Levenson

Crowd Control

The positive power of the masses is something that is praised and discussed extensively. Swarm intelligence, crowdfunding, crowdsourcing, and crowd innovation are some of the keywords that promise economic and social progress thanks to the bundling of the power of individuals. Social media platforms make it easy to combine individuals into masses, just as frequent and cheap international transportation mobilizes masses all around the world.

On the flip side, mass tourism is resulting in chaotic situations at major sites, the threat of terrorism at crowded urban spots puts pressure on urban security, and mass urbanization combined with mass migration demands ever more refined methods of managing and controlling streams of people.

Six people per square meter is the threshold at which bodies are jammed so tightly that they begin to behave like a fluid.[1] Pressure waves can travel through them and they can lose control. Yet in most cases, crowd control is not about avoiding a disaster through overcrowding but about avoiding disastrous media coverage. The police also have to watch out since, through the use of smartphones, helmet cameras, and even drones, participants in demonstrations monitor the police continuously. Additionally, feeling safe is at the top of the list for people choosing to visit or live in a specific place. Thus, crowd control is important not only to the masses involved, but much more to the masses not involved but potentially bothered by them.

All this is resulting in an ever more sophisticated set of crowd-control strategies by event organizers, tourist boards, and especially police forces. The smallest sign of an unusual gathering rings alarm bells, and even the smallest demonstrations (which always need to be announced and permitted weeks beforehand) result in a massive police operation. Orchestrated handling and professional communication to the crowd, the public, and the citizens is key. To restore confidence in safety, the public needs to be assured that everything is at any moment "under control," with the downside that this naturally includes each and every one of us.

1 www.theguardian.com, www.gkstill.com

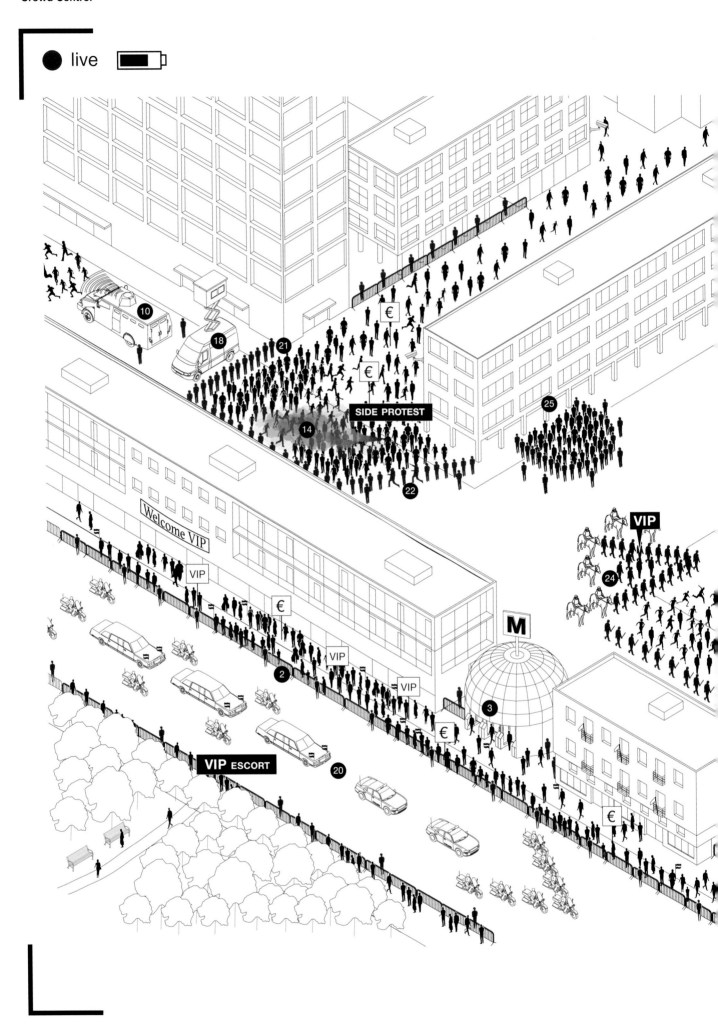

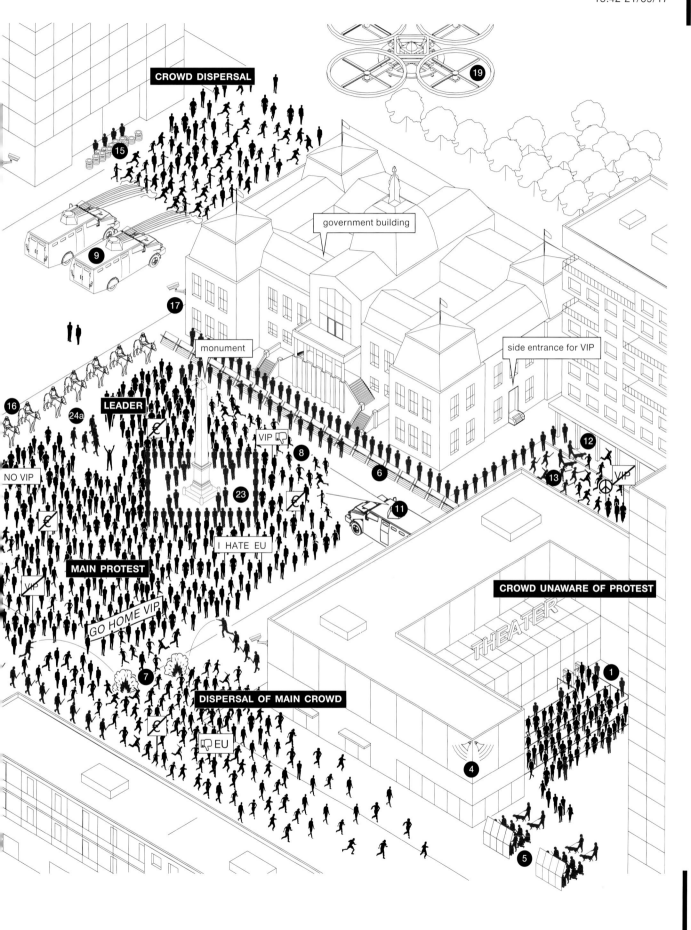

99

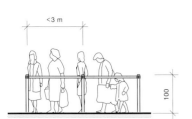

1 Stanchions. Used to create barricaded lines with adequate numbers of breaks and turns at regular intervals to maintain orderly flow and reduce the risk of harm.

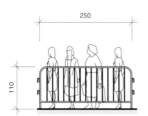

2 Temporary barriers. Used to provide a physical and psychological way to limit movement outside dedicated areas. They interlock to prevent being moved or tipped.

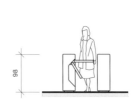

3 Turnstile. Used at entrances and exits to limit entry and restrict flow, preventing overcrowding inside a building/venue.

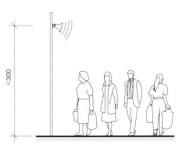

4 Public-address system. A system used to issue clear, compelling commands that help create a sense of calm and facilitate a quick, safe exit.

5 Shield wall formation. Based on ancient Roman techniques, a tight formation allows a compact unit of officers to find protection behind shields.

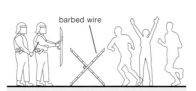

6 Barbed-wire barriers. Metal barriers used to create physical denial of a crowd's access to a suspected target of protest.

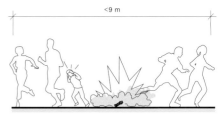

7 Stun grenades. Used as a diversionary tactic, their explosion emits a bright light and a noise of around 175 dB. Causes temporary loss of sight and hearing, as well as confusion.

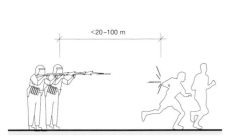

8 Baton rounds. Projectiles intended to strike their target with sufficient force to cause compliance by inducing pain.

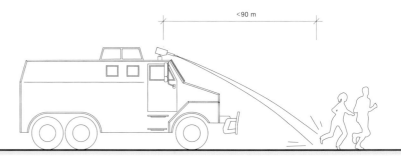

9 Water cannon. A high-pressure pump jets out thousands of liters per minute. The vehicle is armored to resist attack from projectiles and generally has a 9000-liter water reservoir.

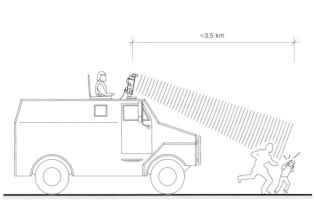

10 Long-range acoustic device. A device that blasts targeted, amplified sound of up to 160 dB, which is extremely painful to human ears, in order to disperse crowds.

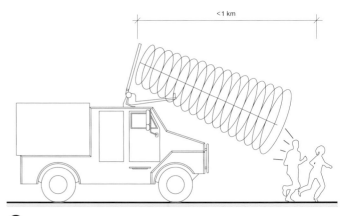

11 Active denial system. A vehicle-mounted system which projects a focused beam of millimeter waves at a frequency of 95 GHz for a very short duration, giving targets a feeling of intense heat, causing crowds to disperse.

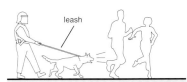

12 Police dogs. Dogs are used to assist with the dispersal of crowds and often to support police cordons.

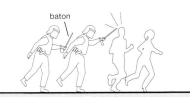

13 Baton charge. A coordinated tactic involving police officers charging with batons and often riot shields, intended to cause pain and disperse the crowd.

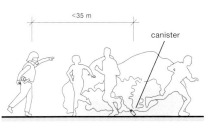

14 Gas fired from guns in grenade canisters which causes severe eye, skin, and respiratory irritation. Used to disperse crowds.

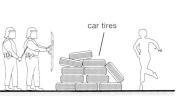

15 Improvised barriers. Vehicles, traffic jams, and items such as car tires are used to create barricades to block or channel crowd movement.

16 Mounted police. Horse-mounted police use height and a strong presence to control crowds. They may also charge at crowds to clear a path through them or to disperse the groups.

17 CCTV video analysis. These systems monitor crowds, counting objects, and detecting humans in order to quickly spot threats.

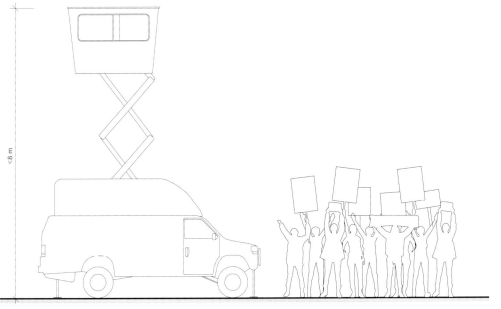

18 Mobile surveillance tower. Vehicle-mounted system which uses automatic hydraulic stabilization to elevate a temporary surveillance tower up to 8 m in order to monitor crowd activity from a height.

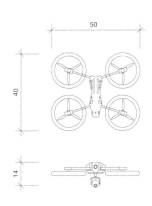

19 Surveillance drone. Video surveillance via drones can provide the police with clear views of the action and the ability to focus on specific scenes and individuals. Lately, there have been indications of police equipping drones with weaponry such as tasers, pepper spray, and rubber bullets.

Sweepers. Motorcycles clear the way so that the speed can remain consistent. The motorcycles form a wedge, gradually knocking everyone to either curb.

Lead car. It works as a guide and a buffer for what lies ahead.

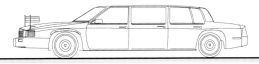

VIP limousine: The limousine rides at the very center of the motorcade "package."

Rear guard. Another set of motorcycles or police cars covers the back of the motorcade to ensure no one launches a sneak attack from behind.

20 Motorcade. Motorcades can be used to transport a very important person (VIP), usually a political figure. Yet motorcades can also be used in protests and demonstrations, as happened in Ukraine in 2013–2014: the Automaidan.

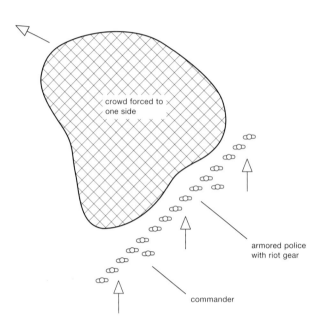

21 Line. The line is a basic formation that has come into frequent use because of its offensive and defensive applications. Used as an offensive formation, the line is deployed in order to drive a crowd straight back, across an open area, or down a city street. As a defensive formation, the line is used to block or contain a crowd and/or to deny access to the crowd.

22 Echelon. An offensive formation consisting of a diagonal line used to turn or divert groups in open or built-up areas and to move crowds away from buildings, fences, and walls.

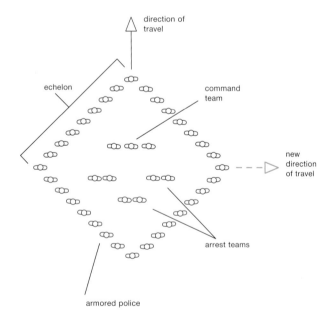

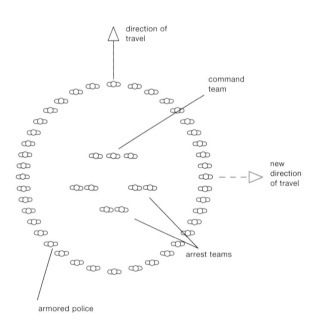

23 Diamond. As a defensive formation, this is used when all-around security is required in open areas. As an offensive formation, it is used for entering a crowd, especially by extraction teams. The symmetrical shape means the direction of travel can easily be changed.

23a Circular formation. The circular formation is used for the same purpose as the diamond formation. The decision to use this formation is based on the shape or structure of the crowd.

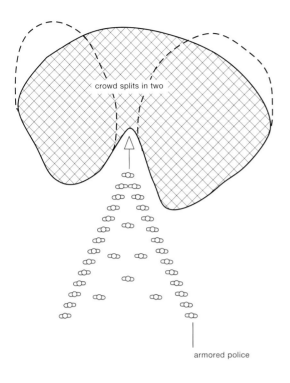

crowd splits in two

armored police

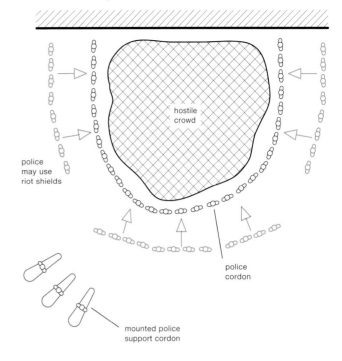

wall / blank building facade

hostile crowd

police may use riot shields

police cordon

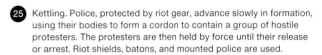

mounted police support cordon

24 Wedge. An offensive formation that is used to penetrate and split crowds into smaller groups.

24a Wedges are used to allow VIPs to pass through a crowd, but can also be used to extract ringleaders.

25 Kettling. Police, protected by riot gear, advance slowly in formation, using their bodies to form a cordon to contain a group of hostile protesters. The protesters are then held by force until their release or arrest. Riot shields, batons, and mounted police are used.

Hand-and-Arm Signals by the platoon commander

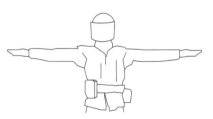

Line. Raise both arms from the sides until they are horizontal. The arms and hands should be extended with the palms down.

Echelon. Extend one arm 45° above the horizontal and the other 45° below the horizontal. The arms and hands should be extended. The upper arm points in the direction of the echelon when the commander faces the troops.

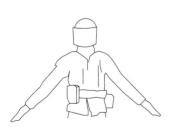

Wedge. Extend both arms downward and to the sides at a 45° angle. The arms and hands should be extended with the palms down and facing inward.

Diamond. Extend both arms above the head. Bend the elbows slightly and touch the fingertips together.

Circular. Give the diamond signal. Then give a circular motion with the right hand.

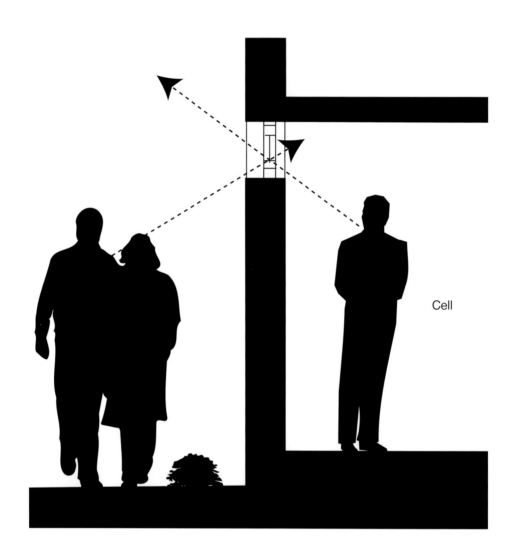

Cell

Window sill height above floor level prevents view conflict.

Prison Cells

The prison cell is a mirror of society. From a cell's size, amenities, and maintenance, one can draw a direct conclusion about a country's level of prosperity, democracy, and humanity. Apparently, wrongdoers need to be locked up or locked away, since there is no country without prisons. Even the most humanist governments lock people away. But there are big differences in the philosophy of imprisonment, symbolized by two extremes: the prison as a place to get rid of people versus the prison as a place that can turn inmates into better people. Cell layouts differ accordingly.

Cell sizes can vary from as little as 2 m² (Guinea) to a quite spacious 12 m² (Switzerland). Some countries have guidelines, but the reality is that in many developing countries space requirements have yet to be established. In the absence of universal standards, international organizations have developed a minimum standard for the architecture of cells. The Red Cross states that a single cell should be at least 5.4 m².[1] Windows have to be the size of at least 10 percent of the floor space and should allow detainees to see part of the external environment.

Today there are more than 10 million prisoners in the world.[2] The United States houses almost one quarter of the world's detainees. But it was not always like that. Since the 1980s, starting with the privatization of prisons, the number of prisoners in the US more than quadrupled, from 0.5 to 2.2 million.[3] Consequently, incarceration went from being a state responsibility to an industry. Today, on Wall Street, the US prison industry is worth $70 billion and the US incarceration industry has an estimated annual cost of $74 billion.[4] This equates to $32 000 per prisoner which is, cruelly enough, the value of a slave in 1850 (in the equivalent of today's money). The privatization of prisons not only influences the jurisdiction, but also the prison cell architecture. The nonstop striving for efficiency by the prison industry results in initiatives like "Windowless is More," proposed by a US architecture firm specializing in correctional facilities.[5] The company proposes windowless-cell architecture as "a strategic prison design approach that offers clear financial, logistical, operational, and social benefits, while keeping security at the forefront." Accordingly, the company's renderings of prison complexes are reminiscent of big-box storage depots.

Stock exchange companies have managed to turn prisoners from humans into tradable commodities. Dictatorial regimes have come to the same conclusion, although from a very different angle. As opposition, architects who design prison cells should design them as a human habitat, no different from a living room. And we, the free part of society, should be aware that it is we who hold the keys to the prison cells and the key to what they ought to look like.

1 www.icrc.org
2 www.prisonstudies.org
3 www.sentencingproject.org
4 www.smartasset.com, www.investigate.afsc.org
5 "Windowless is more: Innovative prison cell designs balance function, form and funding" by L. R. Kimball, www.lrkimball.com

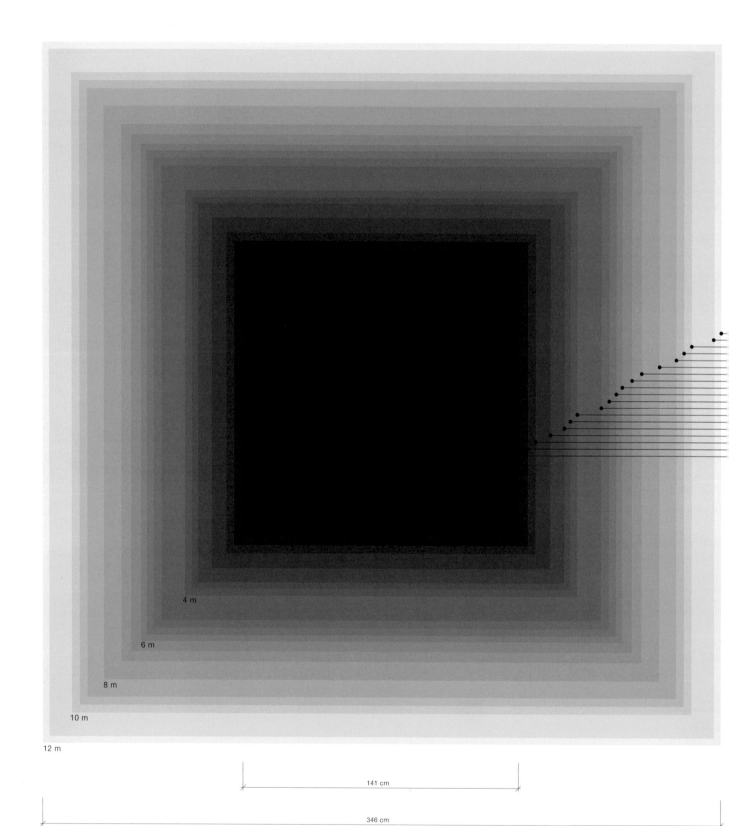

4 m

6 m

8 m

10 m

12 m

141 cm

346 cm

ground section

12.0 m²–Switzerland*

11.5 m²–Greece*, Guatemala

10.0 m²–The Netherlands

9.5 m²–Spain

9.0 m²–France, Germany*, Italy, Latvia*, Mauritius

8.0 m²–China*, New Zealand

7.0 m²–Canada*, Ireland, Scotland*

6.5 m²–Australia*, Mexico, USA

6.0 m²–European Committee for the Prevention of Torture & Brazil*, Chile*

CPT

5.7 m²–South Africa

5.4 m²–International Committee of the Red Cross & England and Wales

ICRC

5.0 m²–Argentina, Japan, Thailand

4.0 m²–Albania*, Hungary*, Ukraine*

3.7 m²–Kenya

3.5 m²–Czechia*, Senegal, Slovakia*

3.0 m²–Estonia*, Israel, Poland*

2.5 m²–Indonesia, Russian Federation*, Romania

2.3 m²–Iran

2.0 m²–Guinea*

* Statutory law applies

141 cm

346 cm

section

107

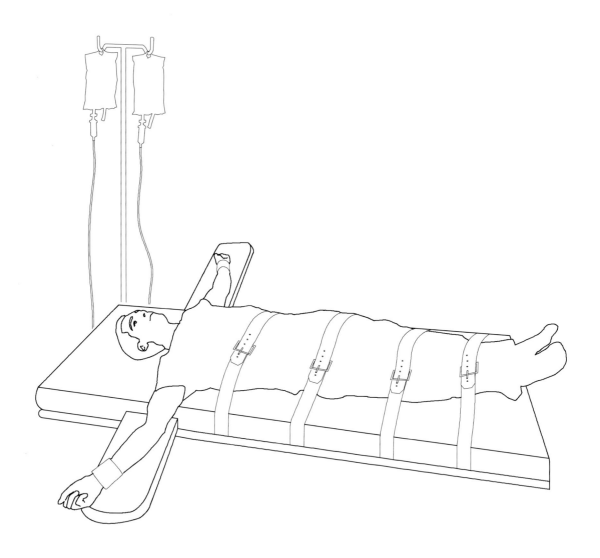

A Vast Conspiracy

Brendan McGetrick

Stanley Tookie Williams awoke for the last time on December 13, 2005. San Quentin State Prison's maximum-security cells had been on lockdown since midnight, as is customary on the day of an execution. Within this environment of intensified imprisonment, Williams was relatively free. He spent the day walking the cell blocks and meeting with friends and family in the prison visiting room.

At precisely 6 p.m., Williams was moved to a death watch cell next to the execution chamber. There, three guards observed him constantly throughout the rest of the evening. Williams was offered a last meal, which he refused. A month earlier, he'd told the *San Francisco Chronicle*, "I don't want food or water or sympathy from the place that is going to kill me. I don't want anyone present for the sick and perverted spectacle. The thought of that is appalling and inhumane. It is disgusting for a human to sit and watch another human die."

At 11:30 p.m., Williams was given a new pair of denim jeans and a new blue work shirt to wear.

At 11:45 p.m., the first group of witnesses was led into a room adjacent to the execution chamber. They were placed in a half-circle around the chamber— 11 in chairs at the window, the rest on risers along the walls. The witnesses included state officials, lawyers, and people who had requested that they observe the execution on behalf of Williams or his victims. At 11:55 p.m., witnesses from the media were escorted in and positioned on risers. Once positioned, no one was allowed to move or speak. In total there were 39 witnesses present, 17 of them from the press.

Among the witnesses were impassioned supporters of Williams, the 51-year-old cofounder of the Los Angeles street gang known as the Crips, who had later renounced violence and written influential books advocating peace. Sharing the room with them were survivors of the four people Williams had been convicted of killing: a 26-year-old convenience store clerk named Albert Owens, motel owners Yen-I Yang and Tsai-Shai Chen Yang, and their 43-year-old daughter Yee-Chen Lin.

At 12:00 a.m., prison officials placed a final call to the headquarters of the state Department of Justice to determine whether a last-minute stay had been issued. That process took less than a minute, and at 12:01 Williams was led into the prison's lime-green execution chamber through an oval door similar to a submarine hatch.

Williams shuffled in with a green-uniformed guard on each side, loosely holding his arms, and three following behind. His wrists were handcuffed to a waist chain. Williams and the guards barely fit inside the 2.3-meter-wide octagonal chamber. Originally designed for two lethal gas chairs, the room had been retrofitted with a lethal injection gurney in 1996.

Williams slowly lay down and the guard team secured him in place, using black straps with buckles at his shoulders, chest, waist, knees, and feet, and brown-leather Velcro straps at his wrists. The process took about two minutes, during which Williams stared at the ceiling, his lips moving rapidly. At one point, a tear slid down his cheek.

A medical technician and an assistant entered and attached a cardiac monitor. They then inserted catheters into two of Williams's veins. The process usually takes around five minutes, but in this case there were complications. The first catheter slid in at the crook of Williams's right elbow, taking just two minutes to seat but spurting so much blood that it soaked a cotton swab, which shone deep red before being taped off.

It took the medical technician, a woman with short black hair, 11 minutes of painful probing before the second needle hit home. At the first attempt, at 12:04 a.m., Williams clenched his toes. At 12:05, he struggled against the restraints to look up at the press gallery behind him, delivering a hard stare for several seconds. By 12:10, the medical tech's lips were tight and white, and sweat was pooling on her forehead as she probed Williams's arm.

"You guys doing that right?" Williams asked in anger. A female guard whispered a reassuring response. Another guard, his jaw clenched tightly, patted Williams's shoulder as if to comfort him.

Outside the chamber, Barbara Becnel, Williams's friend and coauthor of his books, stood with her two companions at the only window with a clear line of sight into Williams's eyes. They thrust their fists upward in what appeared to be a black power salute. One of them called out softly: "Tookie." They whispered "I love you" and "God bless you" as they looked adoringly into Williams's eyes.

Three meters away, Lora Owens, stepmother of one of Williams's victims, sat stiffly, looking through the thick glass at the top of Williams's head. Her red hair never moved, and her mouth remained a tight line. A blond woman sitting next to Owens put her arm around her, then removed it and clasped her hands in her lap.

At 12:16 a.m., the second needle was finally inserted. Williams's hands were taped to the gurney arms. The guards hurried out the door and sealed it, leaving Williams with two clear intravenous lines snaking off his arms and into holes in the back wall of the execution chamber. The prison warden asked Williams if he had any last words to say. Williams declined. The warden left, the door was shut, and Williams was alone.

At 12:18 a.m., a female prison guard loudly read off the warrant proclaiming that prisoner number C29300 had been sentenced to die and that "the execution shall now proceed." Williams forced his head up one last time to stare into the eyes of his friends. He kept it raised for 90 seconds before passing out.

From behind the walls of the chamber, out of view of the witnesses, a prison official pressed three plungers in succession to send poison through the intravenous lines into Williams's veins.

The first plunger administered 5 grams of sodium pentothal to put him to sleep. The lines were then flushed with saline solution. The second plunger injected 50 ml of pancuronium bromide to stop his breathing. The lines were flushed again, and the third plunger sent 50 ml of potassium chloride to stop his heart.

Williams's chest heaved several times as he lay with his eyes closed. Sorrow washed over the faces of Becnel and her female companion as his head sank, and they clasped their hands in prayer.

At 12:35 a.m., a doctor watching the cardiac monitor—again, out of view of the witnesses—determined that Williams was dead. A prison official wrote up a short notice announcing that the execution was over. In the witness room, the audience heard someone behind the walls call out, "He's flatlined." A hand slid a paper through a slot in the witness room, and a guard read off a brief statement affirming Williams's death. Thirty seconds later, the room was cleared.

At 12:35 a.m., the prison guards ordered the 39 witnesses to leave. The first to go were the three friends Williams had invited to watch his final moments. The room was so quiet that when one man jangled his pocket change, the sound echoed off the walls.

Just as they crossed the threshold into the chilly outdoors, the three whipped their heads back and screamed in unison: "The state of California just killed an innocent man!" Across the room, a witness for one of Williams's victims stared at them in horror and then burst into tears.

This account is based on an eyewitness report by Kevin Fagan, published in the *San Francisco Chronicle* on December 12 and 14, 2005.

———

I remember reading about Stanley Williams in the days before and after his death. Throughout the winter of 2015, the justness of Williams's sentence was furiously debated by politicians, lawyers, activists, and ordinary citizens for and against the death penalty. Both sides had a compelling case. For: Williams was a convicted quadruple murderer who also happened to be the founder of one of America's deadliest street gangs. Against: Throughout his 24 years of imprisonment, Williams maintained his innocence, renounced gangs, and authored a series of books warning children against the life he had led.

On a practical level, the debate was resolved by California's governor at the time, Arnold Schwarzenegger, who ignored the pleas of his Hollywood friends and rejected Williams's last-ditch appeal for clemency. It was a masterpiece of Californian spectacle: on one side Williams, a black revolutionary and bona fide killer, backed by Bianca Jagger and Snoop Dogg; on the other side Schwarzenegger, a European bodybuilder turned movie star turned tough-on-crime Republican. The headlines wrote themselves: "Tookie v Arnold" was how *The Economist* covered it.

The whole episode is a master class in how an infernally complex, multifaceted issue is boiled down to an easy-to-understand opposition: Tookie vs. Arnold; Good vs. Bad; Life vs. Death. But, of course, Arnold didn't kill Tookie. Not literally. He was nowhere near the execution chamber on that day. Neither were the judge and jury that convicted Williams, nor the manufacturers of the carefully measured cocktail of sodium pentothal, pancuronium bromide, and potassium chloride that ultimately killed him.

It's human nature to attribute a complex action to a single actor. The small amount of drama that we're able to deal with each day is just a glint on the surface of a sea. The great invisible iceberg underneath is the vast association of actors that allow, authorize, and enable anything to happen. Regardless of who administers the process, a state-sanctioned execution is a vast collaboration. To attribute it to any single person or institution is to fundamentally misunderstand political power—and the indispensable roles design and technology play in maintaining it.

As Bruno Latour has pointed out, it is by mistake or through unfairness that our headlines read, "Man flies," "Woman goes to space." Flying is a property not of individuals, but of the whole association of entities that includes airports and planes, launch pads and ticket counters. "B-52s do not fly; the US Air Force flies," Latour has said. "Action is simply not a property of humans but of an association of actants."[1] In this sense, Stanley Williams's three witnesses were much closer to the truth than any news account: It was the state of California—

1 Bruno Latour, "On Technical Mediation: Philosophy, Sociology, Genealogy," *Common Knowledge*, vol. 3, no. 2 (1994), 35.

including its prisons, its hospitals, and gun shops, its governor, and the 52%
of its citizens who voted against a 2012 ballot initiative that would have repealed
the death penalty—that killed their friend.

——

This is a book about tyranny. It joins a tremendous volume of works on the
subject, but its contribution is unique in its insistence on the role of nonhuman
entities in making and maintaining society. These entities include objects—walls,
benches, and bunker busters—as well as operations—controlled demolition,
crowd control, slaughter, and execution. In doing so, this handbook closes the
escape routes often taken by architects, engineers, and the rest of us to avoid
responsibility for the tyrannical features of modern life.

The customer is as culpable for the horrors of the slaughterhouse as the
foreman overseeing its operation, the architects who design its form, and the
multinational corporation that orchestrates the slew of other agents needed
to serve our massive appetite. Instinctively, we know this. But it's easy to ignore,
and this is why this book's emphasis on nonhuman elements—the tools of
tyranny, whether chiseled from stone or genetically engineered—is so valuable.

For hundreds of thousands of years, we humans have extended our social
relations to nonhuman entities with which—with whom—we form collectives.
This is most obvious in our intense socialization and reconfiguration of plants
and animals—so intense that their shape, function, and genetic makeup are
changed. This redesign provides previously wild fauna and flora with the social
characteristics necessary to contribute to collectives, such as the "defensive
landscape" so brilliantly detailed at the end of this book.

When within the collective, all participants lose their individual identities. No one,
including the human apparently at the center of it all, has a fixed role. There
are no subjects or objects, only composites created when two or more entities
come in contact. It is the contact itself, the link between human and nonhuman,
that turns a dog into a guard dog and bamboo into a fence.

It can, as shown in the chapter on passports, also turn a surgeon into a suspected terrorist. Regardless of her politics, education or intentions, an Afghan
citizen becomes someone else when she holds a passport in her hand.
She is no longer just a person, but a composite—a passport-person—with open
access to only 22 countries. Were this surgeon to one day receive German
citizenship, the German passport itself would change. Through its contact with
someone born in Kabul, the powerful little book that grants German citizens
no-questions-asked access to 159 countries would suddenly weaken and in
some cases no longer guarantee entry at all.

Nonhumans—whether organic or inorganic—stabilize the social order. They
are at once malleable and durable; they can be shaped very quickly but, once
shaped, last far longer than the interactions that produced them. Every day,
we encounter hundreds, even thousands, of invisible administrators who
are remote in time and space yet are simultaneously active and present. The
Camden Bench, for instance, a piece of public architecture described as
"specially crafted to make sure that it is not used as anything except a bench,"
is ultimately not made of matter. It is instead full of engineers and councilors
and concerned citizens, commingling their wills and their agendas with those of
concrete, limestone, and granite.

The bench is a small piece of a vast ecosystem of urban control described
in the Defensive City chapter of this book. For the unseen overseers
who produce them and place them in our cities, the tramp-proof, graffiti-proof,

Death by stoning–Iran

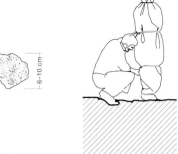  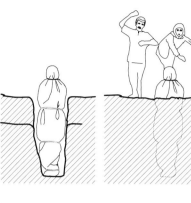 

woman
man

❶ The size of the stone used in stoning shall not be too large to kill the convict by one or two throws and at the same time shall not be too small to be called a stone. The condemned prisoner is counseled by advising clergymen and asked to repent and share his or her last will. The prisoner submits to a preburial washing with lotus water and pure water in advance of the stoning so that the body will be ready for burial after the execution.

❷ The condemned has his or her hands bound and is wrapped in three pieces of white shroud in accordance with Muslim burial practices.

❸ Law enforcement or prison officials are obliged to dig a hole in the place where the punishment will be carried out and provide stones for the stone-throwers. The prisoner is placed in the hole before the stoning. According to Muslim law, the ditch must be deep enough to reach a man's waist or a woman's chest. A judge inspects the execution area for appropriate depth.

❹ Once approved, the condemned is placed in the ditch and the stoning begins. The crowd of stone-throwers is made up of recruited volunteer paramilitary groups. Adult men comprise the bulk of the group, though there are no fixed age or gender restrictions. Iranian law originally intended for stoning to be conducted out in the open, with community participation.

❺ If the stoning sentence is based on the condemned's own confession, then the sentencing judge throws the first stone, followed by the rest of the crowd. If the condemnation is based on the testimony of witnesses, then the witnesses throw the stones first, then the judge, and then the others.

❻ The stoning takes anywhere from twenty minutes to two hours. A doctor recruited to oversee the execution (often against his will), will periodically stop proceedings to check whether the victim is dead. If not, the stoning resumes until the prisoner is finally pronounced dead. The law mandates that the proceedings be recorded and shared via media.

In 2008, Iran's judiciary scrapped stoning in draft legislation submitted to parliament for approval. The 2012 penal code officially ended the punishment of stoning in Iran. Nevertheless, women have continued to be sentenced to death by stoning as late as 2015.

Death by firing squad–China

d = 2000 m

d = 200 m
d = 50 m

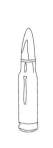 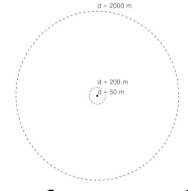   

❶ After receiving an order from the Supreme People's Court, the People's Court at a lower level shall see that a death sentence is carried out within seven days. The criminal's family is made to pay for the bullet.

A death sentence may be carried out on the execution grounds or in a designated place of custody. Executions shall be announced, but not carried out in public.

❷ In some parts of China, there is no specific site for executions. A team of scouts chooses a place in advance to serve as the execution grounds. The grounds will normally have three perimeters: the innermost 50 meters is the responsibility of the execution team; the 200-meter radius from the center is the responsibility of the People's Armed Police; and the 2 km alert line is the responsibility of the local police. The public is generally not allowed to view the execution.

❸ Chinese laws do not specifically state the site of execution grounds, but shootings are usually carried out at military target ranges, along riverbanks, and on remote hillsides, the prisoner being transported in an open vehicle from the public venue where he or she was sentenced.

The judicial officer directing the execution shall verify the identity of the criminal, ask him if he has any last words or letters, and then deliver him to the executioner for the death sentence to be carried out.

❹ The prisoner is made to wear a dark blue jumpsuit. The prisoner's arms are shackled behind his or her body as he is made to kneel down before receiving a single bullet fired at close range into the back of the head or neck by a soldier of policeman. Sometimes a bullet is fired into the heart from behind using an automatic rifle.

❺ After a death sentence is carried out, the People's Court that implemented it shall notify the family members of the criminal. After the prisoner is pronounced dead, the kidneys, heart, and corneas are removed from the dead body and are used in transplants at local hospitals.

Death pentalty per country 2017

■ abolitionist
░ abolitionist in practice
■ retentionist

retentionist countries:

Afghanistan	Botswana	Iraq	Pakistan	Thailand
Bahrain	Chad	Japan	Palestine	United Arab Emirates
Bangladesh	China	Jordan	Saint Kitts & Nevis	United States
Belarus	Egypt	Kuwait	Saudi Arabia	Vietnam
	Ethiopia	Libya	Singapore	Yemen
	The Gambia	Malaysia	Somalia	
	India	Mongolia	South Sudan	
	Indonesia	Nigeria	Sudan	
	Iran	North Korea	Syria	
		Oman	Taiwan	

skateboard-proof public bench offers a way to control others without giving commands. In today's most liberal cities, there is less and less need to rely on signs or slogans to dictate what can and can't be done. The rules are written into the city itself. With the help of their nonhuman collaborators, our leaders have developed a new, postliterate language of control.

To truly understand tyranny, we must expand political and social theory to include these nonhuman agents. We must become conversant in the language of coercive design in both its physical and virtual forms. We must recognize our own roles in the vast collective effort that maintains the scale, asymmetry, durability, power, hierarchy, and the distortion of roles that define the current social order. Doing so is a taxing, dispiriting, indispensable effort for anyone committed to fairness and freedom. Let this handbook be a guide.

The Stoning of St. Stephen by Marx Reichlich, 1506

Death by beheading–Saudi Arabia

❶ Saudi Arabia uses a traditional scimitar that is 1100 to 1200 mm long.

The condemned of both sexes are typically given tranquilizers and then taken by police van to a public square or a parking lot after midday prayers. The prisoner's eyes are covered. The police clear the square of traffic, and a plastic sheet of about 1.5 square meters is laid out on the ground.

❷ Dressed in either a white robe or his or her own clothes, barefoot, with shackled feet, and hands cuffed behind his or her back, the prisoner is led by a police officer to the center of the sheet, and is made to kneel facing Mecca. An Interior Ministry official reads out the prisoner's name and crime to the crowd.

❸ The executioner is handed the sword by a policeman. He raises the scimitar, often swinging it two or three times in the air to warm up his arm muscles before approaching the prisoner from behind and jabbing him or her in the back with the tip of the blade, causing the person to raise his or her head.

❹ With a single swing of the sword, the prisoner is decapitated. Normally it takes just one swing of the sword to sever the head, often sending it flying a meter or more.

❺ Paramedics bring the head to a doctor, who uses a gloved hand to stop the blood spurting from the neck. The doctor sews the head back on, and the body is wrapped in the plastic sheet and taken away in an ambulance. Burial takes place in an unmarked grave in the prison cemetery.

Death by hanging–Kuwait

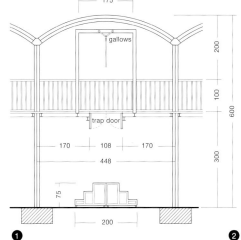

❶ In Kuwait, for each prisoner, a gallows pavilion is provided with a common stairway that leads to the upper level.

For the "long drop" hanging method typically practiced in Kuwait, a measured drop of approximately 2.2 meters is given. The trap door is sprung by a lever, and the impact of the fall causes the dislocation of the third or fourth vertebra. The body goes limp immediately and death is instantaneous. However, if the ratio of the drop and rope length are out of sync with the weight of the prisoner, the victim is strangled–an episode that can last up to fifteen minutes. Too far a drop can result in decapitation. For this reason, the British Home Office issued the "Official Table of Drops," which was in use until the suspension of capital punishment in 1965. It calculated a drop energy of roughly 1000 foot-pounds, which when divided by the prisoner's weight in pounds, resulted in the drop height in feet.

❷ The noose used in Kuwait hangings was developed by William Marwood in the 1870s. It is a brass eyelet that allows the rope to run more freely; this has been shown to cause a quicker death. The eyelet is held in place by a rubber washer. The hemp rope is usually 4 m long and 1.9 cm in diameter, with a leather-bound part where the rope meets the neck.

❸ The condemned prisoner is given time to prepare and pray before the execution.

❹ The prisoner, dressed in a brown boilersuit, with leather straps holding the wrists and arms behind him or her, is led to a gray-painted metal and wood gallows by an execution team shrouded in ski masks. Here, he or she is made to climb the steps up to the platform some three meters above the ground and is placed on a trap-door. A leather strap is placed around the ankles, and the noose is placed around the prisoner's neck. A black hood is placed over his or her head to minimize rope burn and scarring of the skin on the neck.

❺ Once the prisoner is pronounced dead, the body is displayed to onlookers and an announcement is published in the following day's papers.

Death by electric chair–USA

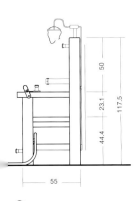

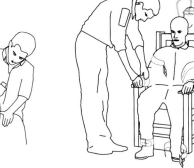

❶ The design of the electric chair emerged from that of the dental chair, since one of its early developers, Alfred P. Southwick, was a dentist. After its first use in 1890, electrocution soon became the prevalent method of execution in the United States, replacing hanging. It remained the most prominent execution method until the mid-1980s, when lethal injection became widely accepted.

❷ Prior to execution, the inmate's head and legs are shaved.

❸ The inmate is led into the execution chamber and strapped into the chair with leather or webbing straps across the chest, thighs, legs, and arms. A metal or leather helmet is then placed on the inmate's head. The leather helmet contains one or two copper electrodes, which are placed in direct proximity to a brine-soaked sponge to improve contact with the prisoner's skull.

The leg electrode, which typically forms part of the chair, may be coated with Electro-Crème gel, increasing conductivity and reducing burning.

❹ The helmet or headpiece is connected to the wiring. The prisoner will also be wearing a diaper. At the signal from the prison warden, the executioner presses a button on the control panel to deliver an initial shock of between 1700 and 2400 volts at 7.5 amperes, which lasts between 20 and 30 seconds, followed by a second shock of 240 volts at 1.5 amperes for 30 to 60 seconds. The process is automatically timed and controlled.

After a short interval, the process is repeated and the body allowed to remain in the chair with the electricity off for five minutes before being examined by the doctor and pronounced dead. If any heartbeat is still found, a further shock cycle can be administered. Smoke frequently emanates from the inmate's legs and head while the current is flowing.

Death by lethal injection–USA

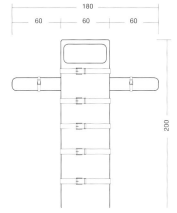

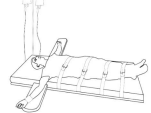

❶ Lethal injection protocols vary from state to state. Typically, the prisoner is strapped to a gurney or a fixed execution table, rather like an operating-room table fashioned with leather or webbing straps.

❷ The prisoner's bare arms are strapped to boards projecting from the sides of the gurney. Two IV lines, one primary and one backup, are initiated, one in each arm. Trained technicians use 14-gauge (4.7 mm diameter) catheters, the largest commercially available needles for a human vein.

❸ Once the catheters are in place, they are flushed with 10 ml of a heparin solution, to prevent clots forming inside the catheter. Then a 1000 ml bag of saline solution is connected to the catheter ends and the inmate is either wheeled into the execution chamber or the curtains surrounding it are drawn back to allow witnesses to see the procedure. The condemned is allowed to make a final statement.

❹ The prison warden gives the signal for the execution to begin, and the technician begins to manually inject the drugs. Typically, five grams of sodium thiopental is administered, a barbiturate that puts the condemned to sleep. The line is flushed with saline solution, and then 50 ml of pancuronium bromide is administered through the IV. This paralyzes all the muscles but the heart. Breathing ceases as the muscles controlling the rib cage and the diaphragm are affected. The IV line is once again flushed with saline, and 50 ml of potassium chloride, an electrolytic interrupter, is administered. This drug blocks nerve impulses to the heart, stopping it from beating.

The amount of sodium thiopental used is between eight and ten times the amount used for medical anesthesia. The condemned may have a peaceful outward appearance, but internally, because of the barbiturate and relaxant, his lungs are imploding and his organs are writhing. Death usually occurs in six to thirteen minutes.

In the United States, a scarcity of lethal-injection drugs for death-row inmates has forced states to bring back other execution methods. Oklahoma reintroduced the gas chamber (2015), Utah the firing squad (2015) and Tennessee the electric chair (2014).

Death Penalty

In general, laws are established to organize a society. In democracies, we believe that laws are implemented by us, the people, and that these laws are necessary in order to protect us from one another.

A state comprises a territory with a very specific set of laws and rules which everyone within this territory must obey. The power of law may be exercised upon anyone who is within this territory. For example, being caught with 15 grams of heroin in one's possession in the Netherlands results in 120 hours of community service,[1] while in Singapore the same offense leads to the death penalty.[2] It's the same heroin and the same person, just different soil under one's feet.

Death sentences are forms of cultural expression as well as public events. Beheading, stoning, shooting, and electrocution each bear an entirely different cultural connotation. The loudest and most violent of all is the gunshot. The sound of the gun is the final heartbeat; it is a lethal firework that cannot be overheard. Injection or electrocution, by contrast, is silent and sterile. No sound is heard; the body retains its shape. This method symbolizes a clean and efficient authority that shies away from a critical public. Stoning conceals the individual murderer. Stone sizes are chosen in a way that a single stone barely kills a person, but the quantity of stones does. As a result, nobody knows the real killer, since it was a group—and, in the broader sense, the denizens of the state. The sword is the most symbolic instrument. It takes the bloodstream into account and plays with the chilling effect of the execution.

Justice is at the heart of the matter. If a crime is committed, if somebody killed my mother or my child, I ask for justice. What should be done to compensate what can't be compensated? To define what justice is, a state authority is established. The definition and implementation of justice are transferred from the individual to the general body of the authority. Real justice is defined not by the system of government (democracy, despotism or monarchy), but by the fact that for each and every person the same crime results in the same punishment.

A state authority that uses its right to kill, does so in the name of all its people. It is a Leviathan that takes up the gun, sword, or stone—and terminates the life of a person. In western Europe and especially in Germany, the memories of an authority that had the right to kill are still very vivid. And it wasn't the Nazis who introduced the death penalty in Germany; a prior law was still in effect,[3] as in most European countries in the 1930s. It was just after World War II when most of the world's nations abolished the death penalty, since it became obvious what danger it poses to a country if the wrong party or the wrong person comes to power.

1 www.om.nl
2 www.cnb.gov.s
3 www.wissen.de

Countries without death penalty by date of abolishment

Of the world's 203 sovereign states, 114 have abolished the death penalty as of the end of 2016; in 89, the possibility of a death sentence is mentioned in their constitution, while 38 of those countries have actively implemented it within the last ten years. China makes by far the most aggressive use of capital punishment, but does not disclose the number of executions, which, according to Amnesty International, are in the thousands. The United States is the only country that elects a president democratically and also implements the death penalty.

The 1990s and the 2000s have been two exceptional decades. 60 countries, or more than half of all abolitionist countries, got rid of the death penalty during this period. Three more such decades and the 92 countries that currently still have the death penalty in their legal system would renounce it and the world would be free of the death penalty.

Unfortunately, the speed of abolition does not appear to be continuous. President Recep Tayyip Erdoğan is right now considering reintroducing the death sentence in Turkey after it was abolished in 2004.[4] In the Philippines, President Rodrigo Duterte's government will very certainly bring back the death penalty for drug-related crimes in 2017.[5]

Yet a trend has started, and the majority of countries are abolitionist. These countries and time prove that there is no need for any authority that possesses the power to decide to end someone's life.

4 www.independent.co.uk
5 www.aljazeera.com

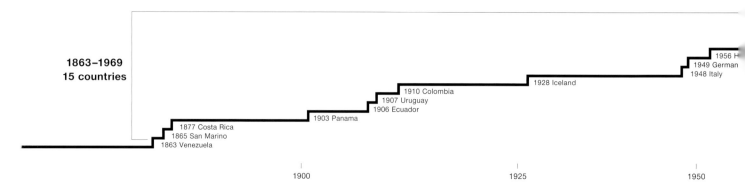

1863–1969
15 countries

1877 Costa Rica
1865 San Marino
1863 Venezuela
1903 Panama
1910 Colombia
1907 Uruguay
1906 Ecuador
1928 Iceland
1956 F
1949 German
1948 Italy

1900   1925   1950

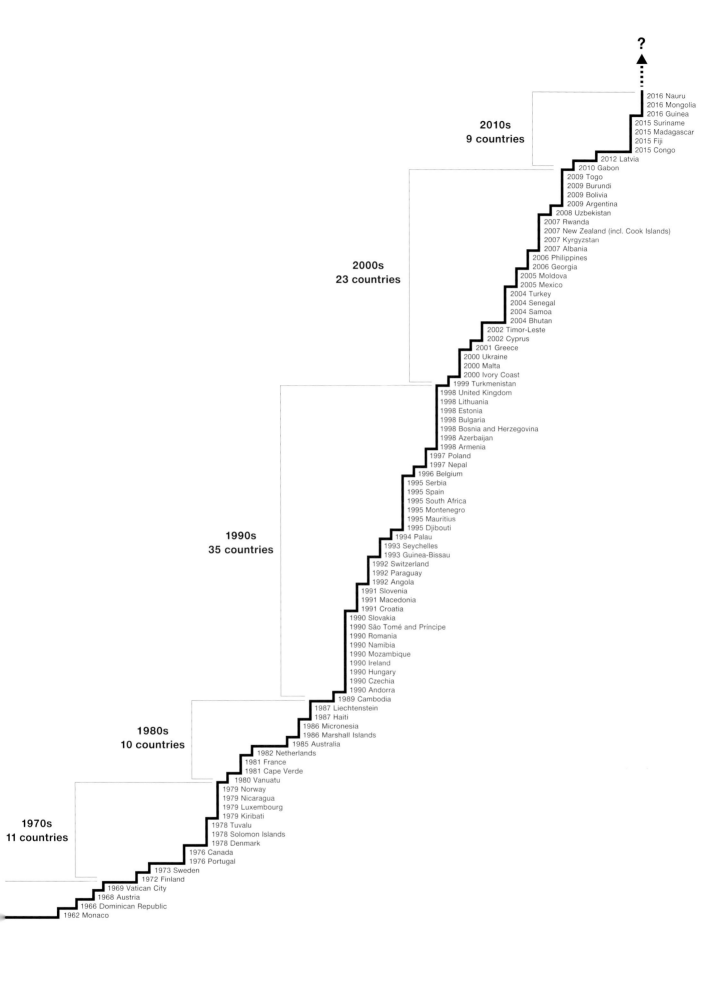

2016 Nauru
2016 Mongolia
2016 Guinea
2015 Suriname
2015 Madagascar
2015 Fiji
2015 Congo

2010s
9 countries

2012 Latvia
2010 Gabon
2009 Togo
2009 Burundi
2009 Bolivia
2009 Argentina
2008 Uzbekistan
2007 Rwanda
2007 New Zealand (incl. Cook Islands)
2007 Kyrgyzstan
2007 Albania
2006 Philippines
2006 Georgia
2005 Moldova
2005 Mexico
2004 Turkey
2004 Senegal
2004 Samoa
2004 Bhutan
2002 Timor-Leste
2002 Cyprus
2001 Greece
2000 Ukraine
2000 Malta
2000 Ivory Coast

2000s
23 countries

1999 Turkmenistan
1998 United Kingdom
1998 Lithuania
1998 Estonia
1998 Bulgaria
1998 Bosnia and Herzegovina
1998 Azerbaijan
1998 Armenia
1997 Poland
1997 Nepal
1996 Belgium
1995 Serbia
1995 Spain
1995 South Africa
1995 Montenegro
1995 Mauritius
1995 Djibouti
1994 Palau
1993 Seychelles
1993 Guinea-Bissau
1992 Switzerland
1992 Paraguay
1992 Angola
1991 Slovenia
1991 Macedonia
1991 Croatia
1990 Slovakia
1990 São Tomé and Príncipe
1990 Romania
1990 Namibia
1990 Mozambique
1990 Ireland
1990 Hungary
1990 Czechia
1990 Andorra

1990s
35 countries

1989 Cambodia
1987 Liechtenstein
1987 Haiti
1986 Micronesia
1986 Marshall Islands
1985 Australia
1982 Netherlands
1981 France
1981 Cape Verde

1980s
10 countries

1980 Vanuatu
1979 Norway
1979 Nicaragua
1979 Luxembourg
1979 Kiribati
1978 Tuvalu
1978 Solomon Islands
1978 Denmark
1976 Canada
1976 Portugal

1970s
11 countries

1973 Sweden
1972 Finland
1969 Vatican City
1968 Austria
1966 Dominican Republic
1962 Monaco

1970   1980   1990   2000   2010   2020

Theseus and the Minotaur in the Labyrinth
by Sir Edward Burne-Jones, 1861

Slaughterhouse

1.3 billion chicken wings are chowed down by Americans during the Super Bowl event alone.[1] Thus it should come as no surprise that in order to satisfy our appetite for meat, 6 million chickens have to be slaughtered worldwide every hour, as well as several million cows, pigs, and sheep.[2] And our craving for meat is only increasing.

Due to livestock epidemics (classical swine fever and avian flu) in the 1990s, rules have been adapted in such a way that it has become virtually impossible for the average European butcher to keep slaughtering on a small scale. Consequently, the alternatives to large-scale slaughterhouses have diminished. This has fueled the emergence of killing factories that have slaughtering lines with a maximum processing capacity of 150 cows per hour, 300 sheep per hour, 350 pigs per hour, and about 13 500 chickens per hour.[3] The current push toward automation will gradually eliminate the human factor in the production line and will make it up to five times as fast.

As cruel as this may sound, it won't change. Since it is not likely that humans will change their eating habits rapidly, one can only make this process less brutal and stressful. The layout and design of most slaughterhouses was influenced by the work of the world's most respected expert in animal science, Temple Grandin. She designed curved corrals with high walls that prevent animals from seeing what is around them or glimpsing what lies at the end of their walk.[4] Moreover, it plays to their natural tendency to circle and return to where they came from. This design, along with the design elements of solid sides, a solid crowd gate, and reduced noise at the end point, work together to encourage animals to move forward in the chute.

Sure, the end result of a slaughtering line is always the same: a piece of meat on a Styrofoam plate covered in plastic wrap. But as Dr. Grandin has shown, good design is able to create circumstances that give death more dignity.

1 www.forbes.com
2 www.fao.org
3 marel.com
4 www.grandin.com

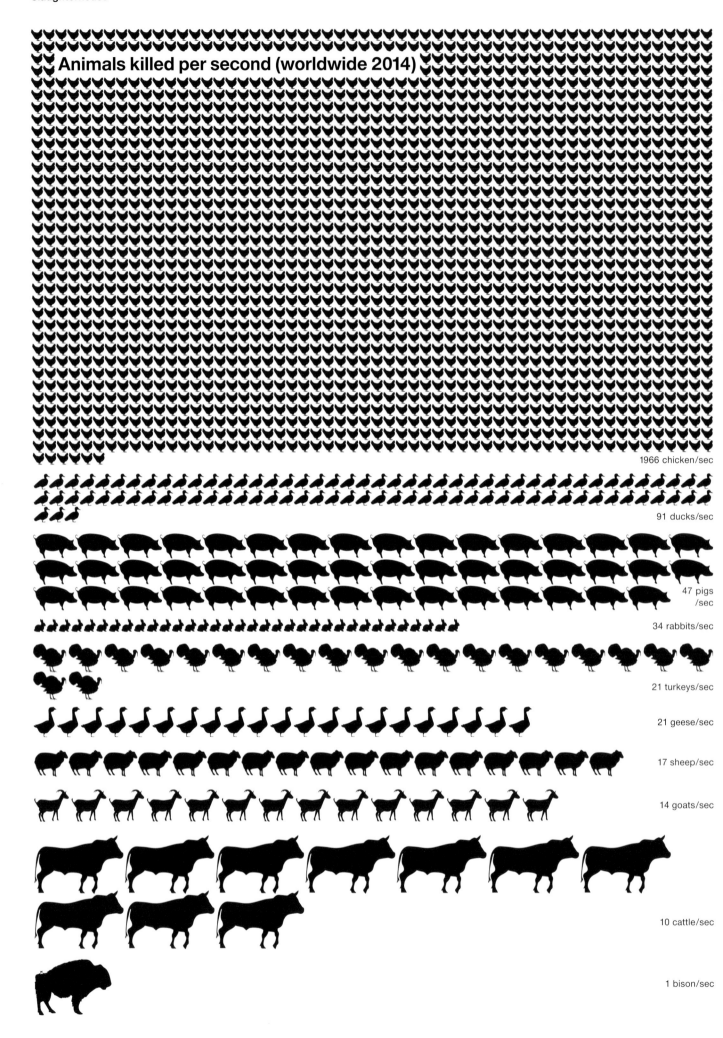

Animals killed per second (worldwide 2014)

1966 chicken/sec

91 ducks/sec

47 pigs /sec

34 rabbits/sec

21 turkeys/sec

21 geese/sec

17 sheep/sec

14 goats/sec

10 cattle/sec

1 bison/sec

Slaughterhouse
floor plan

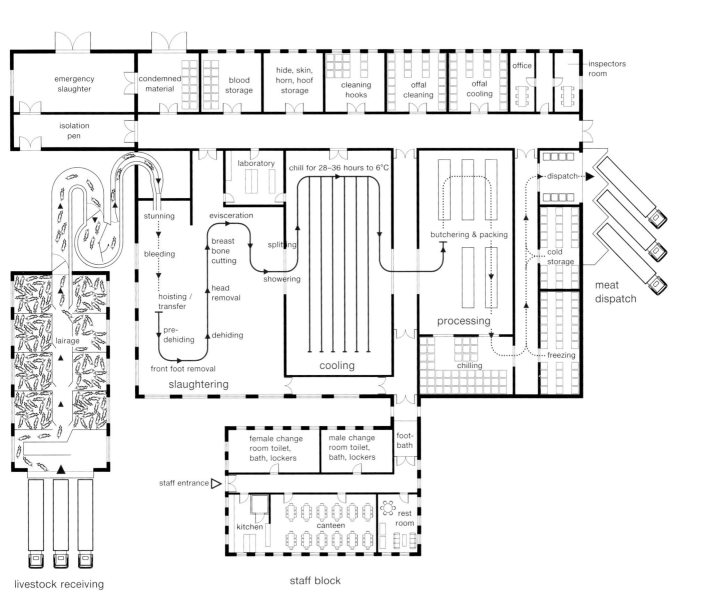

emergency slaughter

condemned material

blood storage

hide, skin, horn, hoof storage

cleaning hooks

offal cleaning

offal cooling

office

inspectors room

isolation pen

laboratory

chill for 28–36 hours to 6°C

dispatch

stunning

evisceration

bleeding

breast bone cutting

splitting

butchering & packing

cold storage

meat dispatch

hoisting / transfer

head removal

showering

pre-dehiding

dehiding

lairage

processing

front foot removal

cooling

chilling

freezing

slaughtering

livestock receiving

female change room toilet, bath, lockers

male change room toilet, bath, lockers

foot-bath

staff entrance

kitchen

canteen

rest room

staff block

Poultry

1500 m² slaughter hall
3000 heads per hour

Due to increased automation and mechanization, the maximum line speed quadrupled from 3000 birds in 1970 to 13 500 in 2015.[5] This resulted in ever-cheaper consumer prices and subsequently an increase in consumption that rose worldwide between 2000 and 2011 from 11.0 kg to 14.4 kg per person per year.[6] That's an increase of 31%, while the world population grew by only 14% in the same period.

Parallel to speeding up the poultry production line, the industry worked on speeding up the growth process of the chicken itself. In the 1920s it took an average of 112 days to grow a chicken to the market weight of 1.1 kg, while in the 2010s it takes only 47 days to grow it to 2.6 kg.[7]

To increase poultry consumption in well-fed, rich countries like the United States, which went from an annual poultry consumption of 18 kg per person in the 1960s to 50 kg per person today,[8] new products like chicken nuggets were invented. It seems there will be more to come: It is expected that by 2020, poultry production will surpass production of all other meats including pork.[9]

stainless steel shackle

can cause bruising to feet and legs

guide rails

jugular vein & carotid artery severed

circular knife

max. 1 min.

125 V

2 min.

shackling   water bath stunning   killing   bleeding

Pig

1500 m² slaughter hall
250 heads per hour

Food consumption habits depend very much on food culture and religion. There is hardly any other food that divides human society as much as pork. Described by Islam as haram, meaning forbidden by the Koran, and described by the Jewish dietary laws or kashruth as nonkosher, pork is banned by at least two influential world religions.

Globally, enough pork eaters are left to enjoy a piece of one of the 1.5 billion pigs that are slaughtered for meat in the world each year.[10] China in particular, where pork has long been considered a luxury, now accounts for about half the pigs consumed in the world.[11] Also in the case of pig slaughtering, ever-faster line processing capacities (up to 1400 pigs per hour)[12] and more marketable meat per pig have reduced prices tremendously throughout the past 100 years.

5   www.poultryandmeatprocessing.com
6   www.thepoultrysite.com
7   download.poultryandmeatprocessing.com
8   www.nationalchickencouncil.org
9   www.fao.org
10 www.fao.org
11 www.foeeurope.org
12 www.marel.com

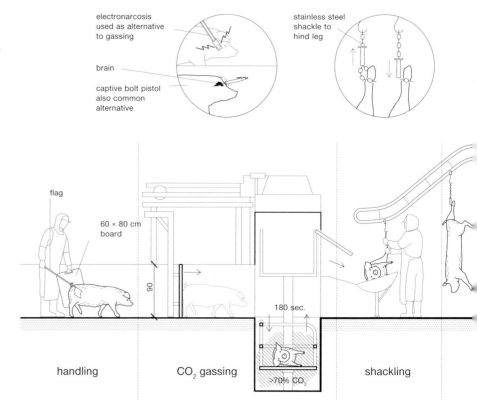

electronarcosis used as alternative to gassing

brain

captive bolt pistol also common alternative

stainless steel shackle to hind leg

flag

60 × 80 cm board

90

180 sec.

>70% CO_2

handling CO_2 gassing   shackling

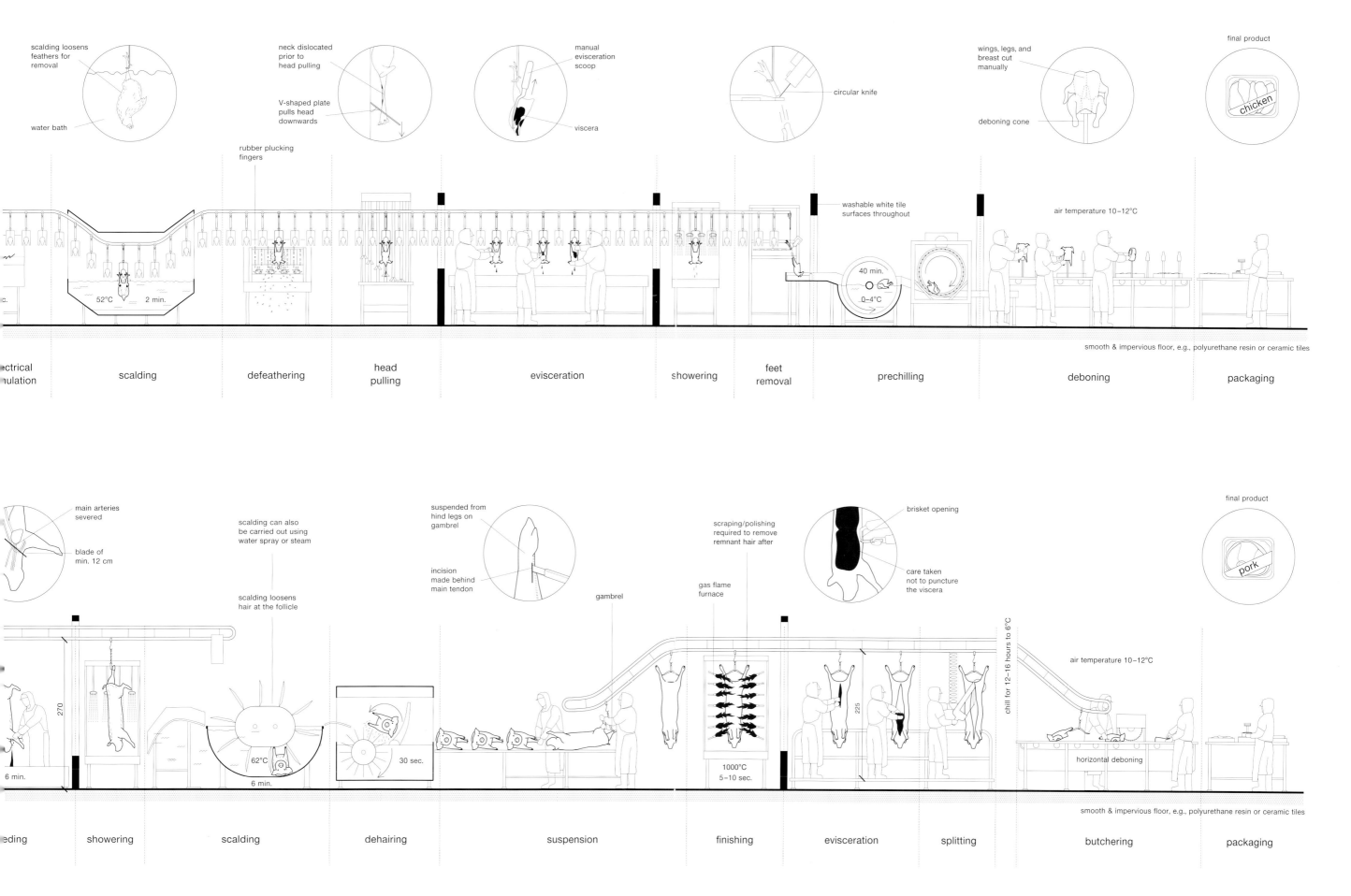

scalding loosens
feathers for
removal

water bath

rubber plucking
fingers

neck dislocated
prior to
head pulling

V-shaped plate
pulls head
downwards

manual
evisceration
scoop

viscera

circular knife

washable white tile
surfaces throughout

wings, legs, and
breast cut
manually

deboning cone

final product

chicken

air temperature 10–12°C

52°C   2 min.

40 min.

0–4°C

smooth & impervious floor, e.g., polyurethane resin or ceramic tiles

ctrical
ulation   scalding   defeathering   head
pulling   evisceration   showering   feet
removal   prechilling   deboning   packaging

main arteries
severed

blade of
min. 12 cm

scalding can also
be carried out using
water spray or steam

scalding loosens
hair at the follicle

suspended from
hind legs on
gambrel

incision
made behind
main tendon

gambrel

gas flame
furnace

scraping/polishing
required to remove
remnant hair after

brisket opening

care taken
not to puncture
the viscera

final product

pork

270

62°C

30 sec.

1000°C
5–10 sec.

225

chill for 12–16 hours to 6°C

air temperature 10–12°C

horizontal deboning

6 min.

6 min.

smooth & impervious floor, e.g., polyurethane resin or ceramic tiles

eding   showering   scalding   dehairing   suspension   finishing   evisceration   splitting   butchering   packaging

Cattle

**1500 m² slaughter hall
30 heads per hour**

The number of animals raised for beef increased just slightly from 97 million in 1950 to 100 million in 1999, while the amount of beef produced increased by about 62% during this time span.[13] This is largely due to the breeding of faster-growing beef animals. As with poultry, where egg-producing chickens have been separated from meat-producing chickens, the same has happened in beef production, where meat cows today are raised to be very different animals from milk cows.

While parts of the industry might still be concerned with the speed of killing or with breeding super cows, beef production faces a new challenge: global warming. Beef requires 160 times as much land as pork or chicken and produces 11 times the amount of greenhouse gases, which makes it one of world's largest air polluters.[14]

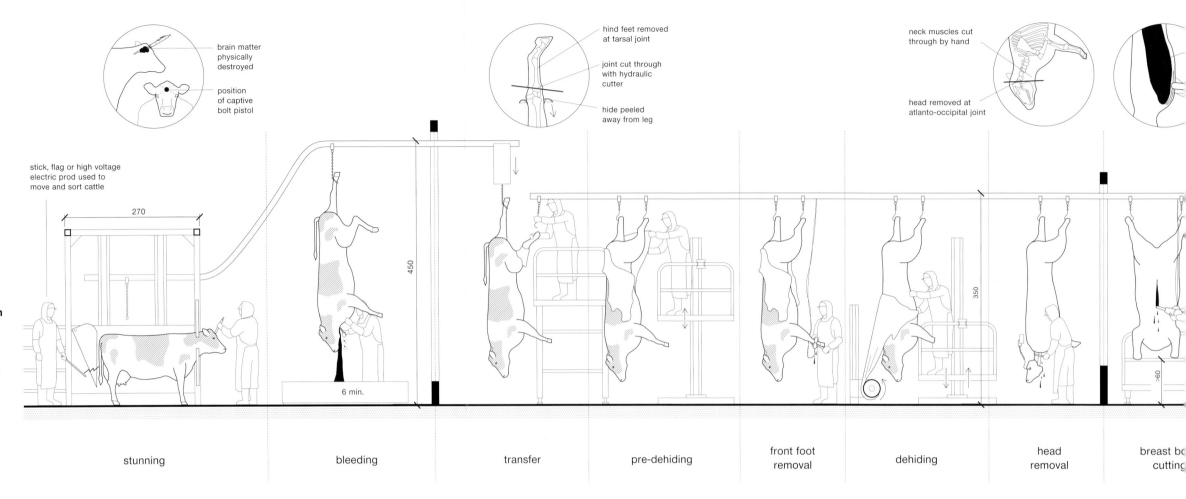

brain matter
physically
destroyed

position
of captive
bolt pistol

hind feet removed
at tarsal joint

joint cut through
with hydraulic
cutter

hide peeled
away from leg

neck muscles cut
through by hand

head removed at
atlanto-occipital joint

stick, flag or high voltage
electric prod used to
move and sort cattle

270

450

350

6 min.

stunning   bleeding   transfer   pre-dehiding   front foot removal   dehiding   head removal   breast bo cutting

Sheep

**1500 m² slaughter hall
300 heads per hour**

62 billion chickens, 1.5 billion pigs, 300 million cattle, and 550 million sheep that have been raised for food production are killed each year.[15] In total, 70 billion nonmarine animals are killed for their meat each year.[16] Not only will the killing continue; it is expected to increase by 10% in the coming ten years.[17]

High tech brought us here, and "higher tech" could lead the way out. After reaching the limits in killing speed and in breeding highly efficient animals, the next step could be to produce meat, milk, and eggs without animals through "cellular agriculture," which uses cell cultures for production. In the future, farming could be reduced to a hobby and it might sound absurd that animals had to be killed to nourish us.

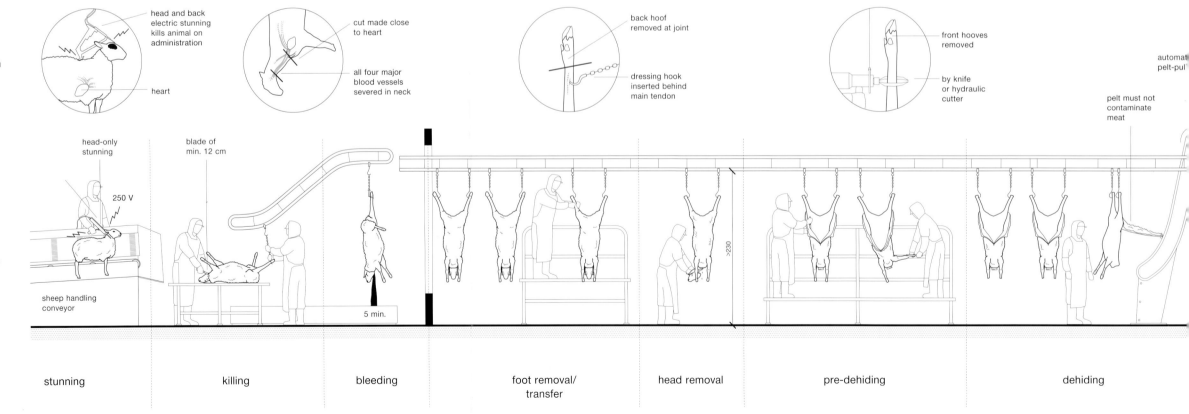

head and back
electric stunning
kills animal on
administration

heart

cut made close
to heart

all four major
blood vessels
severed in neck

back hoof
removed at joint

dressing hook
inserted behind
main tendon

front hooves
removed

by knife
or hydraulic
cutter

automat
pelt-pul

pelt must not
contaminate
meat

head-only
stunning

250 V

blade of
min. 12 cm

sheep handling
conveyor

5 min.

230

stunning   killing   bleeding   foot removal/ transfer   head removal   pre-dehiding   dehiding

13 www.lohmann-information.com
14 www.theguardian.com
15 www.fao.org
16 www.fao.org
17 www.fao.org

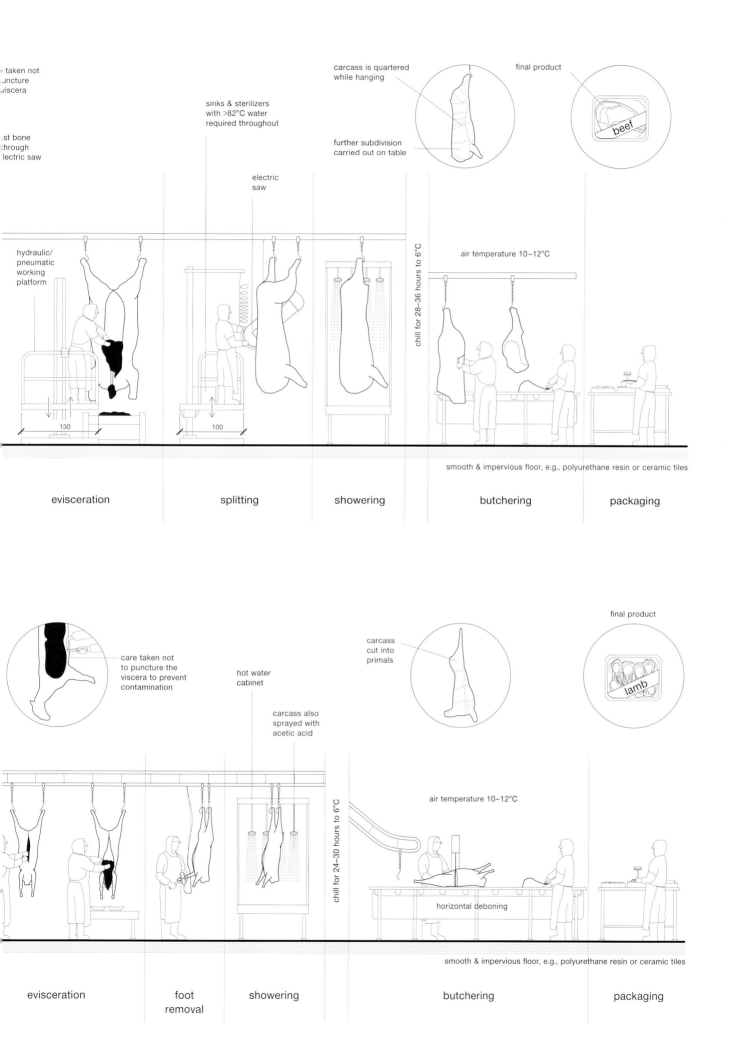

The Ha-Ha landscape design concept

Green Fortress

Nothing is more deceiving than human preconceptions. One of the most persistent of these is the idea that beauty is good and ugliness is evil. Today, hardly anything can compete with nature's image as good and beautiful. Nature is elevated as something that is so pristine and fragile that it needs to be protected from human actions. Therefore, using nature against humans is a fantastic and unexpected twist. What looks like a lovely garden is in fact a very smartly designed low-tech fortress.

Landscape elements can be placed carefully to make noise, cause pain, and block entry. A good fortress consists of a series of lines of defense, and so does a private house. The first line of defense is the one most remote from the building, yet already defined according to the building's position within the landscape, the direction the front door faces, and the distance to the street. Along this outer ring, landscaping can define the territory without using fences or walls. The oldest, most well-known landscaping element is the ha-ha,[1] a recessed landscape design element that creates a vertical barrier while preserving an uninterrupted view of the landscape beyond.

The second line of defense consists of elements such as vegetation, bodies of water or dams that prevent trespassing. Especially prickly plants help to keep intruders away, since the danger of being identified via drops of blood (DNA samples) and shreds of cloth might come in handy for the police. Within the second line of defense is the garden. Gravel walkways help to alert people to possible intruders by making a sound when walked upon. Sand may reveal footsteps.

The third line of defense is along the walls of the house. Here, vegetation and other materials can prevent intruders from climbing to the upper levels of the house and reaching the windows.

It is of utmost importance that this green fortress be well-maintained. The lawn must always stay trimmed, otherwise it might indicate to burglars that people are away. Trees, shrubs, and bushes should always be kept trimmed so that intruders have no place to hide. The pond needs to be cleaned and the gravel walkways smoothed and cleared of leaves. All in all, walls and fences are much cheaper, yet the cheapest response of all is optimism.

1 www.theenglishgarden.co.uk

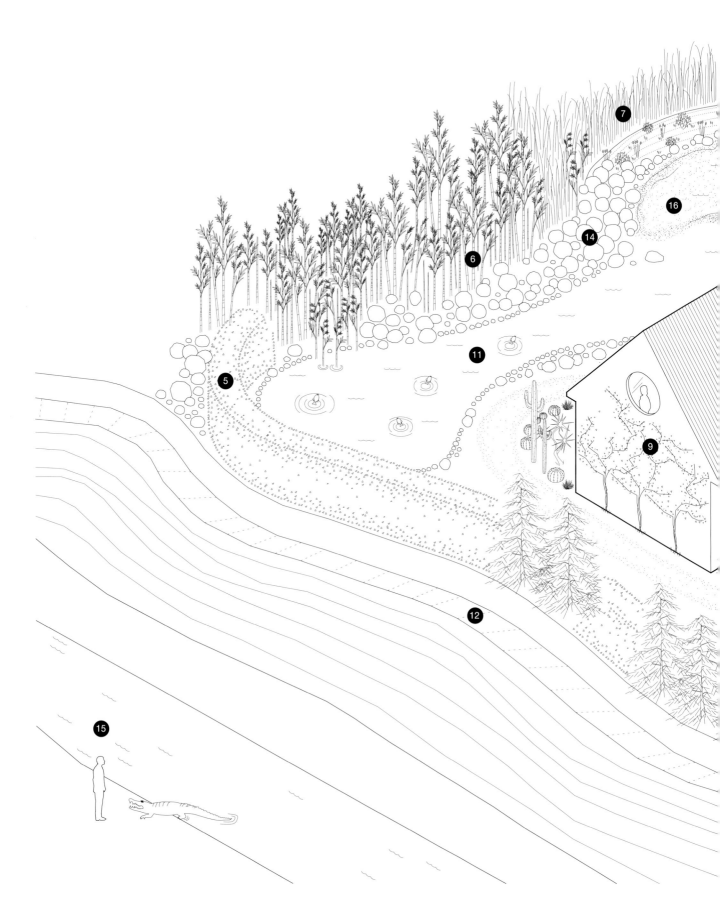

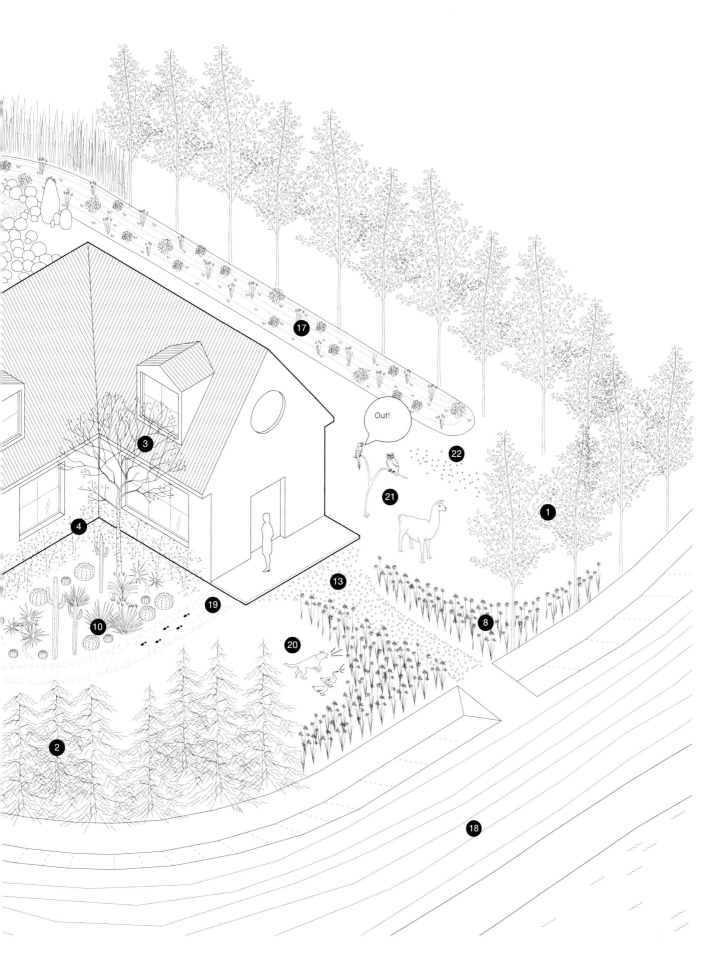

Vegetation

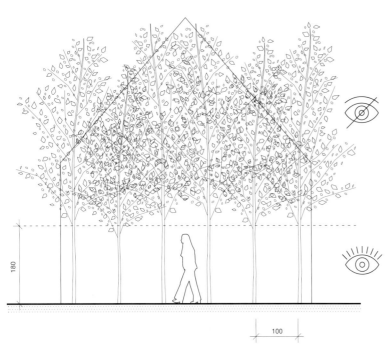

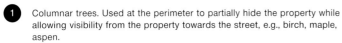

1 Columnar trees. Used at the perimeter to partially hide the property while allowing visibility from the property towards the street, e.g., birch, maple, aspen.

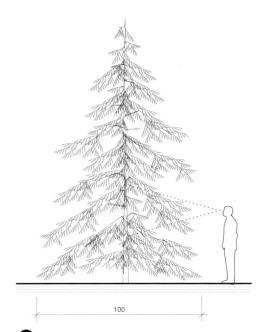

2 Dense trees. Used at the perimeter to hide the property and block access, e.g., spruce, pine.

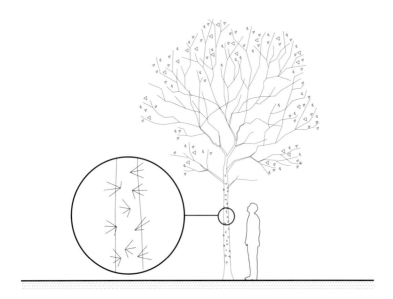

3 Prickly trees. Used outside upper-floor windows to deter intruders from climbing and entering.

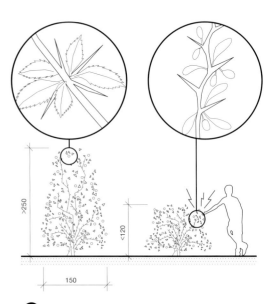

4 Prickly shrubs. Used at the perimeter, below windows, and around walkways to deter intruders from entering, e.g., barberries, roses, holly.

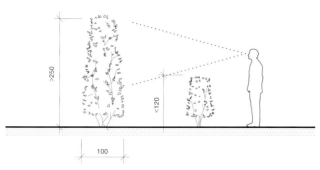

5 Hedges. Used at the perimeter and around walkways to block visibility and access, e.g., boxwood, privet, Canadian hemlock.

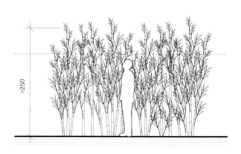

6 Bamboo. Ideal for fencing due to its high density, extremely strong properties, and fast growing rate. It can reach a height of 30 meters.

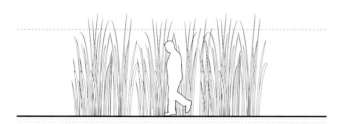

7 Reed grass. Very high and dense grass that can reach heights of 2 to 6 meters, e.g., giant reed, Burma reed.

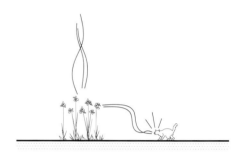

8 Scented plants. Used at the perimeter to deter animals from approaching, e.g., lavander, mint, rue.

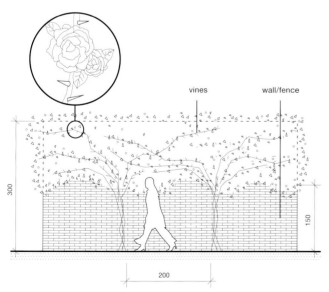

9 Prickly vines. Used at the perimeter with the support of another element such as a wall or fence to prevent intruders from climbing, e.g., roses, bougainvillea, bristly greenbrier.

10 Prickly plants. Used at the perimeter, below windows, and around walkways to deter intruders from entering, e.g., cactus, agave, yucca.

Landscaping

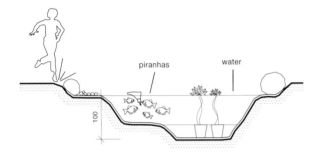

11 Pond. Used at the perimeter to deter intruders from entering. Piranhas can be added for an extra deadly effect.

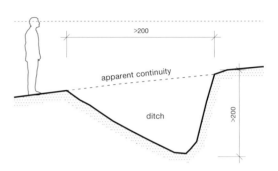

12 Ha-ha. Used at the perimeter, usually around big properties, to block intruders from entering while respecting the continuity of the landscape.

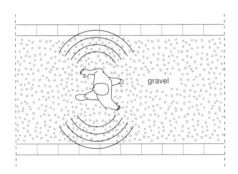

13 Gravel walkway. Helps to alert people to possible intruders by making a sound when walked upon.

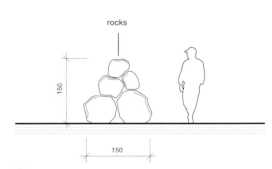

14 Rocks. Used at the perimeter to block access.

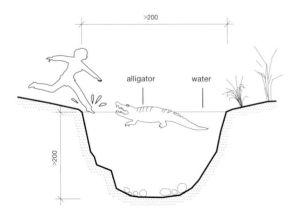

15 Moat. Used at the perimeter, usually around big properties, to block intruders from entering.

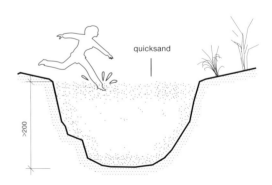

16 Quicksand. Potential intruders will slowly sink into the quicksand, making it an ideal barrier for blocking access and slowing down intruders.

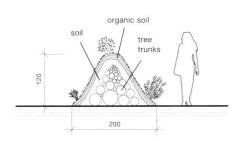

17 Raised garden bed. Used in perimeters to block access.

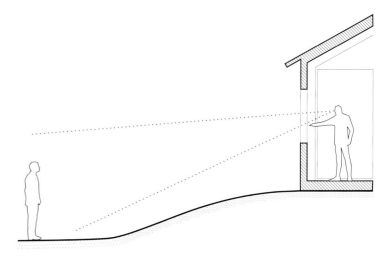

18 Hill. If the house is built on top of a hill, it can provide a better panoramic view of possible intruders.

Animals

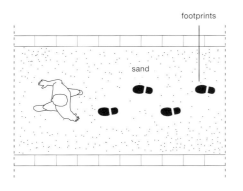

19 Sand walkway. Used to detect an intruder's footprints.

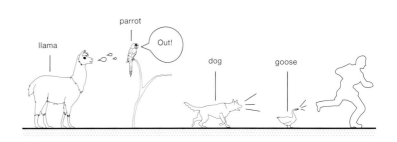

20 Guard animals. There is a wide range of animals that can be used for guarding a property. Some are aggressive and bite, while others make sounds that alert the owners, e.g., dogs, geese, donkeys, llamas, ostriches, parrots, screamers.

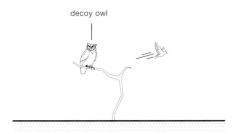

21 Plastic decoy owls. Used to scare small birds away.

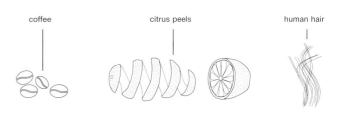

22 Waste products. Used to deter small animals from approaching, due to their distinct smell.

Register and Sources

Walls & Fences

Anti-Vehicle Barriers

a/a	Barrier	Elements	Length	Height/Depth	Purpose	Status	Sources
1	USA–Mexico	a. PV-4 metal "floating fence"	470 km anti-vehicle barriers already completed	3 m (est.)	Anti-smuggling & anti–illegal immigration	Partially completed (1100 km of 3200 km)	1. www.cbp.gov 2. fourwinds10.com 3. www.globalsecurity.org
		b. Metal posts filled with concrete		3 m (est.)			
		c. Metal posts		1.5 m (est.)			
		d. Normandy–style metal barrier		1.2 m (est.)			
2	Ukraine–Russia	2 ditches, electrified metal mesh fence, mines, flares, watchtowers, weight sensor alarms, cameras	2000 km (proposed)	3–3.5 m (est.)	Conflict zone barrier, anti–illegal weapons smuggling, anti-terrorism	Under construction; 230 km completed by 2016 (started in 2015)	1. www.globalsecurity.org 2. sputniknews.com
3	Morocco–Sahrawi Arab Democratic Republic (Western Sahara)	Sand berms, stone fortification, ditches	2735 km	2 m tall berms	Anti-smuggling & anti–illegal immigration	Completed	en.wikipedia.org
4	Saudi Arabia–Yemen	Pipelines filled with concrete, electronic detection system	75 km	3 m	Anti-infiltration & anti-terrorism	Construction stopped in 2004	1. en.wikipedia.org 2. www.middle-east-online.com
5	Tunisia–Libya	Sand banks, ditches filled with water	200 km	3 m deep ditch 2 m tall banks	Anti-terrorism	Completed in 2016	www.bbc.com
6	Kuwait–Iraq	Anti-vehicle ditch 4.6 m wide and 4.6 m deep, sand berms	190 km	3 m tall berms 4.6 m deep ditch	Anti-terrorism	Completed	1. en.wikipedia.org 2. www.middle-east-online.com
7	Pakistan–Afghanistan	HESCO bastion prefabricated walls, barbed wire, ditches up to 3.4 m deep and 4.2 m wide	1100 km (first phase) 2400 km (second phase)	2.5–3 m tall (est.) 3.4 m deep ditch	Anti-smuggling & anti–illegal immigration	First phase completed; second phase under construction	1. en.wikipedia.org 2. www.pakistantoday.com.pk

Fence Barriers

	Barrier	Elements	Length	Height/Depth	Purpose	Status	Sources
8	USA–Mexico	a. Metal mesh, metal studs	650 km (anti-pedestrian barrier already completed)	3 m (est.)	Anti-smuggling & anti–illegal immigration	Partially completed (1100 km of 3200 km)	1. www.cbp.gov 2. fourwinds10.com 3. www.globalsecurity.org
		b. Metal studs, concrete wall		6 m (est.)			
		c. Metal bars, metal studs		4 m (est.)			
		d. Wooden poles		5 m (est.)			
		e. Wire, metal studs, USA flags		1.5 m (est.)			
9	USA–Cuba (Guantanamo Bay)	Double metal mesh fence, Y-shaped metal studs, barbed wire, nontransparent fabric, watchtowers, security lights, cameras, and gravel that allow patrols to listen to intruders	Unknown	3 m (est.)	Border security, detention facility	Unknown (prison as of 2002)	1. panampost.com 2. en.wikipedia.org 3. www.indiatvnews.com
10	Spain–Morocco (Ceuta/Melilla)	Triple metal mesh fence, metal studs, barbed wire, motion detectors, sand strip that helps detect footsteps	19 km 11 km in Melilla & 8 km in Ceuta	3–6 m	Anti–illegal immigration, anti-smuggling	Completed in 1998 (renovated in 2005)	en.wikipedia.org
11	UK–France (Great Wall of Calais)	Double metal mesh fence, barbed wire, metal studs	Unknown (border length 50.5 km)	4 m (est.)	Anti–illegal immigration	Completed in 2015	www.mirror.co.uk
12	Austria–Slovenia	Threaded rod studs, hexagon metal mesh	3.7 km	2.2 m	Anti–illegal immigration	Completed in 2016	1. en.wikipedia.org 2. sputniknews.com
13	Hungary–Croatia & Serbia	Double metal mesh fence, barbed wire, metal studs	175 km	3.5 m 4 m (originally planned)	Anti–illegal immigration	First phase completed in 2015	en.wikipedia.org
14	Slovenia–Croatia	a. Barbed wire, metal bars	211 km	2.2 m (est.)	Anti–illegal immigration	Completed	1. en.wikipedia.org 2. www.total-croatia-news.com
		b. Metal mesh, Y-shaped metal studs		3 m (est.)		Partially completed	
15	Bulgaria–Turkey	a. Double metal mesh fence, barbed wire, Y-shaped metal studs	166 km (proposed)	3.5 m	Anti–illegal immigration	Under construction (100 km out of 166 km)	1. www.express.co.uk 2. uk.reuters.com
		b. Barbed wire, metal studs		2 m			
16	Greece–Turkey	double metal mesh fence, barbed wire, metal studs, mines	10 km	4 m	Border security and anti–illegal immigration	Completed in 2012	1. www.globalsecurity.org 2. www.huffingtonpost.com
17	Macedonia–Greece	Double metal mesh fence, barbed wire, metal studs, patrol route	100 km 300 km (envisioned)	3 m	Anti–illegal immigration	Under construction 100 km completed in 2016	1. en.wikipedia.org 2. www.criticatac.ro
18	Norway–Russia	Metal mesh, metal studs	0.2 km	3.4–3.7 m	Anti–illegal immigration & anti-smuggling	Completed in 2016	1. en.wikipedia.org 2. www.bbc.com
19	Latvia–Russia	Metal mesh, barbed wire, metal studs	91 km	2.7 m (est.)	Anti–illegal immigration	Under construction (started in 2016)	1. www.unian.info 2. www.youtube.com
20	Russia–Poland	a. Concrete posts, barbed wire	Unknown (border length 210 km)	1.8 m (est.)	Anti–illegal immigration	Unknown	1. 112.international 2. borderhunting.blogspot.nl
		b. Wooden posts, barbed wire		1.8 m (est.)			
21	Ukraine–Russia	Metal mesh, barbed wire, metal studs	2000 km (proposed)	3–3.5 m (est.)	Conflict zone barrier, anti–illegal weapons smuggling, anti-terrorism	Under construction; 230 km completed by 2016 (started in 2015)	1. www.globalsecurity.org 2. sputniknews.com
22	Russia–Georgia (Abkhazia/South Ossetia)	Double barbed-wire fence, metal bars	63 km	1.5 m (est.)	Illegal occupation barrier in violation to human rights	Completed in 2013	1. agenda.ge 2. www.rferl.org
23	Morocco–Algeria	Metal mesh, metal studs	100 km	3.5 m (est.)	Conflict and anti-terrorism	Under construction	www.moroccoworldnews.com
24	Kenya–Somalia	Double metal mesh fence, prefabricated concrete posts, barbed wire, metal studs	708 km (proposed) 3 km completed	3.5 m (est.)	Anti-terrorism	Under construction (started in 2016)	1. www.algemeiner.com 2. allafrica.com

	Barrier	Elements	Length	Height/Depth	Purpose	Status	Sources
25	Botswana–Zimbabwe	Electrified (turned off) metal mesh fence, barbed wire, metal studs	483 km	2 m	Anti–illegal immigration, animal control	Completed	1. news.bbc.co.uk 2. www.earthtripper.com
26	South Africa–Zimbabwe	Electrified 35 000 volts metal mesh fence, barbed wire, metal studs, patrol route	Unknown (border length 225 km)	3 m (est.)	Anti–illegal immigration, anti–drug smuggling, anti–weapon smuggling	Partially completed	1. www.newscientist.com 2. www.news24.com
27	Israel–Egypt	Double metal mesh fence, barbed wire, metal studs	Approx. 245 km	5–8 m	Anti–illegal immigration	Completed in 2014	1. en.wikipedia.org 2. www.jpost.com
28	Turkey–Syria	Prefabricated concrete posts, barbed wire	900 km (proposed)	3 m (est.)	Anti–illegal immigration & anti–terrorism	Completed in 2017	www.dailymail.co.uk
29	Israel–Jordan	Metal mesh, metal studs	30 km	3 m	Anti–illegal immigration & anti–terrorism	Completed in 2017	www.timesofisrael.com
30	Israel–Gaza Strip	Electrified metal mesh fence, barbed wire, metal studs	60 km	3 m (est.)	Anti–illegal immigration	Completed in 1996	en.wikipedia.org
31	Israel–Syria	Metal mesh, barbed wire, metal studs	Unknown	4 m (est.)	Anti–illegal immigration, anti–terrorism	Completed in 2016	www.ft.com
32	Jordan–Syria & Iraq	Metal mesh, barbed wire, metal studs, watchtowers, radar, patrol routes, helicopter patrols	442 km	4 m (est.)	Anti–illegal immigration, anti–terrorism	Under construction (started in 2014)	1. www.thegatewaypundit.com 2. news.vice.com
33	Saudi Arabia–Iraq	Double metal mesh fence, Y-shaped metal studs, razor wire pyramid, underground motion detectors, watchtowers, cameras, radar, patrol route, helicopter patrols	900 km	4 m (est.)	Conflict zone barrier, anti–illegal immigration, anti–terrorism	Under construction (started in 2014)	1. en.wikipedia.org 2. wonderfulengineering.com
34	United Arab Emirates–Oman	Concrete, metal mesh, barbed wire, metal studs	410 km (est.)	3.5–4 m (est.)	Anti–smuggling, anti–terrorism & anti–illegal immigration	Nearly completed	1. www.youtube.com 2. www.globalsecurity.org
35	Tajikistan–Afghanistan	T-shaped wooden posts, barbed wire	Unknown (border length 1 300 km)	2.5 m (est.)	Anti–smuggling	Unknown	1. www.bbc.com 2. en.wikipedia.org
36	Kazakhstan–Uzbekistan	Metal studs, barbed wire	150 km	1.7 m	Anti–smuggling	Completed in 2012	www.acbk.kz
37	Uzbekistan–Kyrgyzstan	Concrete posts, barbed wire	Unknown	2.5 m	Conflict zone barrier, anti–smuggling	Unknown (started in 1999)	1. query.nytimes.com 2. en.wikipedia.org
38	India–Pakistan (Kashmir)	Double metal mesh fence, barbed wire, metal studs, motion sensors	550 km	2.4–3.7 m	Anti–terrorism, disputed territory	Completed in 2004	en.wikipedia.org
39	India–Pakistan	Double metal mesh fence, barbed wire, metal studs, laser detection system	3323 km	3.5 m (est.)	Conflict zone, anti–terrorism, anti–illegal immigration	Under construction (to be completed in 2018)	1. www.thehindu.com 2. tribune.com.pk
40	India–Myanmar	Double metal mesh fence, barbed wire, metal studs	1624 km	3.6 m (est.)	Border security & anti–illegal immigration	Partially completed	1. en.wikipedia.org 2. www.telegraphindia.com
41	India–Bangladesh	Double metal mesh fence, barbed wire, metal studs	3289 km (proposed)	4 m (est.)	Border security & anti–illegal immigration	Under construction (2536 km completed in 2008)	1. indianexpress.com 2. www.globalsecurity.org
42	Myanmar–Bangladesh	Concrete posts, barbed wire	290 km	3 m (est.)	Anti–smuggling, anti–terrorism	Under construction (started in 2009)	1. aa.com.tr 2. www.globalsecurity.org
43	Russia–Mongolia	Double metal mesh fence, metal studs, T-shaped wooden posts, barbed wire	Unknown (border length 3 485 km)	3 m (est.)	Anti–illegal immigration	Unknown (built in the Soviet era)	1. en.wikipedia.org 2. billandsamthebigadventure.wordpress.com 3. www.transmongoliano.com
44	China–Hong Kong	Metal mesh fence, barbed wire, metal studs	32 km	4 m (est.)	Anti–illegal immigration	Completed	en.wikipedia.org
45	North Korea–China	Double metal mesh fence, Y-shaped metal studs, concrete posts, barbed wire, patrol route	20 km	2.5–4 m	Border security, anti–illegal immigration	Completed	1. en.wikipedia.org 2. www.globalsecurity.org
46	DMZ (Demilitarized Zone between North Korea and South Korea) Korea	Double metal mesh fence, barbed wire, Y-shaped metal studs, patrol route	250 km	4 m (est.)	Conflict zone	Completed (started in 1953)	en.wikipedia.org

Wall Barriers

	Barrier	Elements	Length	Height/Depth	Purpose	Status	Sources
47	USA–Mexico	a. Concrete bollards, barbed wire	650 km (anti-pedestrian barrier already completed)	4.4 m (est.)	Anti–smuggling & anti–illegal immigration	Partially completed (1100 km of 3200 km) new wall construction starts in 2017	1. www.cbp.gov 2. fourwinds10.com 3. www.globalsecurity.org
		b. Concrete, corrugated metal		4 m (est.)			
		c. Corrugated metal, metal studs, metal mesh		4 m (est.)			
		d. Corrugated metal, metal studs		3 m (est.)			
48	Haiti–Dominican Republic	Stone, concrete blocks, barbed wire	17 km (proposed)	3 m	Anti–smuggling	Partially completed	www.ieee.es
49	UK–France (Great Wall of Calais)	Concrete panels, barbed wire	10 km	4 m	Anti–illegal immigration	Completed in 2016	1. www.express.co.uk 2. www.dailymail.co.uk 3. www.gettyimages.nl
50	Cyprus UN Buffer Zone between the Greek and Turkish side of Cyprus	a. Stone, concrete, barbed wire	180 km	3.5 m (est.)	Demilitarized zone	Completed (1964–1974)	en.wikipedia.org
		b. Sand-filled oil drums, barbed wire		1.7 m (est.)			
51	Turkey–Syria	a. Prefabricated concrete, barbed wire	900 km (proposed)	3 m	Anti–illegal immigration & anti–terrorism	Completed in 2017	1. www.reuters.com 2. www.dailymail.co.uk 3. www.middleeastmonitor.com
		b. Prefabricated concrete wall, barbed wire, patrol route, border lights, predator drones, surveillance balloons, watchtowers		4 m (est.)			

52	Israel–Lebanon	Prefabricated concrete	79 km	8 m (est.)	Anti-terrorism	Completed	en.abna24.com
53	Israel–West Bank / Jordan	Prefabricated concrete, metal mesh	708 km	8 m	Anti-terrorism	Partially completed	en.wikipedia.org
54	Egypt–Gaza Strip	Corrugated steel	10–11 km	8 m (est.) extents 18 m underground	Anti–illegal immigration	Completed	1. en.wikipedia.org 2. news.bbc.co.uk
55	Iran–Pakistan	Reinforced concrete barrier, barbed wire	700 km (proposed)	3 m	Border barrier, anti–illegal immigration	Under construction (started in 2007)	1. en.wikipedia.org 2. news.bbc.co.uk
56	Malaysia–Thailand	Reinforced concrete, metal mesh, barbed wire, metal studs	650 km (proposed)	3 m (est.)	Anti-terrorism	Under construction (started in 2007)	1. en.wikipedia.org 2. www.theborneopost.com 3. www.thestar.com.my

Barriers with No Visual Material Available

	Barrier	Elements	Length	Height/Depth	Purpose	Status	Sources
57	Algeria–Libya	Metal mesh, barbed wire	120 km	3 m	Anti-terrorism, anti-smuggling	Under construction (started in 2016)	www.middleeastmonitor.com
58	Estonia–Russia	Metal mesh, patrol route, animal barriers, turnpikes, border posts, caution signs, illumination	90 km	2.5 m	Anti–Russian intrusion, anti-smuggling, anti–illegal immigration	Under construction (started in 2016)	1. www.reuters.com 2. upnorth.eu
59	Lithuania–Russia	Unknown	130 km	Unknown	Anti–Russian intrusion, anti-smuggling	Proposed	www.bbc.com
60	Turkey–Iran, Armenia & Iraq	Prefabricated concrete	Unknown (border length 268 km)	3 m	Anti-terrorism, anti–illegal immigration, anti-smuggling	Proposed	www.azernews.az
61	Uzbekistan–Afghanistan	Barbed-wire fence	209 km	3 m	Anti–illegal immigration	Completed in 2001	argalinetwork.wordpress.com
62	India–Bhutan	Metal mesh or barbed wire	35 km	Unknown	Anti-terrorism	Unknown (proposed in 2015)	www.indiandefensenews.in
63	China–Vietnam	Fence typology unknown, monitoring devices	8 km	Unknown	Anti-smuggling	Unknown (proposed in 2015)	www.ecns.cn

Rumors

	Barrier	Elements	Length	Height/Depth	Purpose	Status	Sources
1	Mexico–Guatemala	Plan Frontera Sur 2014	Unknown	Unknown	Anti–illegal immigration, anti-smuggling	Proposed	1. www.dailymail.co.uk 2. www.coha.org 3. elpais.com
2	Brazil–Paraguay	Proposal cancelled	Unknown	Unknown	Anti–illegal immigration, anti-smuggling	Proposed	www.ultimahora.com
3	Argentina–Paraguay	Customs wall (Posadas, Argentina)	Unknown	Unknown	Anti–illegal immigration, anti-smuggling	Proposed	www.lanacion.com.ar
4	Argentina–Bolivia	No wall (deputy proposal)	Unknown	Unknown	Anti–illegal immigration, anti-smuggling	Proposed	1. www.thebubble.com 2. internacional.elpais.com
5	Brazil–Argentina	SISFRON	Unknown	Unknown		Proposed	1. www.upi.com 2. logo-americas.com
6	Brazil–Colombia	"	Unknown	Unknown		Proposed	"
7	Brazil–French Guiana	"	Unknown	Unknown		Proposed	"
8	Brazil–Guyana	"	Unknown	Unknown		Proposed	"
9	Brazil–Peru	"	Unknown	Unknown		Proposed	"
10	Brazil–Suriname	"	Unknown	Unknown		Proposed	"
11	Brazil–Uruguay	"	Unknown	Unknown		Proposed	"
12	Brazil–Venezuela	"	Unknown	Unknown		Proposed	"
13	South Africa–Mozambique	Wall	Unknown	Unknown		Rumored	www.news24.com
14	Namibia–Angola	Unknown	Along entire boder	Unknown	Animal health	Proposed	allafrica.com
15	Oman–Yemen	Fence, details unkown	Unknown	Unknown		Construction started 2013	1. www.youtube.com 2. country.eiu.com

Bunker Buster

Weapon system	Add-on	Penetration through reinforced concrete (m)	Weight (kg)	Length (m)	Diameter (mm)	Range (km)	Accuracy CEP (m)	Delivery method	Manufacturer	Developed by	Year of Introduction	In operation by
GBU-57A/B Massive Ordnance Penetrator (MOP)	–	61.0	13 600	6	800	32	5	B-2 and B-52 bomber	Boeing	USA	2010	USA
DF-15C	–	20.0	6 200	9.1	1 000	700	15	Ground-launched	ARMT	China	1995	China, Pakistan
BLU-122 Penetrator	GBU-28C/B	7.2	2 270	8	390	10	9	F-15, B-2	Raytheon	USA	2005	USA, Singapore
BLU-113 Super Penetrator	GBU-28	6.0	2 270	6	370	10	9	Strike & fighter aircraft: F-111, F-15E, B-2 Spirit	Raytheon	USA	1991	USA, Israel, South Korea
KAB-1500Kr-Pr-E	–	4.0	1 525	5	580	20	7	Su-24, Su-34, Tu-22M3M, Su-30MK, Su-30MKI, Su-35, Su-35UB	KTRV	Russia	1995	Russia
BLU-116 AUP	AGM-130	3.7	1 650	4	370	10	3	F-15E, F-111, F-4, B-52	Lockheed Martin	USA	–	USA, France, UK
BLU-116 AUP	GBU-15	3.7	980	4	370	20	9	Strike & fighter aircraft: F-117A, F-16, F/A-18E, F/A-18F, Tornado, Mirage	Lockheed Martin	USA	–	USA, France, UK
BLU-116 AUP	GBU-24	3.7	1 050	4.4	370	20	9	A-6, A-10, F-14, F-15, F-16, F/A-18, F-111	Lockheed Martin	USA	–	USA
BLU-116 AUP	GBU-27	3.7	900	4.2	711	19	1	Strike & fighter aircraft: F-117A, F-14D, F-16, F/A-18E, F/A-18F, Tornado, Mirage	Lockheed Martin	USA	–	USA, France, UK
AGM-86D CALCM	–	3.7	1 430	6	620	1 100	3	B-52	Boeing	USA	2001	USA
BLU-118/B Thermobaric Warhead	GBU-24	3.4	1 650	4	370	10	3	F-15E, F-111, F-4, B-52	Lockheed Martin	USA	–	USA
BLU-118/B Thermobaric Warhead	GBU-15	3.4	1 050	4	370	20	9	A-6, A-10, F-14, F-15, F-16, F/A-18, F-112	Lockheed Martin	USA	–	USA
BLU-118/B Thermobaric Warhead	AGM-130D	3.4	1 320	4	370	65	3	F-15E	Boeing	USA	–	USA
AGM-158A JASSM	–	2.1	1 020	4	450	360	2	B-1, B-2, B-52, F-15E, F-16, F/A-18	Lockheed Martin	USA	2003	USA, Australia, Finland, Poland
NEB	–	2.1	1 160	3	460	27	6	F-4E 2020, F-16	TÜBİTAK	Turkey	2013	Turkey
PB-500	–	2.0	435	3	290	–	–	Fighter and long-range attack aircraft	IMI	Israel		Israel
GBU-39/B SDB (Small Diameter Bomb)	–	1.8	110	2	190	110	8	F-15E Strike Eagle, Panavia Tornado, JAS-39 Gripen, AC-130W	Boeing	USA	2005	USA, Israel, Italy, Saudi Arabia
BLU-109 Penetrator	GBU-10	1.8	1 160	4	370	15	9	A-7, A-10, B-52, F-111, F-117, F-15E, F-16 , F/A-18 C/D, A-6, F-14	Lockheed Martin	USA	1977	Australia, USA, UK, UAE, Taiwan, Spain, South Korea, South Africa, Singapore, Saudi Arabia, Oman, Egypt
BLU-109 Penetrator	GBU-15	1.8	1 650	4	370	10	3	F-15E, F-111, F-4, B-51	Rockwell International	USA	1975	USA
BLU-109 Penetrator	GBU-24	1.8	1 050	4	370	20	9	A-6, A-10, F-14, F-15, F-16, F/A-18, F-111	Raytheon	USA	1983	USA, UK, Spain, France, South Korea
BLU-109 Penetrator	GBU-27	1.8	980	4	370	20	9	Strike & fighter aircraft: F-117A, F-16, F/A-18E, F/A-18F, Tornado, Mirage	Raytheon	USA	1987	USA, France, UK
BLU-109 Penetrator	GBU-31 (JDAM)	1.8	1 070	4	630	24	10	Long-range attack aircraft, strike & fighter aircraft	Boeing	USA	1999	USA, UAE, Singapore, Saudi Arabia, Portugal, Poland, Oman, Norway, Netherlands, Italy, Israel, Denmark, Belgium, Australia
BLU-109 Penetrator	AGM-130	1.8	1 320	4	370	65	3	F-15E Strike Eagle, F-15K Slam Eagle	Boeing	USA	1994	USA
BLU-111/B (Broach)	AGM-154C (JSOW)	1.5?	450	4	330	130	3	F-16C/D, F/A-18, B-1, B-2, B-52, F-15E, F-35	Raytheon	USA	2005	USA, Turkey, Singapore, Poland, Greece, Australia
KAB-500L / Kr	–	1.5?	525	3	400	17	7	Long-range attack aircraft: Su-24, Su-34, Tu-22M3M; strike & fighter aircraft: MiG-27, etc.	KTRV	Russia	1995	Russia, China
LT-3	–	1.5	560	4	380	24	–	Fighter and long-range attack aircraft	EOTDC	China	2008	China
AGM-84H SLAM-ER	–	1.2	725	4	340	280	3	Strike & fighter aircraft: F-15K, F-15SA, F-16E, F-16F, F/A-18.	Boeing	USA	2000	USA, Turkey, South Korea
BetAB-500	–	1.2	500	2	350	–	–	Long-range attack aircraft: Su-24, Su-34, Su-30MKI	KTRV	Russia	2014	Russia
MPR-500	–	1.0	230	3	270	15	–	Fighter and long-range attack aircraft	IMI	Israel	2012	Israel
B61-11 (Thermonuclear)	–	–	544	3.7	340	–	100	Long-range attack aircraft: B-2A, B-1B, B-52H, F-16	–	USA	1997	USA

Register and Sources

	Handheld Firearms			
RPG-7 grenade launcher	0.11		40	0.5
Medium machine gun	0.05		7.62	0.2
Assault rifle	0.03		5.56	0.2
Pistol	0.02		5.56	0.2

Abbreviations:
Boeing = Boeing Integrated Defense Systems
Lockheed = Lockheed Martin Missiles
TÜBİTAK = The Scientific & Technological Research Council of Turkey
KTRV = Tactical Missiles Corporation
IMI = Israel Military Industries
EOTDC = Luoyang Electro-Optics Technology Development Centre
ARMT = Academy of Rocket Motors Technology

Sources:
www.globalsecurity.org
www.ausairpower.net
www.defense-aerospace.com
www.jpost.com; www.deagel.com
mengnews.joins.com
www.sage.tubitak.gov.tr
tonnel-ufo-english.tk
www.fi-aeroweb.com
en.wikipedia.org
www.airpower.at

Total Demolition

The demolition methods described below may not align perfectly with the illustrations in this section,
because a single demolition method may make use of various techniques.
The list of sources is arranged by the type of technology used, in order of increasing intensity.

Preparation before Demolition

Method	Description	Links
Asbestos abatement	An asbestos-containing building that is to be torn down may have to be sealed and have its asbestos safely removed before ordinary demolition can be performed. Due to its highly toxic state, the asbestos removal may take longer and cost more than the actual demolition.	en.wikipedia.org www.epa.gov
Decontamination	Decontamination and removal of any chemical or harmful substances is particularly relevant in the demolition of industrial buildings.	www.arcadis.com
Soft strip	Taking the structure back to construction materials, including the removal of windows and door frames. Non-load-bearing walls are also usually removed at this stage.	www.spectra-analysis.co.uk

Manual Demolition

Method	Description	Links
Sledgehammer	Used to manually break up elements such as partition walls, timber structure, concrete and masonry.	en.wikipedia.org
Jackhammer	A pneumatic or electro-mechanical tool combining a hammer and a chisel, used to break up rock or concrete, usually in a vertical position.	en.wikipedia.org
Drill	Drills, including diamond drills, can be used to weaken and break apart hard elements of a structure such as concrete or masonry. Can easily be used in a horizontal position.	en.wikipedia.org
Hand-held crunch	A hydraulic device which provides an almost silent controlled-demolition technique for crushing concrete or masonry into manageable pieces without vibration.	www.johnfhunt.co.uk
Thermic lance	Thermic lancing is the process of cutting and removing stubborn materials by means of a thermochemical reaction. When ignited, the lance will burn at a high temperature and be capable of cutting or boring through almost any material, such as concrete, steel or cast iron. This is ideal for demolition work, where noise and vibrations are unacceptable, or where speed is essential, particularly on reinforced concrete.	www.colemetal.co.uk
Pressure jet	High-pressure water, used mainly in the demolition of reinforced concrete to loosen the aggregate by washing out softer mortar. Abrasive compounds may be added for cutting reinforcing steel.	www.hydroblast.co.uk

Machine Demolition

Method	Description	Links
Concrete saw	Large, circular, diamond-tipped saws are used to cut through concrete, enabling significant cost savings compared to conventional concrete-removal methods.	en.wikipedia.org
Diamond wire saw	A diamond wire is passed around the structure and, working through a set of pulleys attached to a tensioned drive unit, gradually drawn through the object. Ideal for cutting through large sections of reinforced concrete, such as bridge sections, jetties, columns or beams. Diamond-wire cutting is particularly useful when extremely thick or awkward shapes need cutting or the structure is underwater.	www.johnfhunt.co.uk
Diamond drilling	Used in the preparation of bursting or implosion as a demolition technique. Two main types of diamond drilling are in use: wet and dry drilling. Both techniques create precise holes in all types of base materials such as mass concrete, reinforced concrete, brick masonry, and block work.	www.castle-pryor.co.uk
Pusher arm technique	Pusher arms and deflector plates are fitted on excavators. Small sections of a structure are pushed over one at a time in order to reduce the overall height of the structure. This allows speedy and safe demolition.	www.thehindu.com
Bulldozer	Used to demolish smaller buildings of 1–2 stories. Used both to knock down the building and to clear debris from the site.	en.wikipedia.org
Mechanical plant	Power shears may be used to crop and cut through concrete and metal, such as reinforcing steel or beams, particularly where there might be a risk of fire. On-site noise is also reduced. Power grapples may be used to handle waste material, either to move it about the site or to load other vehicles when disposing of the waste.	nebula.wsimg.com
High-reach excavator	A high-reach excavator is one that has a particularly long boom, allowing controlled deconstruction of multistory or tall structures down to a safe height at which conventional excavators can continue. Boom lengths can vary in size from 19 to more than 50 meters. These come with a variety of specialized attachments to allow the operator precision and accuracy during the demolition process.	www.volvoce.com
Wrecking ball	A steel ball weighing between 500 and 1000 kg is suspended from a crane by a steel rope and swung by a drag rope. The building is dismantled by the force of the steel ball coming into contact with the structure. This method is effective for demolishing multistory structures that have suffered structural damage, after all other methods have been considered.	en.wikipedia.org
Mechanical bursting	Large concrete structures such as foundations, pillars, bearers and concrete walls can be removed easily and effectively by hand or crane, by installing hydraulic bursters in diamond-drilled holes. The bursters expand to induce controlled cracking of the structure. The method breaks up concrete structures with a minimum of noise and flying debris.	www.concretenetwork.com
Cut-and-lift process	The structure is initially cut into individual pieces or segments using one or more of the abovementioned methods. Then the pieces are lowered by crane onto the ground to be demolished further or to be hauled away. The technique may be applied to safely remove projections such as canopies, architectural features, balconies, and bay windows.	jmciqatar.com
Robotic demolition	Electrically powered, remote-controlled hydraulic power packs produce no harmful fumes and very little noise, and can alleviate hand-arm vibration problems. These machines are very versatile and come with a variety of attachments including powerful percussive breakers, hydraulic crushing jaws, loading buckets, and concrete milling heads. This method is Ideal when a building may have a risk of falling debris, as no human needs to be in close proximity.	www.johnfhunt.co.uk

Deliberate Collapse

Method	Description	Links
Wire rope pulling	Cables and wire ropes are fixed to key structural members, then pulled down by tractors or winches. This method is suitable for detached buildings, where there is plenty of surrounding space. It can be used on timber-framed buildings, bridges, brick, masonry or steel chimneys, and on spires and masts. The rope should be at least 16 mm in diameter, and the method should be limited to buildings less than 15 m tall.	www.demolitionhub.my
Implosion	Implosion or explosion deconstruction is an effective and efficient method that can reduce both the cost and time needed to bring dangerous multistory structures to the ground. In many cases, implosion can reduce the demolition period by as much as 80%, with the majority of time being spent in both the preparation period and the clean-up following implosion. The usual method is to cut or disintegrate key structural members by loading drilled holes with explosives, or by fixing plaster charges to the outside of these members.	www.demolitionhub.my
Undermining	Hydraulic excavators may be used to topple one- or two-story buildings in an undermining process. The strategy is to undermine the building while controlling the manner and direction in which it falls. The demolition project manager/supervisor will determine where undermining is necessary so that a building is pulled in the desired manner and direction. The walls are typically undermined at a building's base, but this is not always the case if the building design dictates otherwise.	en.wikipedia.org
Hydraulic jack collapse	Engineers use remote-controlled powerful hydraulic jacks to push supporting walls sideways on a mid-level floor. With the walls gone, the top portion of the building immediately drops down with enough force to pulverize, in rapid succession, the stories below. This method generates a bit less dust than explosives.	www.economist.com
Gas cartridge collapse	The cartridge is triggered electrically from a lead, causing a proprietary mixture containing an oxidizer to react rapidly, producing a high-pressure gas. Because the gas is tightly contained within the borehole, its expansion splits the surrounding material. Gas-generating cartridges are increasingly used to help demolish buildings, reducing noise, and being much less dangerous to handle than explosives.	www.economist.com

Other Methods

Method	Description	Links
Chemical bursting	Poured into diamond-drilled holes, an expanding agent cracks reinforced concrete and rock safely and quietly. This method provides controlled demolition and makes it easy to break reinforced concrete and all kinds of stone into desired sizes and shapes without noise, vibration or dust.	en.wikipedia.org
Cut & take-down method	This method works by starting at the bottom, gutting one floor, and then lowering the entire building on computer-controlled hydraulic jacks, one floor at a time, meaning all the work can be performed safely at ground level. Noise pollution and dust emission are reduced, and the sorting of material for recycling can be performed efficiently at ground-floor level. Floors can removed at a rate of two every ten days.	www.kajima.co.jp
Top-down method	An exoskeleton "hat" that encloses the top three floors is attached to the central core of the building and lowered as the structure is reduced in size. This gives workers ample access to the building, reduces noise, contains dust, and prevents debris from falling to the street. Floors can removed at a rate of two a week.	www.economist.com www.fastcoexist.com

Bridge Demolition

Method	Description	Links
Controlled collapse	One of the most common methods of bridge demolition is to use explosives. Explosives are particularly effective in taking down large amounts of concrete, usually placed in boreholes that are drilled into the concrete at strategic points. The advantage of explosives is their adaptability and flexibility in getting the job done.	www.ehow.com
Cut and lift	In some circumstances, bridges can be removed simply by cutting them into sections and removing them by crane. This method can be done relatively quickly and without generating dust, vibrations or noise, or creating problems for surrounding buildings.	www.ehow.com

Defensive City

	Name	Company	Description	Location	Source
1	Glass surface	Unknown manufacturer	Glass surface with metal holders: addition on window ledges to deter people from sitting or littering.	London, UK	–
2	Bird spikes	Bird-X Inc.	Weatherproof stainless steel spikes to deter birds from nesting on ledges, flat roofs, lampposts, etc.	–	www.bird-x.com
3	Anti-sticker garbage bin	Stausberg	Metal litter basket with diamond-shaped bumps to prevent people from affixing stickers and posters.	Linz, Austria	www.stausberg.at
4	Roller Barrier	Insight Security	Recycled polycarbonate cups are installed as rollers around an aluminum tube to deter people from climbing over walls and fences. Designed especially for playgrounds, schools, mental institutions, and youth detention centers.	Philadelphia, USA	www.insight-security.com
5	Noise projection	Zhejiang Haoyuan Electronic Technology Co., Ltd.	The TC-40 40-watt outdoor horn speaker projects loud construction noises outside buildings to keep homeless people from sleeping between 11 p.m. and 7 a.m.	San Francisco, USA	frankaudio.en.alibaba.com
6	Spiked Anti-climb bracket	Insight Security	Weatherproof spiked bracket made out of steel and galvanized components used in poles, lampposts, trees, etc., to deter people from climbing.	–	www.insight-security.com
7	Anti-Sticker coating	CAS	The AS 2010 Anti-Sticker Coating is sticker- and poster-repellent.	Eindhoven, Netherlands	casnederland.nl
8	Round bench	Guangzhou Gavin Urban Elements Co.	This round, backless, galvanized steel bench is used to protect plants but also to deter people from lying down.	–	cngzgavin.gmc.globalmarket.com
9	SkateStop Edge	SkateStop	The SkateStop Edge deters skaters from "grinding". It can be integrated into the project design, but is also suitable for retrofitting. SkateStop Edge is manufactured from marine-grade stainless steel and is also available in brass.	Melbourne, Australia.	www.skatestop.com.au
10	Anti-Climb Paint	Blackfriar	A thick, oily, slippery, nondrying coating for ledges, fences, and walls. It deters potential intruders by making surfaces virtually unclimbable, while rubbing off on hands and clothing. Can be applied to brickwork, concrete, plastic, metal or wood.	–	www.blackfriar.co.uk
11	Anti-litter planter	Unknown manufacturer	A concrete base planter with metal mesh extension prevents people from littering or sitting on its edges.	NYC, USA	–
12	Georgetown Bench	Barco Products	The Georgetown Bench, made of 100% recycled iron and plastic, is designed to face contemporary urban realities with a center arm that discourages overnight stays.	–	www.barcoproducts.com
13	Anti-graffiti coating	D. Adam & Associates/ACTEL Coatings	After applying AG anti-graffiti water-based sacrificial building protection coating, graffiti damage can be removed from any surface without chemicals by using pressured hot water at 1,000 to 1,500 psi and 85 °C.	Edinburgh, UK	www.enviroguard-surface-protection.co.uk
14	Anti-climb barrier	Insight Security	The Vanguard anti-climbing barrier is split and formed aluminium tubing used to deter people from climbing over a wall or fence. Vanguard works more as a visual deterrent; it is unlikely to cause life-threatening or serious injury.	–	www.insight-security.com
15	"Gum Drop" bollard	Dawn Enterprises	The 360 kg moveable "Gum Drop" concrete bollard with natural finish is designed to be portable while still weighing enough to provide an effective security barrier where needed. The "Gum Drop" is commonly used to slow, deter, or direct traffic on public streets.	NYC, USA	godawn.com
16	Mechanical bollard	FAAC (UK) Ltd	The J200 Series bollard is a metal cylindrical bollard resistant to impact and weather. It is provided with a piston mechanism with which it can be moved on command to deter unwanted traffic.	–	www.faacbv.com
17	Anti-Trespass Panels	ROSEHILL POLYMERS GROUP – Rosehill Highway	The anti-trespassing panels are 100% recycled rubber pyramid-shaped panels that provide a physical and visual deterrent to unwanted pedestrian, vehicular or livestock traffic.	–	www.rosehillhighways.com
18	CCTV camera	360 Vision Technology Ltd	The VisionDome high-speed pan, tilt, and zoom camera with 360° coverage in high resolution is a camera disguised as a streetlamp.	Broadway, UK	www.360visiontechnology.com
19	Cone spikes	Unknown manufacturer	Metal cone-shaped spikes are used to deter people from sitting or sleeping on ledges.	London, UK	–
20	Anti-vandal speaker	Moving Sound Technologies, Inc.	The MK4 Multi-Age plastic speaker produces a high-frequency sound (8–17 kHz) to deter people from loitering in public spaces. A frequency of 17 kHz sound is used against teenagers (aged 13–25), while 8 kHz is used against people of all ages.	Manchester, UK	www.movingsoundtech.com
21	Wall spikes	Insight Security	The "Anti Climb Prikla Supa-Strip" is a robust UV (ultraviolet)-balanced, weatherproof, recycled plastic-hinged strip of spikes designed to deter climbing on walls and flat roofs. It causes maximum discomfort but minimum harm. It's also useful against cats and birds.	–	www.insight-security.com
22	Urine deflector	Unknown manufacturer	Steel profile used in public spaces to deter public urination. Similar devices in London date back to the nineteenth century.	Frankfurt, Germany	–
23	Bird netting	BirdBusters	High-density, UV-resistant polyethylene net that forms a strong, impenetrable bird barrier.	–	www.birdbusters.com
24	Half bench	Unknown manufacturer	Metal and wood bench (stasteun) that discourages citizens from staying too long and does not allow sleeping.	Rotterdam, Netherlands	www.publicspaceinfo.nl
25	Anti-suicide light	Unknown manufacturer	Blue LEDs are used to prevent people from committing suicide in train or subway stations. A research paper published in the Journal of Affective Disorders four years after the first lights were installed found that there was an 84% decrease in suicides at stations with blue lights.	Tokyo, Japan	–
26	Anti-injection light	Hikari	Black-light blue fluorescent light bulbs are used in public restrooms to deter people from using intravenous drugs, as they make it harder for users to see their veins.	The Hague, Netherlands	www.1000bulbs.com

Vehicle as Weapon

Natural barriers

Name	Description	Utilization	Dimension	
Rock	Rocks are a landscape design element; they may serve as seating but also as engineered barriers.	Part of landscape design.	Weight and size of the rocks as well as their connection to the ground need to be considered.	**
Water	A channel can be designed to be an effective trap. In combination with walls, it can be engineered to stop a vehicle. Water can also be used in the form of lakes and fountains.	Part of landscape design.	Depth and width of the channel have to be taken into consideration (see ha-ha).	**
Tiger Trap	The Tiger Trap uses collapsible concrete technology below at-grade paving or planting. Under the weight of a vehicle, the material collapses and is stopped by a wall.	The Tiger Trap is used when no visual obstacles are desired. Precondition is that enough space is available.	US Department of State K12 standard.	**, 1
Anti-vehicle ditch	Ditches offer a simple method of securing a lengthy perimeter against moving vehicles. Trapezoidal ditches should be avoided since vehicles could drive in and out of the ditch in a slow attack.	Part of landscape design when enough space is available.	Asymmetric V-shaped ditch; angle >65°, total width ≥5 m and depth ≥1.2 m.	*
Hillside cut	Hillside cuts are easy to construct and can be effective against a wide range of vehicle types.	Part of landscape design when enough space is available.	To be effective, the angle of the sides has to be at least 45°.	**
Berm	Berms are more intrusive than ditches, since they can easily hinder the view and therefore help to fragment public space.	Part of landscape design when enough space is available.	Height needs to be considered in order not to obstruct the line of sight.	**

Artificial barriers

Name	Description	Utilization	Dimension	
Bollard	Cylindrical vehicle barrier made of steel or concrete. Bollards prevent vehicles from passing, but allow the entrance of pedestrians and bicycles. A bollard system connects all bollards underground with one continuous beam.	Part of the architectural or urban design of public space.	Max. clearance 1200 mm. Min. height 500 mm.	**, 4
Bollard 2	If underground utilities make the installation of conventional bollard foundations too difficult, bollards with a wide, shallow base and a system of beams below the pavement are used.	Part of the architectural or urban design of public space.	Max. clearance 1200 mm. Min. height 500 mm.	**
Hidden bollards (in planters and street furniture)	Crash-rated bollards can be concealed between benches and in planters to minimize visual obstruction, save space, and secure the terrain.	Part of the architectural or urban design of public space.	Max. clearance 1200 mm. Min. height 500 mm.	**, 5
"Family" of security elements (e.g., lighting column, traffic signal, seating)	The reinforced foundations of streetlamps, bus shelters, and kiosks add standard street furniture to an additional defense line. Such components would need testing to ensure acceptable performance.	Part of the architectural or urban design of public space.	various	**
Fences	Cable restraints that stop the vehicle are hidden among vegetation. The cable is held in place by bollards and is anchored to the ground by a "deadman."	Part of the architectural or urban design of public space.	Min. height 500 mm.	**
Features with sloped pedestal	For elements with a sloped base, specific heights and angles need to be taken into account so that the measure can be effective.	Part of the architectural or urban design of public space.	Approach angle >50°, height >1250 mm, break-over angle <130°.	***
Stairs and retention walls	Stairs and walls are effective measures that can be incorporated in the design. Sufficient heights and angles have to be taken into account.	Part of the architectural or urban design of public space.	Ideal height 900 mm.	***
Advertisement	In the case of the Emirates Stadium in London, the name of the Arsenal soccer club functions as a massive shield at a critical access point. The letters can allegedly stop a seven-ton truck.	Part of the architectural or urban design of public space.	Size, height, and foundation need to be considered. Should not obstruct pedestrian flow.	
Icons & art in public space	For example, cannons, which feature in the Arsenal soccer club's insignia, are used as disguised "tank traps" to stop car bombers.	Part of the architectural or urban design of public space.		2
Jersey barrier	A Jersey barrier or Jersey wall is a modular concrete barrier that separates lanes of traffic. When used as a permanent measure, the Jersey wall is reinforced by a concrete foundation.	Can be applied temporarily or permanently as part of the general road perimeter design.	www.eliteprecast.co.uk	3

Active barriers

Name	Description	Utilization	Dimension	
Wedge barrier	The barrier ramp is flush with the roadway and does not obstruct pedestrian or vehicular traffic when not active. The system can rise in less than two seconds.	In high-security areas and vehicle entrances.	For example, the DSC501 by Delta Scientific.	**, 6

Road barriers

Name	Description	Utilization	Dimension	
Speed cushions (speed hump)	A speed hump is less obstructing than a bump. For 80 mm high-speed humps without a flat center section, the speed is between 30 and 35 km/h. With a flat center section, that speed may reach 50 km/h.	To supplement existing roads.	Pittman	***, 7
Chicanes and roundabouts	Chicanes or bends encourage drivers to slow down. Roundabouts with ramp-proof elements in their midst can prevent head-on impacts.	Part of the redesign of existing roads or an urban master plan.	Chicanes and roundabouts need space to be implemented.	***
Road blocks (King Tut Blocks)	Well-designed temporary chicanes can help to slow vehicles in the approach to a special-event area.	As a temporary solution against an immediate threat, or at events.	The distance between roadblocks depends on the street width and the expected speed.	*
Inclination	Inclined roads slow down potential hostile vehicles and prevent acceleration, especially of larger, heavier vehicles.	Part of the redesign of existing roads or an urban master plan.	If not available in the surrounding topography, inclines will require a large amount of space.	***

Road design

Name	Description	Utilization	Dimension	
Angled impact	This impact mode is less dangerous than a head-on approach. Due to the angle, the vehicle cannot impart its full momentum.	Part of the redesign of existing roads or an urban master plan.		***
"In-turn" impact	This mode of impact is the least severe. The vehicle is unable to maintain or increase speed while turning.	Part of the redesign of existing roads or an urban master plan.	If space allows, approaches should be designed that are parallel to the building facade.	**, ***

Sources:

*   Document UFC 4-022-02: Selection and Application of Vehicle Barriers, June 8, 2009; Change 1, August 9, 2010, superseding Military Handbook 1013/14: Selection and Application of Vehicle Barriers, US Department of Defense.

**   Site and Urban Design for Security: Guidance Against Potential Terrorist Attacks, Risk Management Series, FEMA 430, December 2007, www.fema.gov

*** Hostile Vehicle Guidelines for Crowded Places: A Guide for Owners, Operators and Designers. ANZCTC, www.nationalsecurity.gov.au

1   "Rogers Marvel Architects & Rock 12 Security Architecture," www.asla.org

2   www.news.bbc.co.uk

3   en.wikipedia.org
    www.eliteprecast.co.uk
    Risk Management Series; Site and Urban Design for Security – Guidance Against Potential Terrorist Attacks; FEMA 430 / December 2007, www.fema.gov

4   Crowded Places Guidance, National Counter Terrorism Security Office, www.gov.uk

5   www.secureusa.net

6   www.deltascientific.com

7   www.pittmantraffic.co.uk

Crowd Control

	Element	Description	Range	Sources
1	Stanchions	Create barricaded lines with adequate numbers of breaks and turns at regular intervals to maintain orderly flow and reduce the risk of harm to visitors and staff, etc.		www.nrf.com
2	Temporary barriers	To contain crowds at organized marches, festivals, rallies, parades, and protests, galvanized metal fences are employed to provide a physical and psychological way to limit movement without dedicated areas. Barriers are interlocking to prevent them from being moved or tipped.		america.aljazeera.com
3	Turnstiles	Used at entrances and exits to arenas, stations, and theme parks to limit entry and restrict flow, preventing overcrowding inside the venue. They can also be used to monitor visitor numbers, important in crowd control.		books.google.co.uk silversecurity.co.uk
4	Shield wall formation	Although largely obsolete as a military tactic due to firearms, a wall of riot shields remains a common formation for riot police where protection is required against large groups using improvised weapons.	arm-length	en.wikipedia.org
5	Barbed-wire barriers	The Rapid Deployment Barrier is used for containing riots and controlling crowds. The system is designed to provide rapid protection: thousands of meters of barbed tape/razor wire coils can be deployed at a speed of 10 meters per second.		www.cochranesteel.com
6	Stun grenades / flash bangs	A diversionary measure, whose explosion emits a bright light and loud noise of around 175 dB, stun grenades are designed to cause temporary loss of hearing and sight, disorientation, and confusion, enabling security forces to overpower protesters.	up to 35 m	www.btselem.org
7	Baton rounds/rubber bullets	The baton round is a projectile, fired from a weapon, which is intended to strike the target with sufficient force to cause compliance through the application of pain.	up to 100 m	www.nihrc.org www.wired.co.uk
8a	Water cannons	High-pressure pump jetting out thousands of liters of water a minute. Typically 9000-liter reservoir. Armored to resist attack from projectiles.	50–90 m	www.newscientist.com www.interarmored.com www.carmor.co.il
8b	Long-range acoustic devices/sound cannons	A device which blasts targeted, amplified sound of up to 160 dB, painful to the human ears, in order to disperse crowds.	up to 3.5 km	www.rferl.org en.wikipedia.org
8c	Active denial systems	A vehicle-mounted system which projects a focused beam of millimeter waves at a frequency of 95 gigahertz for a very short duration, giving targets a feeling of intense heat, causing crowds to disperse.	1000 m	jnlwp.defense.gov
9	Improvised barriers	Improvised barriers are often used as a quick and nasty way to block a road for both vehicles and personnel. A favorite element are car tires, which are placed across a road and set on fire.		archive.org
10	Police dogs	Dogs are used to assist with dispersal of crowds and to support police cordons.	up to 3 m	www.app.college.police.uk
11	Baton charge	A coordinated tactic involving police officers charging at a crowd with riot shields and batons, designed to cause maximum amount of pain and disperse the crowd.	arm-length	en.wikipedia.org
12	Tear gas	Gas fired from guns in grenade canisters which causes severe eye, skin, and respiratory irritation. Used to disperse crowds.	up to 140 m	en.wikipedia.org en.wikipedia.org www.britannica.com
13	Echelon	An offensive formation consisting of a diagonal line used to turn or divert groups in open or built-up areas and to move crowds away from buildings, fences, and walls.		fas.org
14	Wedge	a: An offensive formation that is used to penetrate and split crowds into smaller groups. b: Wedge used to allow VIP, etc., through crowd. c: Snatch squad wedge to extract ringleaders.		fas.org
15	Diamond	As a defensive formation, it is used when all-around security is required in open areas. As an offensive formation it is used to enter a crowd, especially by extraction teams. The symmetrical shape means the direction of travel can be easily changed.		fas.org
16	Kettling	Police, protected by riot gear, advance slowly in formation using their bodies to form a cordon to contain a group of protesters. Access roads and exits can be sealed. Protesters are forcibly held until release or arrest.		flesl.net en.wikipedia.org

Human Stampedes since 2010 with More Than 10 Fatalities

	Place and Date	Description	Deaths	Source
1	Ram Janki Temple stampede, India March 4, 2010	At least 71 were killed and more than 200 injured at Ram Janki Temple, in Kunda, India, in a stampede after the gates of the temple collapsed.	71	en.wikipedia.org
2	Love Parade disaster, Germany July 24, 2010	21 people were killed and more than 500 were injured during crowd turbulence at the Love Parade in Duisburg, Germany.	21	
3	Phnom Penh stampede, Cambodia November 22, 2010	A stampede during a water festival near Cambodia's royal palace in Phnom Penh killed at least 347 people.	347	
4	Sabarimala Temple stampede, India January 15, 2011	102 people died and 100 were injured during a stampede near Sabarimala Temple in Kerala, India.	102	
5	Houphouët-Boigny stampede, Ivory Coast January 1, 2013	60 people were killed, including 26 children, and more than 200 injured in a stampede at the Stade Félix Houphouët-Boigny during a New Year's fireworks celebration in Abidjan, Ivory Coast.	60	
6	Kumbh Mela stampede, India February 10, 2013	During the Hindu festival Kumbh Mela, a stampede broke out at the train station in Allahabad, Uttar Pradesh, India, killing 36 people and injuring 39.	36	
7	Madhya Pradesh Temple, India October 13, 2013	At least 109 people were killed and more than 100 injured in a stampede during the Navratri festivities near a temple in Madhya Pradesh's Datia district triggered by a rumor that a river bridge the devotees were crossing was about to collapse.	109	
8	Patna Stampede, India October 3, 2014	At least 32 people were killed and 26 injured in a stampede shortly after the Dasehra celebrations at the Gandhi Maidan, Patna, India.	32	
9	New Year's Eve celebrations, China December 31, 2014	A crush at New Year's Eve celebrations in Shanghai killed 36 people and injured some 47 others. Social media reports suggest the stampede was triggered by people stopping to pick up fake money thrown from the balcony of a nightclub.	36	
10	Maha Pushkaralu festival, Godavari River, India July 14, 2015	At least 27 pilgrims died in a stampede on the banks of the Godavari River in the southern Indian state of Andhra Pradesh. The Hindu pilgrims had gathered to take a dip in the river at the start of the Maha Pushkaralu festival.	27	
11	30 June Stadium stampede, Egypt February 8, 2015	28 people died after a stampede that occurred at a football game in the 30 June Stadium in Cairo, Egypt.	28	
12	Mymensingh stampede, Bangladesh July 9, 2015	At least 23 people were killed and 50 injured following a stampede at a free clothing drive in the northern Bangladeshi city of Mymensingh.	23	
13	Mecca, Saudi Arabia September 24, 2015	Thousands of Muslim pilgrims were killed and hundreds injured in a stampede in Mina, on the outskirts of the holy city of Mecca. Two waves of people collided, and crowding caused people to suffocate and eventually trample one another.	2 262	
14	Oromo Thanksgiving Festival, Ethiopia October 2, 2016	52 to 300 were killed during the annual thanksgiving festival of the Oromo people in Ethiopia after police confronted protesters during the 2016 Ethiopian protests, resulting in a human stampede.	52–300	

10 Largest Peaceful Gatherings

	Place and Date	Description	No. of gatherers	Source
1	Arba'een pilgrimage, Iraq December 2, 2015	The Arba'een pilgrimage in Karbala, Iraq, is held every year to commemorate the death of Husayn ibn Ali, grandson of the Prophet Muhammad, in 680.	22 000 000	en.wikipedia.org
2	Hindu festival of Kumbh Mela, India January 30, 2001	An estimated 20 million people gathered for the Hindu festival of Kumbh Mela on January 30, 2001, in Allahabad, India. This is the largest peaceful gathering in history.	20 000 000	
3	Arba'een pilgrimage, Iraq December 13, 2014	The Arba'een pilgrimage in Karbala, Iraq, is held every year to commemorate the death of Husayn ibn Ali, grandson of the Prophet Muhammad, in 680.	19 000 000	
4	Arba'een pilgrimage, Iraq January 2013	An estimated 15–18 million people visited the shrine of Husayn ibn Ali in Karbala, Iraq, during Arba'een in January 2013.	18 000 000	
5	Imam Husayn Arba'een symbolic trek, Nigeria November 26, 2015	More than 15 million participated in Imam Husayn Arba'een symbolic trek from Kaduna to Zaria in Nigeria.	15 000 000	
6	Arba'een pilgrimage, Iraq January 14, 2012	An estimated 15 million people visited the shrine of Husayn ibn Ali in Karbala, Iraq, during Arba'een in 2012.	15 000 000	
7	Arba'een pilgrimage, Iraq January 26, 2011	An estimated 15 million people visited the shrine of Husayn ibn Ali in Karbala, Iraq, during Arba'een in 2011.	15 000 000	
8	Funeral of C. N. Annadurai, India February 1969	An estimated 15 million people attended the funeral of C. N. Annadurai, an Indian politician, in Tamil Nadu, India, in 1969.	15 000 000	
9	Processions of M. al-Kadhim, Iraq July 2015	An estimated 12 million people visited the shrine of Imam Musa al-Kadhim in Kadhimiya, Iraq, during the martyrdom processions of Imam Musa al-Kadhim in 2015.	12 000 000	
10	Funeral of Ayatollah Khomeini, Iran June 1989	An estimated 10.2 million people gathered for the funeral of Ayatollah Khomeini, Supreme Leader of Iran, in Tehran in June 1989.	10 200 000	

Prison Cells

a/a	Country	No. of prisoners	Cell area per prisoner (m²)	Official document	Sources
1	USA	2 217 947	6.5 (single cell in detention facilities when prisoners stay in the cell for more than 10 hours) 5.6 (single cell in detention facilities when prisoners stay in the cell for less than 10 hours) 4.6 (single cell in holding facilities)	Yes (ACA)	www.ncjrs.gov
2	China	1 649 804	8 (single cell) 3.6 (shared cell)	Yes (Law)	Book: *Crime, Punishment, and Policing in China*, Børge Bakken
3	Russian Federation	633 826	2.5	Yes (Law)	www.icrcndresourcecentre.org
4	Brazil	622 202	6.0	Yes (Law)	www.hrw.org
5	Mexico	233 469	6.5 (single cell in detention facilities when prisoners stay in the cell for more than 10 hours) 5.6 (single cell in detention facilities when prisoners stay in the cell for less than 10 hours) 4.6 (single cell in holding facilities)	Yes (ACA same as USA)	1. www.ncjrs.gov 2. www.elfinanciero.com
6	Indonesia	197 630	2.5 (single cell) 1.25 (shared cell)	No	www.hrw.org
7	South Africa	161 984	5.7 (single cell) 3.5 (shared cell)	No	www.hrw.org
8	England & Wales	84 857	5.4	Yes (NACRO)	www.icrc.org
9	Poland	71 765	3 2 in some cases for temporary detention of no longer than 14 days	Yes (Law)	www.prisonobservatory.org
10	Argentina	69 060	5 (less than 10 hours) 8 (more than 10 hours)	No	pdf research: S3036-13PL (Argentina law project)
11	France	68 514	9 (single cell) 5.5 (2 ppl cell) 4.5 (3 ppl cell) 4.75 (4 ppl cell) 4.8 (5–6 ppl cell)	Yes (Prison administration)	www.prisonobservatory.org
12	Germany	63 100	9	Yes (Law)	www.rm.coe.int
13	Ukraine	60 771	4	Yes	www.library.khpg.org
14	Spain	59 839	9.5	No	www.prisonobservatory.org
15	Kenya	57 000	3.7	Yes (Law)	www.icrc.org
16	Japan	56 805	5 (single cell) 2 (shared cell)	No	www.hrw.org
17	Italy	55 251	9	No	www.prisonobservatory.org
18	Chile	43 063	6	Yes (Law)	www.icrc.org
19	Canada	40 663	7	Yes	www.cbc.ca
20	Australia	39 152	6.5 (single cell) 8.75 (single cell with toilet and shower) 6 (shared cell)	Yes (Law)	www.icrc.org
21	Czechia	22 565	3.5 (law) (most cells have 1.75)	Yes (Law)	www.theguardian.com
22	Israel	21 072	3	No	www.acri.org
23	Guatemala	20 697	11.5 (single cell) 7 (2 ppl shared) 7.5 (3 ppl shared)	No	www.icrc.org
24	Hungary	18 208	4 (law) 3 (law until 2015) 1.7 (reality)	Yes (Law)	www.budapestbeacon.com
25	The Netherlands	11 603	10	Yes (Law)	www.rijksoverheid.nl
26	Slovakia	10 095	3.5	Yes	www.spectator.sme.sk
27	New Zealand	9 798	4 (shared cell)	No	www.theconversation.com
28	Greece	9 621	11.5 (single cell) 6 (shared cell)	Yes (Law)	www.prisonobservatory.org
29	Senegal	9 422	3.5	No	www.icrc.org
30	Scotland (UK)	7 482	7 (single cell) 4 (shared cell, no toilet)	Yes (Law)	www.heraldscotland.com
31	Switzerland	6 884	12	Yes (Law)	www.icrc.org
32	Albania	6 108	4	Yes (Law)	www.icrc.org
33	Latvia	4 409	9 (single cell) 2.5 (men shared cell) 3 (women/minors shared cell)	Yes (Law)	www.prisonobservatory.org
34	Ireland	3 597	7	No	www.workingnotes.ie
35	Guinea	3 110	2	Yes (Interministerial meeting)	www.data2.unhcr.org
36	Mauritius	2 140	8.75 (single cell) 4 (shared cell) 5.6 (hospital ward)	Yes (Law)	www.icrc.org
37	Fiji	1 555	5.5 (single cell) 3.7 (shared cell)	Yes (Law)	www.unafei.or.jp

Death Penalty

Introduction

This index on capital punishment worldwide divides nation states into three major groups:

A. Abolitionist:
"Abolitionist for all crimes"–Death penalty is abolished for all crimes.
"Abolitionist for all crimes–since independence"–Death penalty is abolished for all crimes since independence.
"Abolitionist for ordinary crimes only"–Death penalty is used only in exceptional circumstances (e.g., wartime).

B. Abolitionist in Practice:
"Abolitionist in Practice–not executed for 10 years"–Permits its use for extraordinary crimes, but has not been used for at least 10 years.
"Abolitionist in Practice–not used since independence"–Permits its use for extraordinary crimes, but was not used since the country's independence.
"Abolitionist in Practice–official moratorium"–Death penalty is under an official moratorium.

C. Retentionist–Maintains death penalty in both law and practice.
The column "Year this step was taken" indicates for group "A. Abolitionist" the most recent date capital punishment was abolished (some countries reintroduced and abolished the death penalty a second time); for group "B. Abolitionist in Practice" the year the country achieved the mentioned status; for group "C. Retentionist," the year of the last implemented execution.
The year of the abolition refers to the time capital punishment was abolished by law (not by constitution). The year of the last execution refers to the last implemented execution itself and not to the last spoken death sentence.

Sources

Source A: *Amnesty International Global Report: Death Sentences and Executions 2016* (available: www.amnesty.org)
Source B: www.capitalpunishmentuk.org
Source C: www.deathpenaltyworldwide.org
Source D: www.icomdp.org
Source E: Book: *The Death Penalty: A Worldwide Perspective,* by Carolyn Hoyle and Roger Hood (2008 Oxford)
Source F: Book: *The International Sourcebook on Capital Punishment,* edited by William Schabas (1997 London)
Source G: en.wikipedia.org

A. Abolitionist

	Country	Last Execcution	Status	Year this step was taken	Sources
1	Albania	1995	Abolitionist for all crimes	2007	1. Source A, 2. Source B, 3. Source G, 4. assembly.coe.int
2	Andorra	1943	Abolitionist for all crimes	1990	1. Source B, 2. Source F, 3. Source G
3	Angola	None since independence in 1975	Abolitionist for all crimes	1992	1. Source G, 2. allafrica.com
4	Argentina	1916	Abolitionist for all crimes	2009	1. Source G, 2. www.icomdp.org
5	Armenia	None since independence in 1991	Abolitionist for all crimes	2003	1. Source B, 2. Source G, 3. www.penalreform.org
6	Australia	1967	Abolitionist for all crimes	1985	1. Source F, 2. Source G, 3. www.bbc.com
7	Austria	1950	Abolitionist for all crimes	1968	1. Source F, 2. Source G,
8	Azerbaijan	1993	Abolitionist for all crimes	1998	1. Source B, 2. Source G, 3. www.penalreform.org
9	Belgium	1950	Abolitionist for all crimes	1996	1. Source A, 2. Source F, 3. Source G
10	Benin	1987	Abolitionist for all crimes	2016	1. Source A, 2. Source C, 3. Source G, 4. blog.deathpenaltyworldwide.org
11	Bhutan	1974	Abolitionist for all crimes	2004	1. Source A, 2. Source F, 3. Source G
12	Bolivia	1974	Abolitionist for all crimes	2013	1. Source A, 2. Source F, 3. Source G
13	Bosnia and Herzegovina	None since independence in 1992 (1)	Abolitionist for all crimes	1998 (1)	1. Source A, 2. Source G
14	Brazil	1876	Abolitionist for ordinary crimes only	1988	1. Source A, 2. Source G, 3. www.executedtoday.com
15	Bulgaria	1989	Abolitionist for all crimes	1998	1. Source B, 2. Source G, 3. assembly.coe.int
16	Burundi	1997	Abolitionist for all crimes	2009 (2)	1. Source C, 2. Source G
17	Cambodia	unknown	Abolitionist for all crimes	1989	1. Source D, 2. Source G
18	Canada	1962	Abolitionist for all crimes	1998	1. Source G, 2. www.cbc.ca, 3. www.capitalpunishmentuk.org
19	Cape Verde	None since independence in 1975	Abolitionist for all crimes	1981	1. Source F, 2. Source G
20	Chile	1985	Abolitionist for ordinary crimes only	2001	1. Source F, 2. Source G, 3. www.ipsnews.net
21	Colombia	1909	Abolitionist for all crimes	1910	1. Source F, 2. Source G
22	Congo (Brazzaville)	1982	Abolitionist for all crimes	2015	1. Source C, 2. Source G, 3. www.amnesty.org
23	Cook Islands	None since independence in 1965	Abolitionist for all crimes	2007	1. Source G, 2. Amnesty International: The Death Penalty Worldwide Developments in 2007 (available: www.amnesty-todesstrafe.de), 3. web.archive.org
24	Costa Rica	1859	Abolitionist for all crimes	1877	1. Source F, 2. Source G
25	Côte d'Ivoire	None since independence in 1960	Abolitionist for all crimes	2000 (3)	1. Source G, 2. www.worldcoalition.org
26	Croatia	None since independence in 1991	Abolitionist for all crimes–since independence	1991	1. Source B, 2. Source F, 3. Source G
27	Cyprus	1962	Abolitionist for all crimes	2002	1. Source F, 2. Source G, 3. assembly.coe.int
28	Czechia	None since independence in 1993	Abolitionist for all crimes–since independence	1993	1. Source F, 2. Source G
29	Denmark	1950	Abolitionist for all crimes	1978	1. Source F, 2. Source G
30	Djibouti	None since independence in 1977	Abolitionist for all crimes	1995	1. Source C, 2. Source G
31	Dominican Republic	Unknown	Abolitionist for all crimes	1966	1. Source G, 2. Amnesty International: Death Penalty In The English-Speaking Caribbean; A Human Rights Issue (available: www.amnesty.org)
32	Ecuador	Unknown	Abolitionist for all crimes	1906	1. Source F, 2. Source G
33	El Salvador	1973	Abolitionist for ordinary crimes only	1983	1. Source F, 2. Source G
34	Estonia	1991	Abolitionist for all crimes	1998	1. Source B, 2. Source G, 3. assembly.coe.int
35	Fiji	None since independence in 1970	Abolitionist for all crimes	2015	1. Source C, 2. Source G
36	Finland	1944	Abolitionist for all crimes	1972	1. Source B, 2. Source G
37	France	1977	Abolitionist for all crimes	1981	1. Source D, 2. Source G

38	Gabon	1981	Abolitionist for all crimes	2010	1. Source E, 2. Source G, 3. www.handsoffcain.info
39	Georgia	1995	Abolitionist for all crimes	1997	1. Source B, 2. Source G, 3. www.penalreform.org
40	Germany	1951	Abolitionist for all crimes	1949 (4)	1. Source F, 2. Source G
41	Greece	1972	Abolitionist for all crimes	2004	1. Source E, 2. Source F, 3. Source G
42	Guinea	2001	Abolitionist for ordinary crimes only	2016	1. Source A, 2. Source C, 3. Source G
43	Guinea-Bissau	1986	Abolitionist for all crimes	1993	1. Source F, 2. Source G
44	Haiti	1972	Abolitionist for all crimes	1987	1. Source F, 2. Source G, 3. Amnesty International: Death Penalty In The English-Speaking Caribbean; A Human Rights Issue (available: www.amnesty.org)
45	Honduras	1940	Abolitionist for all crimes	1956	1. Source F, 2. Source G
46	Hungary	1988	Abolitionist for all crimes	1990	1. Source F, 2. Source G
47	Iceland	None since independence in 1944	Abolitionist for all crimes–since independence	1944	1. Source B, 2. Source G
48	Ireland	1954	Abolitionist for all crimes	1990	1. Source F, 2. Source G
49	Israel	1962	Abolitionist for ordinary crimes only	1954	1. Source F, 2. Source G
50	Italy	1947	Abolitionist for all crimes	1994	1. Source G, 2. Source G
51	Kazakhstan	2003	Abolitionist for ordinary crimes only	2007	1. Source G, 2. www.handsoffcain.info
52	Kiribati	None since independence in 1979	Abolitionist for all crimes–since independence	1979	1. Source E, 2. Source G
53	Kosovo	unknown	Abolitionist for all crimes	unknown	Source A
54	Kyrgyzstan	1998	Abolitionist for ordinary crimes only	2007	1. Source G, 2. Amnesty International: The Death Penalty Worldwide Developments in 2007 (available: www.amnesty-todesstrafe.de), 3. www.worldcoalition.org
55	Latvia	1996	Abolitionist for all crimes	2012	1. Source C, 2. Source G
56	Liechtenstein	1785	Abolitionist for all crimes	1989	1. Source F, 2. Source G
57	Lithuania	1995	Abolitionist for all crimes	1998	1. Source E, 2. Source G, 3. www.executedtoday.com
58	Luxembourg	1949	Abolitionist for all crimes	1979	1. Source F, 2. Source G
59	Macedonia	None since independence in 1991	Abolitionist for all crimes–since independence	1991	1. Source F, 2. Source G
60	Madagascar	1958	Abolitionist for all crimes	2015	1. Source C, 2. Source G
61	Malta	None since independence in 1964	Abolitionist for all crimes	2000	1. Source F, 2. Source G
62	Marshall Islands	None since independence in 1986	Abolitionist for all crimes–since independence	1986	1. Source E, 2. Source F, 3. Source G
63	Mauritius	1987	Abolitionist for all crimes	1995	1. Source E, 2. Source G
64	Mexico	1961	Abolitionist for all crimes	2005	1. Source E, 2. Source G, 3. news.bbc.co.uk
65	Micronesia	None since independence in 1986	Abolitionist for all crimes–since independence	1986	1. Source E, 2. Source G
66	Moldova	None since independence in 1991	Abolitionist for all crimes	1995	1. Source F, 2. Source G
67	Monaco	1847	Abolitionist for all crimes	1962	1. Source F, 2. Source G
68	Montenegro	None since independence in 2006	Abolitionist for all crimes–since independence	2006	1. Source B, 2. Source G
69	Mozambique	1986	Abolitionist for all crimes	1990	1. Source F, 2. Source G
70	Namibia	None since independence in 1990	Abolitionist for all crimes–since independence	1990	1. Source F, 2. Source G
71	Nauru	None since independence in 1968	Abolitionist for all crimes	2016	1. Source E, 2. Source G, 3. www.worldcoalition.org
72	Nepal	1979	Abolitionist for all crimes	1991	1. Source C, 2. Source G
73	Netherlands	1952	Abolitionist for all crimes	1982 (5)	1. Source F, 2. Source G
74	New Zealand	1957	Abolitionist for all crimes	1989	1. Source F, 2. Source G
75	Nicaragua	1930	Abolitionist for all crimes	1979	1. Source F, 2. Source G
76	Niue	unknown	Abolitionist for all crimes	unknown	1. Source A, 2. Source G, 3. adpan.org
77	Northern Cyprus	None since independence in 1983	Abolitionist for ordinary crimes only	unknown	1. Source G, 2. wikivisually.com
78	Norway	1948	Abolitionist for all crimes	1979	1. Source F, 2. Source G
79	Palau	None since independence in 1994	Abolitionist for all crimes–since independence	1994	1. Source E, 2. Source G
80	Panama	None since independence in 1903	Abolitionist for all crimes–since independence	1903	1. Source A, 2. Source F, 3. Source G
81	Paraguay	1928	Abolitionist for all crimes	1992	1. Source F, 2. Source G
82	Peru	1979	Abolitionist for ordinary crimes only	1979	1. Source F, 2. Source G
83	Philippines	2000	Abolitionist for all crimes	2006 (2)	1. Source D, 2. Source E, 3. Source G
84	Poland	1988	Abolitionist for all crimes	1998	1. Source B, 2. Source G, 3. assembly.coe.int
85	Portugal	1846	Abolitionist for all crimes	1976	1. Source B, 2. Source F, 3. Source G
86	Romania	1989	Abolitionist for all crimes	1990	1. Source B, 2. Source E, 3. Source G
87	Rwanda	1998	Abolitionist for all crimes	2007	1. Source D, 2. Source G
88	Samoa	None since independence in 1962	Abolitionist for all crimes	2004	1. Source E, 2. Source G
89	San Marino	1468	Abolitionist for all crimes	1865	1. Source F, 2. Source G
90	São Tomé and Príncipe	None since independence in 1975	Abolitionist for all crimes	1990	1. Source F, 2. Source G
91	Senegal	1967	Abolitionist for all crimes	2004	1. Source D, 2. Source G
92	Serbia	None since independence in 2006	Abolitionist for all crimes–since independence	2006	1. Source B, 2. Source E, 3. Source G
93	Seychelles	None since independence in 1976	Abolitionist for all crimes	1993	1. Source A, 2. Source F, 3. Source G
94	Slovakia	None since independence in 1993	Abolitionist for all crimes–since independence	1993	1. Source F, 2. Source G
95	Slovenia	None since independence in 1991	Abolitionist for all crimes–since independence	1991	1. Source F, 2. Source G
96	Solomon Islands	None since independence in 1978	Abolitionist for all crimes–since independence	1978	1. Source E, 2. Source G
97	South Africa	1991	Abolitionist for all crimes	1997	1. Source D, 2. Source G
98	Spain	1975	Abolitionist for all crimes	1995	1. Source C, 2. Source G
99	Suriname	1982	Abolitionist for all crimes	2015	1. Source C, 2. Source C, 3. Source G
100	Sweden	1910	Abolitionist for all crimes	1973	1. Source F, 2. Source G

	Country	Last execution	Status	Year this step was taken	Sources
101	Switzerland	1944	Abolitionist for all crimes	1992	1. Source F, 2. Source G
102	Tajikistan	2004	Abolitionist for all crimes	2005	1. Source C, 2. Source G, 3. web.archive.org
103	Timor-Leste	None since independence in 2002	Abolitionist for all crimes–since independence	2002	1. Source E, 2. Source G
104	Togo	1978	Abolitionist for all crimes	2009	1. Source E, 2. Source G, 3. www.amnesty.org
105	Turkey	1984	Abolitionist for all crimes	2004 (2)	1. Source D, 2. Source G
106	Turkmenistan	1997	Abolitionist for all crimes	1999	1. Source E, 2. Source G
107	Tuvalu	None since independence in 1978	Abolitionist for all crimes–since independence	1978	1. Source E, 2. Source F, 3. Source G
108	Ukraine	1997	Abolitionist for all crimes	2000	1. Source B, 2. Source G
109	United Kingdom	1964	Abolitionist for all crimes	1998 (6)	1. Source E, 2. Source F, 3. Source G
110	Uruguay	1905	Abolitionist for all crimes	1907	1. Source E, 2. Source G, 3. www.handsoffcain.info
111	Uzbekistan	2005	Abolitionist for all crimes	2008	1. Source E, 2. Source G
112	Vanuatu	None since independence in 1980	Abolitionist for all crimes–since independence	1980	1. Source E, 2. Source F, 3. Source G
113	Vatican City	None since independence in 1929	Abolitionist for all crimes	1969	1. Source F, 2. Source G
114	Venezuela	None since independence in 1830	Abolitionist for all crimes	1863	1. Source C, 2. Source G

B. Abolitionist in Practice

	Country	Last execution	Status	Year this step was taken	Sources
115	Abkhazia	None since independence in 1993	Abolitionist in Practice–death penalty under an official moratorium	2007	1. Source G, 2. www.civil.ge
116	Algeria	1993	Abolitionist in Practice–death penalty under an official moratorium	1993	1. Source C, 2. Source G, 3. www.worldcoalition.org
117	Antigua and Barbuda	1991	Abolitionist in Practice–have not used it for at least 10 years	2001	1. Source C, 2. Source G, 3. antiguaobserver.com
118	The Bahamas	2000	Abolitionist in Practice–have not used it for at least 10 years	2010	1. Source C, 2. Source G, 3. www.amnesty.org
119	Barbados	1984	Abolitionist in Practice–have not used it for at least 10 years	1994	1. Source C, 2. Source G, 3. www.capitalpunishmentuk.org
120	Belize	1985	Abolitionist in Practice–have not used it for at least 10 years	1995	1. Source A, 2. Source C, 3. Source G
121	Brunei	None since independence in 1984	Abolitionist in Practice–was not used since independence	1984	1. Source C, 2. Source G, 3. www.pinknews.co.uk
122	Burkina Faso	1988	Abolitionist in Practice–have not used it for at least 10 years	1998	1. Source C, 2. Source G
123	Cameroon	1997	Abolitionist in Practice–have not used it for at least 10 years	2007	1. Source B, 2. Source C, 3. Source G
124	Central African Republic	1981	Abolitionist in Practice–have not used it for at least 10 years	1991 (7)	1. Source F, 2. Source G, 3. www.worldcoalition.org
125	Comoros	1997	Abolitionist in Practice–death penalty under an official moratorium	2013	1. Source C, 2. Source G
126	Congo (Kinshasa)	2003	Abolitionist in Practice–have not used it for at least 10 years	2013	1. Source C, 2. Source G
127	Cuba	2003	Abolitionist in Practice–have not used it for at least 10 years	2013	1. Source C, 2. Source G
128	Dominica	1986	Abolitionist in Practice–have not used it for at least 10 years	1996	1. Source C, 2. Source G
129	Equatorial Guinea	2014	Abolitionist in Practice–death penalty under an official moratorium	2014	1. Source C, 2. Source G, 3. www.hrw.org
130	Eritrea	None since independence in 1993	Abolitionist in Practice–was not used since independence	1993	1. Source C, 2. Source G
131	Ethiopia	2007	Abolitionist in Practice–have not used it for at least 10 years	2007	1. Source C, 2. Source G
132	Ghana	1993	Abolitionist in Practice–have not used it for at least 10 years	2003	1. Source C, 2. Source G
133	Grenada	1978	Abolitionist in Practice–have not used it for at least 10 years	1988	1. Source C, 2. Source G
134	Guatemala	2000	Abolitionist in Practice–have not used it for at least 10 years	2010	1. Source C, 2. Source G, 3. www.foxnews.com
135	Guyana	1997	Abolitionist in Practice–have not used it for at least 10 years	2007	1. Source C, 2. Source G
136	Jamaica	1988	Abolitionist in Practice–have not used it for at least 10 years	1998	1. Source C, 2. Source G, 3. www.loc.gov
137	Kenya	1987	Abolitionist in Practice–have not used it for at least 10 years	1997	1. Source C, 2. Source G
138	Laos	1989	Abolitionist in Practice–have not used it for at least 10 years	1999	1. Source C, 2. Source G
139	Lebanon	2004	Abolitionist in Practice–have not used it for at least 10 years	2014	1. Source C, 2. Source G
140	Lesotho	1995	Abolitionist in Practice–have not used it for at least 10 years	2005	1. Source C, 2. Source G
141	Liberia	2000	Abolitionist in Practice–have not used it for at least 10 years	2010	1. Source C, 2. Source G
142	Malawi	1992	Abolitionist in Practice–have not used it for at least 10 years	2002	1. Source C, 2. Source G
143	Maldives	None since independence in 1965	Abolitionist in Practice–was not used since independence	1965	1. Source C, 2. Source G
144	Mali	1980	Abolitionist in Practice–have not used it for at least 10 years	1990	1. Source C, 2. Source G
145	Mauritania	1987	Abolitionist in Practice–have not used it for at least 10 years	1997	1. Source C, 2. Source G
146	Morocco	1993	Abolitionist in Practice–have not used it for at least 10 years	2003	1. Source C, 2. Source G
147	Myanmar (Burma)	1988 (8)	Abolitionist in Practice–have not used it for at least 10 years	1998	1. Source C, 2. Source G
148	Niger	1976	Abolitionist in Practice–have not used it for at least 10 years	1986	1. Source C, 2. Source G
149	Papua New Guinea	None since independence in 1975	Abolitionist in Practice–was not used since independence	1975	1. Source C, 2. Source G
150	Qatar	2003	Abolitionist in Practice–have not used it for at least 10 years	2013	1. Source C, 2. Source G
151	Russia	1996 (9)	Abolitionist in Practice–death penalty under an official moratorium	1996	1. Source C, 2. Source G
152	Sahrawi Arab Democratic Republic (Western Sahara)	None since independence in 1976	Unknown	Unknown (10)	1. Source G, 2. www.fiacat.org, 3. www.achpr.org
153	Saint Lucia	1995	Abolitionist in Practice–have not used it for at least 10 years	2005	1. Source C, 2. Source G
154	Saint Vincent and the Grenadines	1995	Abolitionist in Practice–have not used it for at least 10 years	2005	1. Source C, 2. Source G

155	Sierra Leone	1998	Abolitionist in Practice–have not used it for at least 10 years	2008	1. Source C, 2. Source G
156	South Korea	1997	Abolitionist in Practice–have not used it for at least 10 years	2007	1. Source C, 2. Source G
157	South Ossetia	None since independence in 1991	Abolitionist in Practice–death penalty under an official moratorium	1996	1. Source E, 2. wikipedia.org, 3. web.archive.org
158	Sri Lanka	1976	Abolitionist in Practice–death penalty under an official moratorium	1976 (11)	1. Source C, 2. Source G
159	Swaziland	1983	Abolitionist in Practice–have not used it for at least 10 years	1993	1. Source C, 2. Source G
160	Tanzania	1994	Abolitionist in Practice–have not used it for at least 10 years	2004	1. Source C, 2. Source G
161	Tonga	1982	Abolitionist in Practice–have not used it for at least 10 years	1992	1. Source C, 2. Source G
162	Trinidad and Tobago	1999	Abolitionist in Practice–have not used it for at least 10 years	2009	1. Source C, 2. Source G
163	Tunisia	1991	Abolitionist in Practice–have not used it for at least 10 years	2001	1. Source C, 2. Source G
164	Uganda	2005	Abolitionist in Practice–have not used it for at least 10 years	2015	1. Source C, 2. Source G
165	Zambia	1997	Abolitionist in Practice–have not used it for at least 10 years	2007	1. Source C, 2. Source G
166	Zimbabwe	2005	Abolitionist in Practice–have not used it for at least 10 years	2015	1. Source C, 2. Source G

C. Retentionist

	Country	Last execution	Status	Year this step was taken	Sources
167	Afghanistan	2016	Retentionist	2016	1. Source C, 2. Source G, 3. www.afghanistan-analysts.org
168	Bahrain	2017	Retentionist	2017	1. Source C, 2. Source G
169	Bangladesh	2017	Retentionist	2017	1. Source C, 2. Source G
170	Belarus	2017	Retentionist	2017	1. Source C, 2. Source G, 3. www.rferl.org
171	Botswana	2016	Retentionist	2016	1. Source C, 2. Source G, 3. www.amnesty.org
172	Chad	2015	Retentionist	2015	1. Source C, 2. Source G
173	China	2017 (estimated)	Retentionist	2017	1. Source C, 2. Source G
174	Egypt	2017	Retentionist	2017	1. Source C, 2. Source G
175	The Gambia	2012	Retentionist	2012	1. Source C, 2. Source G, 3. www.fiacat.org, 4. www.dw.com
176	India	2015	Retentionist	2015	1. Source C, 2. Source G
177	Indonesia	2016	Retentionist	2016 (12)	1. Source C, 2. Source G, 3. www.hrw.org
178	Iran	2017	Retentionist	2017	1. Source C, 2. Source G
179	Iraq	2017	Retentionist	2017	1. Source C, 2. Source G
180	Japan	2016	Retentionist	2016	1. Source C, 2. Source G
181	Jordan	2017	Retentionist	2017	1. Source C, 2. Source G
182	Kuwait	2017	Retentionist	2017	1. Source C, 2. Source G
183	Libya	2016	Retentionist	2016	1. Source A, 2. Source G, 3. www.libyaobserver.ly
184	Malaysia	2017	Retentionist	2017	1. Source C, 2. Source G
185	Mongolia	2008	Retentionist	2008	1. Source A, 2. Source C, 3. Source G
186	Nigeria	2016	Retentionist	2016 (13)	1. Source A, 2. Source C, 3. Source G
187	North Korea	2017	Retentionist	2017	1. Source C, 2. Source G
188	Oman	2015	Retentionist	2015	1. Source C, 2. Source G
189	Pakistan	2017	Retentionist	2017	1. Source C, 2. Source G
190	Palestine	2017	Retentionist	2017	1. Source C, 2. Source G
191	Saint Kitts and Nevis	2008	Retentionist	2008	1. Source C, 2. Source G
192	Saudi Arabia	2017	Retentionist	2017	1. Source C, 2. Source G
193	Singapore	2017	Retentionist	2017	1. Source C, 2. Source G, 3. www.hrw.org
194	Somalia	2017	Retentionist	2017	1. Source C, 2. Source G
195	South Sudan	2016	Retentionist	2016	1. Source C, 2. Source G
196	Sudan	2016	Retentionist	2016	1. Source C, 2. Source G
197	Syria	2017 (estimated)	Retentionist	2017	1. Source C, 2. Source G, 3. www.washingtonpost.com
198	Taiwan	2016	Retentionist	2016	1. Source C, 2. Source G
199	Thailand	2009	Retentionist	2009	1. Source C, 2. Source G
200	United Arab Emirates	2015	Retentionist	2015	1. Source C, 2. Source G
201	United States	2017	Retentionist	2017 (14)	1. Source C, 2. Source G
202	Vietnam	2016	Retentionist	2016	1. Source C, 2. Source G
203	Yemen	2015	Retentionist	2015	1. Source C, 2. Source G

Footnotes:
(1) Exception: Largely autonomous entity "Republika Srpska"–last execution was in 2000, and it still has capital punishment in the statutes.
(2) Capital punishment expected to be reintroduced soon.
(3) Capital punishment abolished only in constitution, but still remains in penal code.
(4) Last execution in East Germany: 1981; abolition of capital punishment: 1987.
(5) Last abolished in Dutch overseas territory the Netherlands Antilles in 2010.
(6) Last execution at overseas territory Bermuda in 1977, and last abolition at overseas territory Jersey in 2006.
(7) Abolished the death penalty for military crimes in March 2017.
(8) Exception: last execution in self-ruling region named Wa State: 2016.
(9) Exception: last execution in Chechnya (state with limited recognition): 1999.
(10) Banned death penalty. Whether this is equal to total abolition is unknown.
(11) A semi-official moratorium.
(12) Announced official moratorium in March 2017, but did not put it into force so far.
(13) Parts of the southern states did put it under moratorium in 2004.
(14) Depending on the state: some have abolished capital punishment, some are abolitionist in practice.

Green Fortress

Vegetation

a/a	Element	Example	Description	Block	Detect	Scare	Hide	Attack	Sources
1	Columnar trees	Birch tree, maple, aspen	Used around the perimeter to partially hide the property.				X		www.gardenbuildingsdirect.co.uk
2	Dense trees	Spruces, pines	Used at the perimeter to hide the property and block access.	X			X		www.telegraph.co.uk
3	Prickly trees	False acacia, honey locust	Used outside upper-story windows to deter intruders from climbing and entering.	X		X			www.thecrimepreventionwebsite.com
4	Prickly shrubs	Berberis, roses, holly	Used at the perimeter, below windows, and around walkways to deter intruders from entering.	X		X	X		www.telegraph.co.uk
5	Hedges	Boxwood, privet, Canadian hemlock	Used at the perimeter and around walkways to block both visibility and access.	X			X		www.gardenbuildingsdirect.co.uk
6	Bamboo	Golden bamboo	Ideal for fencing due to its high density, extremely strong properties, and fast growing rate. It can grow to a height of 30 meters.	X			X		www.telegraph.co.uk
7	Reed grass	Giant reed, Burma reed	Very tall and dense grass that can grow to a height of 2 to 6 meters.	X			X		en.wikipedia.org
8	Scented plants	Lavender, mint, rue	Used at the perimeter to deter animals from approaching.			X			www.regenerative.com
9	Prickly vines	Roses, bougainvillea, bristly greenbrier	Used at the perimeter with the support of another element such as a wall or a fence to prevent intruders from climbing.	X		X			1. www.thecrimepreventionwebsite.com 2. en.wikipedia.org
10	Prickly plants	Cactus, agave, yucca	Used at the perimeter, below windows, and around walkways to deter intruders from entering.	X		X			en.wikipedia.org

Landscaping

a/a	Element	Example	Description	Block	Detect	Scare	Hide	Attack	Sources
11	Pond		Used at the perimeter to deter intruders from entering. Piranhas can be added for an extra deadly effect.	X		X			www.gardenbuildingsdirect.co.uk
12	Ha-ha		Used at the perimeter, usually around big properties, to block intruders from entering while respecting the continuity of the landscape.	X					en.wikipedia.org
13	Gravel walkway		Helps to warn of possible intruders by creating a sound when walked upon.		X				www.gardenbuildingsdirect.co.uk
14	Rocks		Used at the perimeter to block access.	X					www.sopef.com
15	Moat		Used at the perimeter, usually around big properties, to block intruders from entering.	X		X			en.wikipedia.org
16	Quicksand		Potential intruders will slowly sink into the quicksand, making it an ideal barrier for blocking access and slowing down intruders.	X		X			en.wikipedia.org
17	Raised garden bed		Used at the perimeter to block access.	X					1. www.survivalretreatconsulting.com 2. www.richsoil.com
18	Hill		A house built on top of a hill has a better panoramic view of possible intruders.	X	X				en.wikipedia.org
19	Sand walkway		Used to detect an intruder's footprints.		X				

Animals

a/a	Element	Example	Description	Block	Detect	Scare	Hide	Attack	Sources
20	Guard animals	Dogs, geese, donkeys, llamas, ostriches, parrots, screamers	A wide range of animals can be used to guard a property. Some are aggressive and bite, while others make sounds that alert the owners.		X	X		X	1. en.wikipedia.org 2. www.mnn.com 3. www.adrianflux.co.uk
21	Owls (plastic)	Decoy plastic owl	Used to scare small birds away.			X			www.pigeoncontrolresourcecentre.org

Miscellaneous

a/a	Element	Example	Description	Block	Detect	Scare	Hide	Attack	Sources
22	Waste products	Coffee, citrus peels, human hair	Used to deter small animals from approaching due to their distinct smell.			X			1. www.offthegridnews.com 2. www.scjohnson.com

Illustration Sources

12, 13
javelin en.wikipedia.org
stone www.insidethegames.biz
sling en.wikipedia.org
bow & arrow www.worldrecordacademy.com
bazooka en.wikipedia.org
WW I rifle www.gunsopedia.com
sniper rifle www.edition.cnn.com

18–35
www.passportindex.org, reference date: 3 July 2017

54
www.globalsecurity.org
www.fas.org
www.deagel.com
www.ausairpower.net
www.newatlas.com
www.wikipedia.org

56–69
archive.is
dailycaller.com
english.ahram.org.eg
english.al-akhbar.com
jamestown.org
latimesblogs.latimes.com
mfa.gov.kz
mha.nic.in
news.xinhuanet.com
wam.ae
web.archive.org
www.aljazeera.com
www.almasdarnews.com
www.appledaily.com.tw
www.bbc.co.uk
www.berghof-foundation.org
www.bignewsnetwork.com
www.china-embassy.org
www.dawn.com
www.egyptindependent.com
www.foxnews.com
www.fsb.ru
www.globalsecurity.org
www.gov.uk
www.haaretz.co.il
www.hurriyetdailynews.com
www.kyivpost.com
www.lexology.com
www.mfa.gov.cn
www.mfa.gov.il
www.mofa.go.jp
www.moj.go.jp
www.nationalsecurity.gov.au
www.npa.go.jp
www.nydailynews.com
www.publicsafety.gc.ca
www.redian.org
www.rediff.com
www.resmigazete.gov.tr
www.reuters.com
www.rferl.org
www.rt.com
www.sankei.com
www.spa.gov.sa
www.sponichi.co.jp
www.state.gov
www.sunstar.com.ph
www.theguardian.com
www.thehindu.com
www.treasury.gov
www.tunisia-live.net
www.un.org
www.webcitation.org
www.wsj.com

The following groups are not included in the illustrations
due to missing founding date:
Environs of Jerusalem
Jamaat Ul-Furquan
National Liberation Army
Palestine al-muslima
People's Congress of Ichkeria and Dagestan
Supreme Military Majlis ul-Shura of the United
Mujahideen Forces of Caucasus
United Muslim World

58–60
en.wikipedia.org

72–77
www.popstats.unhcr.org
www.unhcr.org

86
www.theguardian.com
www.news.bbc.co.uk
www.dismalgarden.com
www.architectures.danlockton.co.uk
www.unpleasant.pravi.me
www.wikipedia.org
www.flickr.com/photos/7211263@N02

98
www.wikipedia.org
www.theguardian.com
jnlwp.defense.gov
www.theprepperjournal.com
www.hse.gov.uk
www.btselem.org
www.globalsecurity.org

124
FAOSTAT 2014

125–131
www.fao.org
www.efsa.europa.eu
www.hsa.org.uk
www.topkip.com
www.meyn.com
www.gov.uk
www.butina.eu
en.wikipedia.org
www.nfacc.ca
www.grandin.com
www.fao.org
www.poultryandmeatprocessing.com
www.avma.org

Image Credits

17
"Migratory connectivity and population-specific migration
routes in a long-distance migratory bird" by Christiane
Trierweiler, Raymond H. G. Klaassen, Rudi H. Drent,
Klaus-Michael Exo, Jan Komdeur, Franz Bairlein and Ben
J. Koks; Published 15 January 2014. DOI: 10.1098/
rspb.2013.2897

36
"Stützwandelement UL 12.11," Bundesarchiv DVH
50/127905, folio 53

52
Inside a Citadel of the Static War–One of the Bastions of
Maginot's Mighty Line; *The War Illustrated: A Permanent
Picture Record of the Second Great War,* December 16,
1939, vol. 1, no. 14 (Specially prepared from French
semi-official sources for *The War Illustrated* by Haworth)

70
UNRRA D.P. Operations Germany, situation as of May 8th,
III-6-U, 10.15.590, ITS Archives, Bad Arolsen. Copy in
conformity with the ITS Archives

78
Hitachi ZAXIS-5 series, High-reach Demolition 27 meter;
Hitachi

84
Camden Bench; Factory Furniture Ltd.

96
United States Patent, Levenson, Mar. 5, 1974;
1 Tear Gas Grenade
Inventor: Michael K. Levenson, 2591 Queenston Rd,
Cleveland Heights, Ohio 44118
Filed: July 27, 1972
Application No.: 275 509

104
Jail Design Guide, Third Edition, Dennis A. Kimme
(Project Director), Gary M. Bowker (Associate Project
Director), Robert G. Deichman (Project Staff), March
2011, NIC Accession, Number 024806, for the U.S.
Department of Justice, National Institute of Corrections,
320 First Street, NW Washington, DC 20534

114
Jacobus and Stephen's Altar, right inside wing, lower
scene: The *Stoning of St. Stephen,* Marx Reichlich,
1506; original located at the monastery of Novacella
(Brixen); current location: Alte Pinakothek, Munich

122
Sketch for a tile design: *Theseus and the Minotaur
in the Labyrinth,* Sir Edward Burne-Jones, 1861; current
location: Birmingham Museums & Art Gallery

132
Luca Deutinger

Production

Free Entry
Theo Deutinger, Stefanos Filippas, Marilia Kaisar,
Liam Cooke, Joan Alcobé Alonso

Walls and Fences
Theo Deutinger, Stefanos Filippas

Bunker Buster
Theo Deutinger, Stefanos Filippas, Liam Cooke,
Ekaterina Vititneva

Terrorist Groups
Theo Deutinger

Refugee Camps
Theo Deutinger, Stefanos Filippas, Tomasz Świetlik,
Ekaterina Vititneva

Total Demolition
Theo Deutinger, Stefanos Filippas, Liam Cooke

Defensive Cities
Theo Deutinger, Stefanos Filippas, Vasiliki Mavrikaki,
Eliza Mante

Crowd Control
Theo Deutinger, Stefanos Filippas, Liam Cooke

Prison Cells
Theo Deutinger, Stefanos Filippas, Joan Alcobé Alonso

Death Penalty
Original by Brendan McGetrick, remixed by
Theo Deutinger, Jolande Kirschbaum

Slaughterhouse
Theo Deutinger, Stefanos Filippas, Liam Cooke

Green Fortress
Theo Deutinger, Stefanos Filippas, Joan Alcobé Alonso

Special thanks to Stefano Filippas for all his work
and effort

Theo Deutinger

Is an architect, writer, and illustrator of
sociocultural concepts. He keeps lecture
and teaching engagements with various
institutions, among them Harvard GSD,
Strelka Institute Moscow, and the Bauhaus
in Dessau.

Brendan McGetrick

Brendan McGetrick is a writer, curator,
and designer. His work has appeared in
publications in more than thirty countries,
including the *New York Times, Wired,* the
*Financial Times, Art Review, Der Spiegel,
Domus,* and *Vogue Nippon.*

Theo Deutinger
Handbook of Tyranny

Essays: Theo Deutinger, Brendan McGetrick
Fact-checking: Jolande Kirschbaum, Ekaterina Vititneva
Coordination: Manuel Müller
Design: Theo Deutinger in collaboration with Integral Lars Müller /
Lars Müller and Esther Butterworth
Copyediting: Michael Pilewski
Proofreading: Keonaona Peterson
Production: Martina Mullis
Printing and binding: Kösel, Altusried-Krugzell, Germany
Paper: Allegro matt, 150 gm²

Lars Müller Publishers is supported by the Federal Office for Culture with
a structural contribution for the years 2016–2020.

Lars Müller Publishers
Zürich, Switzerland
www.lars-mueller-publishers.com

ISBN 978-3-03778-534-8

Printed in Germany

For their support we thank:

creative industries fund NL

BUNDESKANZLERAMT █ ÖSTERREICH

Also supported by de Architekten Cie. – droog – Monique Leenders